WETLANDS
TEALHAM MOOR

ROBIN WILLIAMS

IMMEL
Publishing

Wetlands, Tealham Moor is published by Immel publishing

Copyright text © 1995 Robin Williams
Copyright photographs © 1995 Robin Williams

The right of Robin Williams to be identified as the author of this work has been asserted in accordance with the English Copyright Designs and Patent Act 1988, Section 77 and 78.

Design and Typesetting: Jane Stark
Reprographics: Icon Publications Limited, Kelso
Printed by Butler & Tanner Ltd, Frome and London

British Library Cataloguing in Publication Data
A CIP catalogue record for this book is available from the British Library

First Edition 1995

ISBN 0907151 92 2

Immel Publishing Limited
20 Berkeley Street
Berkeley Square
London W1X 5AE

Tel: 0171 491 1799
Fax: 0171 493 5524

For Romey, with love,
and Fiona, Jessica and Candi;
as well as Merlin, Tam and Brock,
constant companions on the moors.

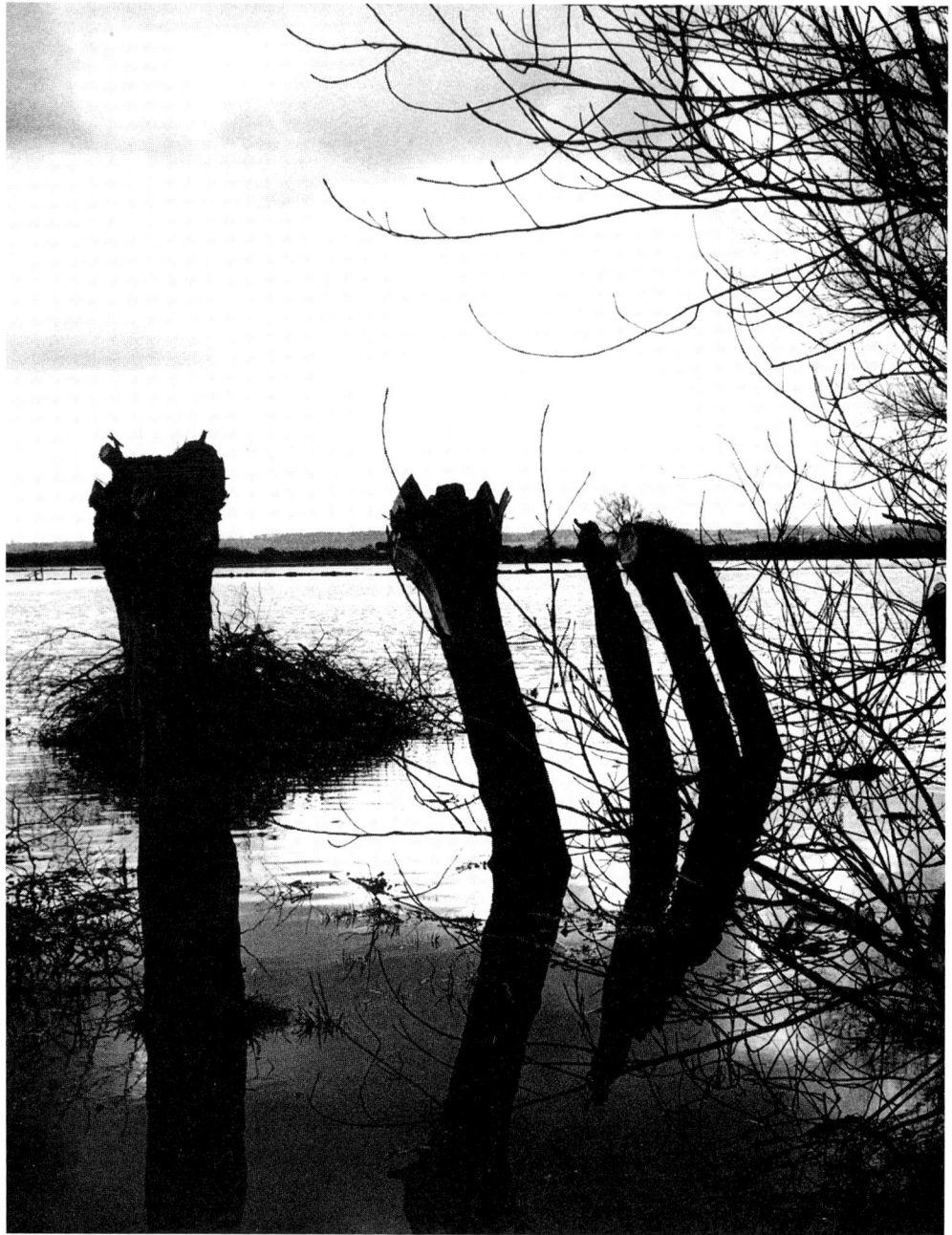

Pollard willows
silhouetted against
the shallow,
spreading waters
of Tealham Moor
in winter.

CONTENTS

Runnels fill and join and sheets of water form miniature lakes.

A WATER-BOUND LANDSCAPE

This book started many years ago as a purely private record of my own special piece of England. Gradually it evolved into a search for the history of a small piece of countryside important to those who live in, above and around it. A period of twenty-seven years enables you to put the seasons in perspective, to appreciate the scale of the country and to see the changes taking place. I am fortunate in being able to walk up to the top of my garden, out across the hill and down into the heart of Tealham Moor, without crossing a road or track. There are not many places where this is still possible.

The story concentrates on a small area but in many ways reflects the experiences of a much larger part of Somerset and of England as a whole. It is certainly typical of most of the great area of the Somerset moors and Levels, nearly 70,000 acres of water-bounded land, at or near sea-level, which penetrates into the heart of inland Somerset, kept from flooding only by sea-walls and pumped drainage systems.

The Levels and moors of Somerset are divided into three main areas, one of which – around Clevedon and Nailsea – is quite separate from the main, better-known Levels. Although these latter now fall into the district of Sedgemoor, it is generally taken that the name 'Sedgemoor' covers that part which lies south of the Polden Hills, running up the basin of the River Parrett and along the present King's Sedgemoor Drain.

I am concerned with the third area, which follows the valley of the River Brue, and is generally known as the 'moors'. It is divided from Sedgemoor by the low line of the Polden Hills, which can barely be seen from a distance, although there are some wonderful views over both moors and Levels from the top, at just over 200 feet. The two areas always were separated and there was no navigation between them, forming two distinct water systems. A Parliamentary report in 1872 estimated the Brue watershed as 136,000 acres and that of the River Parrett as 360,000 acres.

Our particular area comprises Tealham, Tadham and Aller Moors, above which I live and have walked most days in more than twenty years. This clearly defined wetland, quite different from surrounding lands, is better known by its generic name of Tealham, which has come to cover the whole area.

Tealham – often referred to as the moors, or the heath locally – is roughly 2½ miles long by over 1½ miles deep – around 4 square miles of countryside or 2,750 acres. This is a small area but it takes a great deal to know it well, for the interior is varied and access is not always obvious. Farmers know each blade of grass but only in that particular part surrounding their holding or along which their cows are driven up to the farm. After all the years I have lived here, I still feel I am only touching the surface. A particular magic about the place is the sense that there are few other people around and that, somehow, you are discovering something new – nonsense, I know, but a feeling that I have had on many an occasion. I find there are numbers of people who say that it is a very special place, with its own unique feel.

Perhaps because we have not lived above the moors all our lives we look at them with a greater intensity, a hunger for crowding in every changing aspect, for detail, for recording it as it happens. This may be just one of those pretensions which comes to those who move into an area and see it drawn as

Tealham Moor from Keyton Hill. From above, a network of silver ditches is seen.

if in fluorescent colours, so deeply does it impact, but I think not. If that were the case the novelty should have worn off after over twenty years, the colours dimmed and fact taken over from the romance of the new. The reality is that it is my home, where there are everyday chores to be carried out, mud lies underfoot in the winter and all manner of things go wrong. Besides we are not from the city, but have lived in the country for most of our lives.

Within days of arriving, the spell started to exert itself and has not lost its grip to this day. I became instilled with a passionate sense of attachment to something fixed and definite and ancient. At the same time I like to think it is a practical attachment of familiarity, not the sentiment of the over-romantic. I live and work here. I am not a visitor here for the occasional weekend.

When we moved in, we were convinced we had made the right choice, but the viewpoint was still the rim of hills at the edge. We failed to see the flat sweep of moorland, water-edged and fringed with the remains of willows and alders. We looked beyond at the skyline and not at that which was right under our nose.

The first day set the scene, although we were not to realise it until later. As the furniture vans moved up to the bottom of the drive and stopped their engines, we heard a singing in the distance, like the vibration of distant harp-strings. Twelve great swans flew majestically across the sun-clear landscape in front, the light catching their wing-tips and outlining them sharply against dark thunder clouds in the background. We stood and watched them as they swung southwards and landed out of sight behind the distant flood banks of the Brue. The great expanse of green landscape lay open in front of us. Silver ditches etched the outline of some fields, a few willows edged others. The black and white dots of Friesian cows were everywhere. How strange and different it looked, but how peaceful.

This was my first impression of what was to be our home. It did not disappoint, although it was to be some while before it looked as beautiful as that again. It rained virtually the whole time for the next few weeks and we wondered what we had let ourselves in for!

Our cottage is on a spur of the Isle of Wedmore. It looks down on an area known by a variety of names, depending on your interests and background. To the romantic it is the Vale of Avalon, leading up to the distant hill of Glastonbury with its legendary Arthurian connections. The birdwatcher and conservationist uses the less evocative name of the Levels and this is the name by which it is usually known outside. The locals call it the heath or the moors – a name which visitors regard as ridiculous since, "everyone knows that moors are covered with heather and are found on high ground"! Our 'moors' are mostly grass, part rush and wild iris, but mainly at sea-level. Nevertheless moor is the ancient name for these areas as is shown by maps and ancient records, while 'heath' is commemorated in the village name, Heath House. From our cottage we look across Tealham, Tadham and Aller Moors, while

The black and white dots of Friesian cows were everywhere.

11

Mark and Westhay Moors lie to each side. Glastonbury Tor is seen on the left and the long, low line of the Polden Hills lies in front, in the distance.

Our moors are set below and to the south of the Isle of Wedmore, a gently rising ridge which separates them from Cheddar Moor to the north. The outline is seen better from above than when out on the moor, even though the highest point is only a couple of hundred feet up. The southern boundary is formed by the Brue, a canalised river with raised banks which has had its course changed considerably over the centuries. Another broad stretch of water, the North Drain, runs across the middle, parallel with the Brue, while the north is bounded by Little Rhyne, where the land starts to rise. The eastern edge is marked by the main road from Wedmore to Glastonbury along a stretch known as Blakeway, while to the west is a small road running south from Westham which eventually winds its way to Bridgwater. Above the northern contours are various little hamlets looking down on the moor: Westham, Heath House, Sand and Mudgley. All along the slopes of the hill are farmhouses and cottages which either are or were tied to land out on the moor. Wedmore is the local centre.

From above, a network of silver ditches etch the landscape, the water surrounding each field. Each eventually leads into the North Drain. Over to the south-west, on the very edge of our selected area, lies the North Drain Pumping Station, operated by the National Rivers Authority and responsible for rendering the effects of floods as harmless as possible. Flooding cannot be entirely prevented, because of natural phenomena such as wind and the enormous range of local tides, but the water table of the area is now under tight control.

The whole area has become well known as a special habitat for wildlife, both in summer and winter, and has been internationally recognised as such under the Ramsar Agreement.

So I am talking about a rather special piece of our country. It is beautiful in a particular and distinctive way, has good access for those who want to walk over it and is renowned for its wildlife. Its history is equally spectacular. King

Arthur, King Alfred, and the great monastery of Glastonbury figure largely, with Judge Jeffries and Hannah More coming later. But above everything lies the history of farming, of great exploits of drainage and the evolution of one of the finest natural grasslands in Britain, which supported many famous dairy herds in its day.

What does the moor consist of? Of the total area of 2,750 acres, just over 2,400 acres remain untouched permanent pasture. This land is used traditionally as summer grazing for farms which have most of their land on the hills round the perimeter. Around 23 acres have permission for peat working, most of which is either in production or worked out. The peat is processed through a small peat works on Blakeway. Five blocks of land are underdrained in one way or another. Two hundred and twelve acres are deep-drained, with private diesel pumping stations, of which there are now three, while 92 acres are drained by gravity. Of this drained ground, around 70 acres have been ploughed and either planted with root crops or reseeded. The grassland supports milking herds, beef cattle, sheep and even a few domestic geese. Ponds at one end are used to breed and raise ornamental fish and there is a boarding kennel for dogs and cats.

Conservation bodies own around 7 per cent of the moors. The Somerset Trust for Nature Conservation has title to just under 100 acres, but unfortunately this is in several blocks. English Nature owns 69 acres, which it uses for testing various farming practices and seed mixes, and this land is an official part of the Somerset Levels National Nature Reserve. Some 2,267 acres have been declared Sites of Special Scientific Interest (SSSIs), of which 641 acres are the subject of management agreements with 18 people. The whole area is designated as an Environmentally Sensitive Area (ESA). A small wood contains an active heronry.

Tealham remains an enclave of very different countryside within the general agricultural lands of the Level, with many virtues. Because the fields are divided by long, rough-surfaced tracks called droves, there is access to even the most remote parts. The air is fresh and unpolluted, although the wind

13

occasionally brings a whiff of the cellophane plant at far-off Bridgwater. The wildlife is splendid, ranging from Bewick's swans in winter to drumming snipe in spring and yellow wagtails flirting their tails on the gates for much of the summer. Although the air may be heavy and humid for much of the time because of the high water table, the weather is kinder, the sun more consistent, than in other parts of the West Country. All in all it makes an impressive package. Add to that the friendliness and kindliness of the local people and it is one of the most delightful places in which to live.

TRADITION AND CHANGE - A BACKGROUND TO THE MOORS

Tealham Moor forms a low-lying, distinctive, separate area on its own. It used to be peaty marsh grazing, much of it permanently flooded and still has a hint of the wilderness behind its grazed surface. It is a land of contrasts and tradition which has a sense of being apart from surrounding areas, so Tealham and Tadham still retain that sense of unity and apartness, although for how long this will continue has concerned many people in recent years.

This part of the Levels remains traditional. Most of it is permanent pasture, farmed in the old way. It is fed with farmyard manure, and most of it has remained unploughed throughout its known history and produces fine hay. Up to a few years ago this grassland was a source of great quantities of milk and the Friesian cow was the producer of that liquid gold.

In recent years, however, a number of changes have occurred, changes which seem dramatic to anyone who has lived here while they take place. Beef cattle and sheep appear to have taken over from the milking herds. When we first came you could hear the engines on the bails (mobile milking sheds) running every morning and the black and white shapes of Friesians

15

dominated the landscape. Now we have cross-bred herds of beige and brown cattle running in the fields, of Charolais and other alien blood, and you are liable to meet a flock of sheep on the road at anytime as they are moved around the moors. Cows are still milked but they are concentrated on larger dairies and in sizable herds. The European Community (EC) milk quotas have had their effect and things will never be quite the same again. But for all that it remains a land of green grass and huge open spaces. Lapwings pour up into the great open skies in huge twists like ascending spirals of smoke from some unseen bonfire. The heron still fishes the open rhyne.

Wedmore, a quiet village overlooking the moors, where Alfred signed a peace with Guthrum the Dane in 878 AD.

16

The Somerset Levels have a long and fascinating history and have been at the heart of the development of this county. Waves of rebellion, religion and teaching have swept up to their edges or started from their centre while King Arthur dominates the countryside in legend. The first real bringing together of the major parts of the English nation took place at Wedmore, a quiet village sitting above our moors, where King Alfred signed a peace with Guthrum the Dane in 878 AD, which led to a considerable period of stability. Joseph of Arimathea is said to have planted his stick at Glastonbury, where it grew and flowered on Christmas Day. A ceremony is still held to this day, when sprigs are cut from the Holy Thorn and sent to the Queen, and they do indeed flower at Christmas. Here too is the scene of one of the last battles on English soil, when the followers of the Duke of Monmouth, the 'pitchfork' army, were defeated by the Royal forces.

The Levels run from the mouth of the River Parrett, in Bridgwater Bay, to the great dominant island of Glastonbury on one side of the Polden Hills, and to West Sedgemoor and Langport on the other. They form a great depression running into the heart of Somerset. The area is at sea-level, only prevented from flooding by artificial means. The tide range in the Bristol Channel is nearly 40 feet at spring tides, so a nominal elevation of 10 feet or so means the land is well below sea-level for part of the time.

Since time immemorial they have been known as the 'Summer Lands', a place of rich grazing once winter floods dropped and the enriching silts from upland rivers had settled into the soil. Somerset is said to have taken its name from this early practice.

Drainage of this vast area started with the monks of Glastonbury Abbey some 800 years ago and continues to this day, but it is only since the Second World War that the pace of change has accelerated. In the last few years it has moved so fast that many people have become worried about the consequences. The system is based on canalised rivers, straightforward canals or drains, rhynes and pumping stations. It has continued over the centuries with even the ubiquitous Dutch involved at some stage, though they have not always

17

been popular here. The great Admiral Blake, who was born in Bridgwater, sailed the seas with a broom tied to his masthead to show his determination to rid the seas of those Dutch. He was a noted Parliamentarian, fighting doughtily under the leadership of Oliver Cromwell, for the people hereabouts have always held the middle ground, conservative in many matters, but prepared to fight for freedom.

Tealham and Tadham Moors are set to the south and west of the growing and prosperous village of Wedmore. They form a quite distinct entity though they may appear like the surrounding areas. The fields look not dissimilar but there are considerable differences in their character, sward and general feel, as well as in the wildlife. The main reason for this is that they form a lower-lying basin than the moors around. It may only be a matter of inches but it is enough to give them a distinct character. Ditches show how high the water table is, while small boreholes drilled in the centres of the fields sometimes show water lying only 2 or 3 inches down.

The northern boundary is formed by the Isle of Wedmore, a gently rising ridge which divides the moors from Cheddar to the north, never exceeding 200 feet and much of it a mere 60 feet or so above sea-level. In medieval times this was a true island in a vast sea of reeds and stagnant marshes. When we first came here it was more liable to flooding in the winter than it is now, and the Isle was, at times, seen to stand above a silver, shining sea which ran up from Mark to Glastonbury. The Tor, the Isle of Wedmore and Brent Knoll were outposts, refuges where villages could be built with safety. All else was insubstantial, liable to disappear under the waters, not suitable for putting down roots.

Every winter, before the pumping station was completed more than 30 years ago, the whole area flooded, and remained flooded until the long winter rains stopped. Autumnal and vernal equinoxes, with their exaggerated tides, increased the flood plain until the island stood in a great inland sea stretching as far as the eye could see. On rare occasions we have woken to this sight, when the place is like some enchanted, faerie scene, glittering, silver, with

willows rising from the reed-fringed and hidden bounds of the fields. It is as if the house has been moved overnight to some new corner of England: an estuary newly emerged from an earthquake-altered land-mass. Swans float where they grazed but hours before, and great flights of wigeon tear across the huge, open skies.

To the south the ground starts rising, at first imperceptibly, beyond the line of the River Brue, with its flood banking, to the low but commanding ridge of the Polden Hills. This separates the two arms of the Levels and is lined with dormitory villages serving the market and industrial town of Bridgwater. They have splendid views northward to us and south over the battlefield of Sedgemoor at Bussex, near the villages of Westonzoyland and Middlezoy – fine old Somerset names.

Tadham Moor ends on the road from Wedmore to Glastonbury; beyond lies Godney, a tiny settlement of ancient cottages strung along the River Sheppey, a branch of the Brue. To the east of that, the character of the land changes. It can be seen to be different, higher by a few inches, more conventionally

The Isle stands above a silver, shining sea. Bewick's swans in winter floods, Tealham Moor.

19

agricultural. The visual boundary, the edge of the Levels themselves, comes with the great cone of Glastonbury Tor, its stark church-tower on the very top dominating one end. To the west, another hill catches the eye – Brent Knoll, a well-known landmark on the M5 on its way down to Devon.

The natural boundaries of Tealham and Tadham Moors are of water. The ancient rhynes, ditches and drains define the area, setting it between the Brue in the south and Little Rhyne, which follows the bottom contour of the Isle of Wedmore. The area between, 'our' moors, is the original, unimproved flood-pasture of ancient Somerset. It has a special vegetation and bird-life of its own.

The grass is not green in summer, it is a curious red-brown shade, from the sorrel and various types of grass and herbs in the 'unimproved' sward. In spring it dances and waves with untold numbers of palest lilac cuckoo flowers. Before that, each rhyne is lined with the brilliant yellow of kingcups. Later a richer shade of yellow edges the water, that of yellow iris. Only in winter

In spring the moors dance and wave with untold numbers of palest lilac cuckoo flowers.

do you see brilliant greens, when shallow pools of water snake up the fields after prolonged rain, and sunlight catches the tips of grass growing through the water. When the background is dark with storm, and the light pierces through to the grass below, the colour is brilliant emerald – brighter even than the fabled greens of Ireland. But for most of the time the pastures give no hint of the high water table beneath. Its natural russet is the dry, dusty colour of high summer in drier parts.

Before the war, the moors must have looked in winter as they had for the past century. Floods continued for much of the winter and the waters were home to vast numbers of wildfowl, as they were in pre-historic times. When excavating the famous lake-villages at nearby Meare, archaeologists discovered the remains of 27 varieties of bird. One of the most numerous was the pelican, which is no longer found in Britain but is very much a wetland bird. The rest included many different ducks, two types of heron, several seabirds and the white-tailed sea-eagle. It is interesting to see that the swan species found was the whooper. Our present-day wild swan is the Bewick.

The area's connection with wildfowl is shown by some of the names of farms and localities: Tealham, Decoy Pool Farm, and Decoy Pool Wood. In times gone by, many people must have made their living from the ducks and geese pouring in during the autumn and the meat must have fed a great many families. A hundred years ago one particular man was said to have made his living solely from collecting and selling wild duck eggs. Older people recall when boats were a part of life on the moors and the adventures they had in winter, making their way across the water to court girls who lived out on the heath.

The great hordes of birds now visit only at times of great flooding, or hard weather on the coast, and many of the farms and cottages on the heath have been abandoned, but the same spirit still exists in the people who remember it all.

Our cottage is only 50 feet or so above sea-level but the house, and more particularly the orchard, command an extensive sweep of country. The little bump of Keyton Hill, below which we stand, is 117 feet high but has some of the

21

finest views anywhere, because of the very flatness and spread of these moors. The apparent height gives an aerial view of a magic kingdom of miniature black and white cows, crawling tractors and silver threads of water. On a clear day the Poldens look close enough to touch, the toy houses three-dimensional and clear-cut. Glastonbury Tor is magnified, but shimmers with the distance.

But the real importance, the excitement, the interest, lies down below, not at the edges of our vision. Long lines of silver divide the fields horizontally and vertically into a coloured patchwork, green in winter and red-brown in high summer. These fields are permanent pasture, owned individually by a scattering of farmers. Access to many is along the droves that dissect the moors. Few parcels of land have a ring-fence. Ownership is divided and has changed continually over the years, as land is parcelled out amongst sons and daughters with the death of the farmer.

The area is rich in local history. Once, poking around in a tangle of brambles near the North Drain, we were amazed to find a broken-down wall, then more signs of life. A fireplace appeared and perhaps the slope of an outhouse. As the eye became adjusted to the shapes within the scrub and brambles, we saw that the remains of several cottages were scattered throughout this particular part. In this enclosed, wooded, scrub-covered area we noticed a couple of ancient, convoluted and lichen-covered apple trees and other cultivated shrubs gone wild, showing that this must have been a settlement at some time.

We asked Mrs Hazel Hudson of Wedmore, who is an expert on local history, about this 'deserted village', and discovered that these ancient-seeming ruins had in fact been inhabited within living memory. The hamlet can be seen on the map of 1886, and an earlier census showed John Veal and William Roper, Joseph Roper, George Row and Charles Hill living there between 1820 and 1840. But the settlement and farm could have been in existence before the start of the last century as enclosures took place in 1791. Before then Tealham and Tadham Moors were common land, preserved as such with great rigidity, and no one could build there. After enclosure anyone who was able to obtain

The remains of the 'deserted' village, long since abandoned in favour of a kinder living up on the hill.

title or who could build a house and light a fire in it within 24 hours, was entitled to possession. Tealham Moor remained free from houses and cottages, since it was controlled by Blackford Manor, but Tadham became dotted with cottages and farms, few of which have survived.

Sand Drove Farm was the heart of the hamlet we had found. Around it were a number of small enclosures, each with an apparently minute cottage on it. One of these was an ale-house, selling beer and cider. Some of the cottages may have been insubstantial, but the farm was stone-built, large and solid – yet it is gone with the rest, just a hump beside the drove. Why?

23

One reason may have been emigration. It seems that no less than one in four parish inhabitants emigrated to America and Australia after the mid-1800s. The poor were very poor and lived in damp and uncomfortable conditions with extremely low wages, so many left when the opportunities in the New World became known and ships offered a chance to escape. However, this particular group of houses remained inhabited until just before the Second World War. You can still see the apple tree bearing fruit outside one of these cottages.

In the old days people living out on the moors expected to be flooded for much of the winter. Kitchens were moved upstairs and a boat was tied to an upper window, as people made ready for the transformation of the moors into a flooded lake. Two or three of these old houses still exist. One person told me that he courted a young lady down on one of these small farms. He would bicycle down Jack's Drove and if, by a certain point, the water had risen no higher than the wheel-spindle, he knew he could get through. Otherwise it was too dangerous except by boat. The names of the inhabitants have not changed much over the years. Some years ago there was an exhibition of records and relics from the past in the village hall. Among these was a school register from a couple of hundred years ago. The names of the pupils included many found in my daughter's class at the primary school and those which figure on the deeds of present-day moorland fields. This is a situation that is changing, however. Farms are reducing and paring what little labour force they have and larger ones absorb the smaller. Now many local children look to London and Bristol for work. My daughter's fellow pupils are scattered throughout Britain and some abroad, and a structure that held from medieval times has been splintered in one generation.

The moorland fields appear normal grassland, such as is found anywhere in the West Country, but the chocolate-coloured edges to the ditches betray the alien soils beneath. Between 4 and 15 feet of peat sits on an impermeable clay subsoil, the rich pressings and harvests of aeons of prehistoric scrub and forest. In nearby Shapwick, peat is dug in huge quantities. Some commercial peat-digging also takes place on one small part of Tadham Moor. The world appears to have an insatiable appetite for this inert material, which is used for breaking down heavy soils, producing potting composts and even burning – although that is far less common nowadays.

Out on these fields it is the essential ingredient, the sponge which holds the water in the pastures to provide our rich summer grazings. Although the moors are all peat, they are not violently acidic like the peat bogs of Ireland or the Highlands. The Mendips nearby, and the underlying rocks, are limestone and this, in conjunction with the acid conditions natural to peat, produce a near-neutral pH, as is shown by the mix and richness of the herbage.

Water is the dominating feature of moorland life. It dictates when the beasts may be put out to graze and the yield of individual fields. Water levels, flooding and drought still determine how the Levels are farmed and define also the charm of the area for those who enjoy it for its own, unique sake.

Though some of the more remote parts are hedged, much of Tealham and Tadham is edged only by water. Rhynes and drainage ditches surround

The mix and richness of the herbage indicates the near neutral PH of the moors.

each field and every walk takes you along and across water. There is a wave of movement a constant few feet in front of anyone walking along a ditch, caused by an army of sticklebacks and other creatures disturbed by the vibration of their feet. This vibration is a feature of the moors. Cattle moving along a field, even small children tapping their feet, can set up a movement which makes one realise that the topsoil is floating on a spongy, semi-liquid underpan. This may be demonstrated in a rather nerve-racking manner on the roads. As a tractor or lorry passes, the whole surface will be felt to ripple. It is like standing on a trampoline with someone bouncing on the other end.

The roads are literally floating, as their foundations consist of stone rafts hanging in the soft peat soil. In drought years this soil dries out, in spite of the high water-table, and sections of the road subside. Part of the problem must arise from the capillary effects which cause the water-table to vary considerably within the same field and surrounding ditches. Dips and hills appear and the Council has to level these with stones and tarmac. This is a continuing and, no doubt, expensive process. A small road running up to the Polden Hills has had no such treatment in the last few years and one section is just like a switchback, causing low-slung cars to ground unless driven gently.

Some years ago, archaeologists dug up an ancient roadway through the moors. It was discovered by a peat digger after whom it is named – the Sweetway. It consisted of mats of willow floating on the peat, supporting logs, stones and other materials which formed the path. The structure was flexible enough to provide a practical causeway across the worst of the ancient marshes before drainage had been thought about. On a recent trip to Holland I found this ancient method was still in use for a project involving the latest in high technology. The massive earthworks for the Delta Plan, an ambitious attempt to shut off a major part of the Maas, are stabilised with mats of willow in exactly the same manner.

In summer we look across from our windows at fields with browning centres and bright green edges where the ditches surround them. Beyond the first few fields lies the wide line of the North Drain, the key to the complicated man-made drainage system. This is a broad canal that converges with the River Brue, via a pumping station down on the moors and flows thence to the sea at Highbridge. The Brue is seen as a line of banking in the far distance, running across the moor behind raised flood-banks. It is a muddy, featureless river, which rises quickly with rains in the Mendips and subsides even more quickly when the great tidal gates are opened near Highbridge at low water.

The Ordnance Survey map shows the complexity of the system that keeps the area drained and workable, enabling a great many people to live effectively below sea-level. With such a huge range of tidal height – second only to the Bay of Fundy in Canada – median sea-level means little. Someone living at sea-level in the conventional sense, will find themselves 15 or 20 feet below actual sea-level at spring tides – not a comforting thought on a stormy night! Maps of the region show an amazing network of ditches and rhynes. In parts the veining of blue on the map dominates everything, the lines appearing to touch and blend into each other, more water than land.

Normally the great sluices on the Huntspill River near Highbridge are opened for a few hours round low water, then the accumulation of fresh water surges out into the Severn Estuary. In certain conditions, when the sea is piled up in the estuary by a combination of neap tides and south-westerly gales, there may be no differential between the levels on either side of the sluices. In extreme cases there may even be pressures in the opposite direction. Then the waters remain in the inland network of drains, rhynes and ditches and are swollen further by rain or the run-off from the hills, finally rising to overflow the banks. Then all the pumping capacity is useless and we are back to the medieval conditions of flood-swamp.

Flash floods occur extremely rapidly in dry summer weather if the downpour is sufficient. The crusted-over peat below the surface is temporarily impervious to the water and there is no capacity to absorb the surplus, for peat has quite different properties when wet and dry. If it is allowed to dry off completely, it forms a rock-like crust which is virtually impermeable. It does not then suck in water like blotting paper, as it does when it is in a moist state – quite the

When the great reservoir of the Levels has absorbed as much as it is able, the waters rise quickly and overflow the banks.

opposite. It is as if the peat changes its chemical formula and becomes a different substance.

Normally the process of water build-up is slow and deliberate. If you observe closely, the whole cycle may be forecast, for there are optimum conditions for flooding. This may occur in early February, for instance, when there has been a period of hard rain followed by a big freeze. Then the surface of the ground ceases to absorb more moisture. Further heavy rain completes the process. Often there is a gap of a day between the heavy rains and the flooding. The run-off from the hills seems to take this much time to come down. During this period, the waters rise in the fields, runnels fill and join, sheets of water form shallow lakes to one side, but the river and drains remain low. Then a surge rushes down river and it quickly brims the banks. Water flows over the top from swollen rhynes and drains and erstwhile isolated lakes spread into a continuity of water.

It is a wonderful sight when the floodwaters cover all the moors. You wake up to a completely new landscape. Tealham has become an estuary, and for a few hours it is as if you live by the sea. You imagine a sail creeping round the corner, drifting in with the tide.

This happens less and less now, as control becomes greater, with new, improved equipment. When we first came, flooding was frequent and long-lasting. Sometimes Jack's Drove, the road bisecting the two moors, vanished completely in winter, particularly during that second long spell of rain which so often occurs around Christmas. All that could be seen were the gates on either side and the occasional tree. In the old days this state was so common that most droves and roads had a line of willows planted along one side to show where the hard standing was to be found. On either side of the road are deep, muddy ditches, and when everything is hidden beneath the water, it is easy to step off the solid ground and vanish into the hidden ditch.

The floods are shallow out on the fields, though sometimes deep enough for a canoe to navigate. The place is so large, so flat, that the water spreads out for miles and is rarely more than Wellington-boot deep, except in the dips and tussocks of the rougher pastures. Those few alders and willows which are still left stand in a shining silver lake, forming the line marking a drove. The positions of the rhynes are indicated by fringes of dead grass and reeds which catch the late slanting rays of the winter sun and momentarily glow golden-bright. It is an enchanted scene.

Sometimes it has its tragic moments. In 1968 there were flash floods in June and an old man was drowned in his upstairs bedroom in nearby Blackford when the brook broke its banks after extremely heavy, continuous rain. Wedmore was very badly flooded and damaged at the same time. I was away and my

29

My eldest daughter, Fiona, standing in what remained of the road after the great summer floods of 1968.

wife spent a harrowing night trying to hold off rising waters from coming into the house. At first she thought it was simply the rain filling the ditch round the house because of blocked drains, but it was far worse than that. Water was pouring out of the ground from springs on the top of and on the sides of the hill. There have always been such springs on the hill; one runs continuously in the yard of a neighbour, its volume never varying, however great the rainfall. It is said that these springs form a system common with neighbouring Wales. The waters run under pressure beneath the Bristol Channel.

Eventually, after keeping the inrush at bay by all sorts of means, including brooms, buckets and bags, Romey gave in when water started coming up the

bath and through the old flagstones. It is a sobering thought that whatever technological devices are installed, however the basic drainage is improved, the occasional act of God will wreak its will, regardless.

Nowadays, our moorland floods last but a few hours before the pumps catch up and send the water on its way. With increasingly controlled and directed pumping, there has been a considerable reduction in the number and duration of floods. It is argued by some older people that this regime has caused the loss of some positive benefits to agriculture. The old, regular winter flooding brought with it life-giving silt from other areas. This fed the neutral peat and produced wonderful crops of grass from otherwise unfertilised land. In some parts of Somerset this deliberate flooding continues, with benefit to the land. In midwinter our area still seems like wild and untamed country to our visitors, but we have watched the changes over the years, and it is tamer, more controlled, more scientifically farmed than previously.

Long periods of flooding bring with them times of breathtaking beauty, as well as grey, windlashed days when only a masochist, or someone with work to do outside, ventures forth. Days of screaming winds whipping across the great shallow floods, or times of silent tranquillity when not a breath stirs, are part of the fabric of life in this special area. We watch entranced as floods freeze, then fall as sluices clear the surplus, while the ice cracks like thunder and the edges round the rhynes darken and yellow with peat stains.

In certain lights the icy landscape assumes this underlying peat-yellow colour across a whole field. It gives a strange, surrealistic appearance, the winter-bare willows gaunt and skeletal against a pale evening sky. It is the quintessential landscape of England, understated, ancient and beautiful through its subtlety. People venture out into it and become something more than their normal, workaday selves. There is a spice of adventure about wandering these deserted crackling-cold fields with water and ice stretching widely on either side. It has a magic of its own.

Others who feel the special atmosphere of the moors, are to be found among the fishermen who haunt the North Drain. Some look upon it only as

31

Two of the great army of fishermen who enjoy the North Drain whatever the weather.

another piece of fine fishing water but others, I know, feel far more strongly about it. Among their numbers are some of the finest naturalists around. They are entertained by sightings of kingfishers and mink, kestrels dropping down onto prey, or a stoat dancing to hypnotise a rabbit before pouncing. One keen fisherman is a skilled wildlife photographer and keeps his camera with him at all times. He has recorded some of these scenes most beautifully. Fishermen are very persistent souls, prepared to sit and wait all day for that one magic moment.

Important in the landscape, they form an essential part of the jigsaw which goes to make up the moors. At times there are many of them – during major angling competitions, when they throng the banks – but mostly they are lost in the total space. The only complaint that can be raised concerns some of the fine line which may be discarded or lost. This near-invisible and virtually indestructible substance can be lethal to wildlife. The fishing community is becoming more aware of this problem and their bailiffs are trying to put the message over that odds and ends of line left lying around may mean agonising death to swans and other water birds. I hope the message gets through.

There are fish in the North Drain and many are sizable, as was seen at the time of the great summer floods of 1968. Large amounts of nutrients were washed into the water and the rich crop of grass rotted under the water. All this combined to rob the water of its natural oxygen. Many fish drowned, and it was amazing to see what appeared after a few days. Huge pike and many other species came to the surface in the rhynes and ditches, gasping and mouthing until they died and, in turn, robbed the water of more oxygen as they decayed. I had no idea that such large creatures were to be found in our waters - some of the pike were over 3 feet long, deep in body and well muscled.

Just occasionally you are vouchsafed a glimpse into another world. One day in early September we came across a freak of light which allowed us, without benefit of polarising glasses, to look into the water and see what was going on in that very different world. It only lasted a few minutes, but it

Just occasionally you are vouchsafed a glimpse of another world – nine-spined stickleback in the dark peat waters.

33

transformed my ideas of the dark and mysterious North Drain. Its peat-black bottom reflects no light in normal times, absorbing even the brightest day – its normal, essential attractiveness is provided by the green duckweed and waterlilies of summer and the patterns of wind or ice in winter. That day the light streamed into the bottom without obstruction, catching the backs of shoals of small fish. There was little colour – only the great banks of submerged plants on the very bottom showed a pale gold and green. They waved and shimmered as the fish swam over and as the slow current tugged at them. Some looked like large under-water lettuces, luscious in their luxuriant growth, while stems of fennel-leaved pondweed grew straight up, forming forests in the depths and fanning out in beautiful clear green shapes on the surface. Small fish swam in and out of these stems, though the occasional larger fish could be seen but they were much more wary, moving off as soon as we saw them. Then, as quickly as this remarkable and unexpectedly busy scene had appeared, it was gone.

One welcome change is that verges and rhyne edges are regenerating once more, after years of heavy cutting. Councils can no longer afford more than the bare minimum dictated by safety. Lawn-like finishes always were inappropriate for the deep countryside.

It has been wonderful to see the first touches of colour appearing among the tangle of grasses – willow-herbs, cranesbill and purple loosestrife, Queen Anne's lace and meadow rue, with many others.

Trees have also profited. Within a year a spike of bright green appeared; an alder seedling had succeeded in maintaining a precarious hold and established itself. Now it is some 10 feet high, even after its top had been lopped. The Drainage Board sent its contractor to clear the ditch and, although he left the naturally regenerated trees, he decided to lop the tops of most of them. I hope this is not a first step in removing them completely. The trees are pleasant to look at and serve a real need. Finches feed on the alder seeds, which are also popular with wild ducks. The trees also provide much needed perches and cover for small birds in an area which is far too bare and desolate nowadays.

Older moor people will tell you that trees help to stabilise the banks of rhynes and reduce the amount of clearing needed.

The next year saw the arrival of three or four more alders, and now there is a row of neat-leaved alders growing all along the rhyne south of the North Drain. At last there is a chance that the bare moorland may return to the appearance of years ago, with willows and alders lining the edges of droves and roads. It is a slim chance, however; machine ditch clearance takes precedence over everything. There is no spare labour to pollard willows regularly and no demand for the willow poles or smaller wands. As in so much of the country, we are dependent on the goodwill of the farmers to keep up or create the beautiful countryside we desire and which is so much more suitable for wildlife than efficient, bare, modern fields. Fortunately, recent ESA payments, and other grants, have made these operations affordable and the situation may change in the future.

Farmers are as fond as anyone of this landscape but they are forced to run their land economically, and have little time for jobs which do not strictly pay. This is the dilemma. However, Government appears at last to be doing something about it, as we shall see.

The moors we look over are special, unique. They form a large area of quite distinct pattern and methods of agriculture. They are flat, not even green, yet they are beautiful, distinctive, fascinating and, above all, largely empty. In the whole area of Tealham and Tadham, there are but half-a-dozen houses on the low-lying moors. From our house we look out at a ring of lights at night, but they are far-off, those of Glastonbury, Bridgwater, the edges of the Quantocks and the Poldens. In between it is dark, empty of people, inhabited only by cows, sheep, drumming snipe and restless lapwings.

The most distinctive features are the huge and varying skies, the ever-changing light, from hazy views to the crystal clarity of vision after rain, and the coming and going of the perimeter of hills which give scale to it all. Other memories come from the infinitely beautiful, infinitely sad calls of the curlew or the skirling, combative sounds of innumerable lapwings, as the cries come up the hill on a summer evening. The moors draw their charm from this infinity of sound, colour and depth of vision, not the siren shapes of great mountains and glens. It is a subtle vision, to be savoured slowly.

Changes

However, when I read through the notes and diaries on which this book is based I realised that I was writing about the past, not the present. It was a lyrical view of something which was gradually vanishing. Like anything with which one is completely familiar, the changes are difficult to comprehend on a day-to-day basis, but they are there. I decided it was time to take another, up to date, and objective look and set out these changes and their effects on the area, to see where it was all leading. I talked to water authorities, conservation groups and individuals and drew conclusions which were not always happy, before reporting on these in the remainder of the book.

The most significant change is the result of more effective drainage. The fields feel different; they no longer quake when cattle or people walk over them, although roads still ripple as 38 tonne vehicles pound their way across, loaded with bagged peat or stone.

The moorland soil is drying out and this has brought with it changes to farming methods, reductions in wildlife and, surprisingly, reductions in some agricultural output – although the latter has certainly not been the aim of those promoting drainage schemes. The basic fact is that technology has introduced the potential to control water levels absolutely. We have seized the opportunity and gone for the kill, without thinking about the consequences.

However, we are now in the middle of a revolution in thinking, arising from the overproduction of so many agricultural products throughout Europe. This has led to a complete reappraisal of subsidies, which were previously geared to encouraging more production, whatever the cost to the land. Up to then there had been a philosophy which led to the continual 'improvement' of marginal land such as marshes, heaths and upland moors. Now farmers are being paid to set land aside, quotas have been introduced for milk and production subsidies are being reduced. And this trend is expected to continue.

The most important catalyst for further change is this new attitude to farming. While still considered a most important industry, it is no longer above market forces, something to be pushed without any thought except increasing production. Farming is now facing the same problems which have been at the heart of industrial thinking over the last decade – how to improve efficiency, while meeting the demands of the market and what it is prepared to pay.

It used to be thought that the way to increase profits was to push continually the edge of production, by increasing the use of fertiliser until returns almost met the extra costs – marginal costing. Now people are examining minimum-cost farming, improving profitability by reducing costs. Much of the Somerset Levels is well suited to this philosophy, as they are naturally fertile and highly productive permanent pastures, provided water levels are kept high.

Fortunately for the moors, this change has not meant abandoning a way of life. Special payments have been made available to help preserve wildlife habitats, or to maintain a way of life, in areas of Britain which are deemed of special value in one form or another. Tealham and Tadham are able to benefit from these payments, as they are included in such an area. However indications are that, in spite of these apparently beneficial payments, which are accepted by a majority of farmers, the destruction of the moors is continuing, as overall drainage bites deeper and the land dries out.

The forces driving these events are not just local, indeed it is fair to say that worldwide, as well as European, politics are likely to affect us more here than purely British events. Some of the payments under these new schemes are EU-inspired. But I am glad to say that I can discern more than a glimmer of light for the future. Although I am cynical about the reasons for the apparent 'greening' of Government, nevertheless it is leading to a new assessment of values. Hopefully Tealham and Tadham will benefit from this fresh view of the value of the environment to people and wildlife.

A LIVING FROM THE MOORS

It has never been easy to make a living out on the moors. Comparatively few people have tried to live purely from this once hostile environment. Most have used the moors as an adjunct to their other lands on the hills or have worked on them as a part of another, more widely-based, occupation.

Farming is the main activity. Few farmers live out on the moors these days, in contrast to the mid-1800s, when many more cottagers and farmers had homes there, mainly on Tadham. Most were casual labourers or people with smallholdings who also worked for other farmers. There are others now. A boarding kennels has been constructed on the site of a smallholding which was sold off when the owner retired in 1989. Another person has an ornamental-fish farm. A small peat works processes peat dug partly on Tadham and partly on Westhay Moor. English Nature and the Somerset Trust for Nature Conservation have reserves on the moors, but even they depend on farming to keep the land in the right state for their birds, mammals, invertebrates and flora to enjoy the perfect conditions. This requires cattle to graze at the right time and in the right numbers. The remainder of the area is

given over to straightforward farming. It is the farmers who have the burden as well as the pleasure of keeping the landscape as beautiful as it is.

There have been enormous changes in lifestyle, farming practices and the comparative prosperity of those who make their living off Tealham and Tadham Moors, even in the last 40 years. The character of the land has changed in stages, from rough and wet ground, much of it with pools of water remaining throughout the year, to almost dry pasture with little water standing even in winter. This has all occurred in living memory.

Farming has changed from limited summer grazing for milk to longer seasons with a mixed population of beef, milking cows and sheep, which are now important users of the grass. Arable farming came briefly and then its further expansion was halted as the unique nature of the environment was realised, while some arable land has reverted to the original permanent pasture after initial trials.

People living out on the moors have changed from a sub-basic existence, with houses flooding every winter to a lifestyle comparable with people

People living out on the moors have moved from a sub-basic existence, with flooding every winter.

living on the higher ground. Newcomers have moved in, rebuilt the old cottages whose walls previously sat in water, and set up new enterprises. The casual labourers, who hired themselves out to ditch, dig peat and cut willows for various uses, no longer live out there. Contractors using bright yellow diggers come in from outside to clear the ditches. But farmers still farm there and the land is still productive and kindly, with its mild climate, low rainfall and maintained water table.

The changes have been so great that it is difficult to view them objectively as an outsider. Twenty-seven years may seem a long time to live in an area, but it is but a moment in the life and evolution of the countryside. Thousands of years of flooded peat wilderness has changed in just over 150 years to green countryside indistinguishable to the casual visitor from the surrounding areas. The last 40 years have seen the most violent change, from stagnant, semi-drained marshes, to a completely man-controlled environment. To try and obtain a better understanding of the impact of these developments on individual lives, I visited and talked to a number of people who have seen this happen.

I selected these people for their widely varying outlooks and differing connections with the moors: a farmer and contractor, with his wife, who now pursue another career after 45 years on the land; a younger dairy farmer who has the special outlook of the cheesemaker and who has seen threats to his livelihood come and go; a self-employed carpenter born and bred in the same house overlooking the heath; and a farmer who has changed over to beef and sheep and is also a district councillor, known for his wide interest in reconciling farming and conservation interests and fitting them into the wider needs of society as a whole. Their stories provide a fascinating snapshot of life in living memory, and adds weight and colour to the recorded history of Somerset and this area.

I found the process fascinating; so many memories of this very different world will soon be lost, and became convinced that the changes in lifestyle on the moors are about as violent as anything observed in this country. The life of the casual labourer, flooded for much of the winter and racked with rheumatism and arthritis in the damp atmosphere, must have been as close to a Third-World peasant existence as it is possible to imagine in our modern country. They have produced a race of sturdy self-reliant people who are now filling a variety of roles and occupations. Looking out over those silver-edged green fields it is difficult to imagine that such a life could have been endured within a mile of the house – and so recently. It needed recording. It is a slice of history our children and grandchildren will never know about otherwise.

John and Doreen Duckett – moorland farmers and contractors
Our friends and neighbours the Ducketts are real moorland people. The deeds of our cottage originated in the late 1800s, when it was bought from Landsend Farm which was then, as now, owned by their family.

John's grandfather was an entrepreneur who ended up owning several farms, including Landsend, Walnut Tree and Splott. He also ran Heath House Mill – a remarkable man. One of his roads to wealth was by leasing out sheep or cattle to people. They paid him by the week and were able to build up herds with little capital. In this he was well ahead of his time. Apparently he was compassionate in this business, assessing repayments according to how much he thought a man could afford. Eventually, after a variety of adventures, including joining the army, John's father went away to Gloucester to farm but returned to Landsend when John was four, where he has been ever since.

It is difficult to appreciate just how people made a living 50 years and more ago. John remembers as many as twenty horses and carts out on the moors early in the morning. In those days many people kept only five cows, and might bring back as little as one churn of milk (17 gallons in those days), yet they survived on this. The milk was taken back to the dairies at the farms and cooled. John and his brother and sister used to harness the horse at six o'clock in the morning, milk out on the moor, bring the milk back, cool it, push the churns ¼ mile to where the communal milk stand was, then run a mile across Keyton Hill to Blackford School, often without time for breakfast, or else eating as they ran. For all that they were a high-spirited lot. One day they came back with

41

the trolley in the evening and decided to ride it down the hill. Inevitably, they crashed into a wall when they were unable to round the corner at the bottom. They arrived home with scratched and bloody heads – as well as a broken handle on the trolley. Their father took one look and insisted that they put a new handle on immediately.

It was a hard life but the boys enjoyed their bit of fun for all that. It came out in all sorts of harmless ways. On his way to milking one day, John found a lapwing's nest, all the eggs pointed end down. While the bird was away John solemnly turned all the eggs pointed side up. The next morning he chuckled to see them turned again.

"She must have felt uncomfortable with them all sticking into her," he grinned.

Before John was born, there was a pub in Heath House, the Grouse and Pheasant, run by a lady who was known as Silver Ginny. When the children were young there were still many stories being told about her. She was a real character and the tale was told that one night she went up over Keyton Hill to Westham to fetch some jars of cider from a farm. She was gone for hours and eventually people went out to look for her. She was found by a gate with her leg broken, helpless. She had visited several farms en route and tasted so many samples that eventually she just could not make it over a gate.

In those days little hay was taken from the fields.

John and Doreen Duckett of Landsend in their tunnel, where so many tomatoes and vegetables are grown for the house and their friends.

Moorland fields were owned or rented by farms based up on the hills, above flood level. Hay was made in cocks on fields close to the farms, and stored in thatched ricks up on the hill. Our previous neighbour, Henry Dean, used to cut thatching spar cocks from roadside willows. These were split into forked ends and twisted in the middle to anchor the thatch.

The moor grounds were only used for grazing and were very heavily stocked during the months it was possible to keep cattle out on them. The moors flooded in October, with the first heavy rain, and stayed marshy and slushy, often completely flooded over, until March. 'February fill-ditch' usually lived up to its name. Normally, cattle were put out again by the end of April. They were left out on the fields until they had 'eaten into the dirt'. Then they were taken off, but moved back on again as soon as the grass had grown, and the process repeated. Productivity was phenomenal for winter flooding brought heavy silting which acted as an excellent fertiliser and allowed this heavy stocking, on ground wet enough to tremble when creatures moved across it. The area had a reputation for high yields of quality milk, though the ground is not so fertile now, in spite of the 'improvements'. When pumping was first proposed, John's father got up at a meeting called to discuss the plan.

"I reckon you'm wasting your money," he said. "The pumping will push it out here and it will go back into the system at Westhay again. It'll go round in a great circle and you'll be pumping the same water several times."

"And," said John, "so it has been ever since."

Peat fuel used to be a recognised part of local life, although cutting had not taken place on Tealham for a long time. John's grandfather had dug three acres close to the bottom of Keyton Hill and for many years this was a huge hollow, full of irises and leathers (reeds). The boys scythed and scythed this and now you would not know it had ever been cut, although it remains a little wetter than the surroundings after periods of rain.

Most labourers were paid monthly, when the milk cheque came. Money was short for everyone, although it is difficult to equate values in the past with those of today. John earned 2/6d a week when he started full-time work

For many years an area once cut for peat was full of 'leathers', yellow flags, which John cut regularly to get rid of them.

on leaving school at fourteen – although he had been milking since he was eight. By the time he was married he was earning £1 week, working for his father. He then approached his father for an increase of 10/-, which was turned down immediately as being unreasonable. He in turn pointed out that this was a bargain.

"I no longer need my shirts washed, and you don't have to provide any food. My wife will be taking it all on." Doreen smiled at this.

"Be off with you. I'll think on it," said his father.

A fortnight later it was agreed. But this still left them short, so Doreen

44

continued to work in the post office in her home village of Ashcott for 1/6d per hour. In summer she might cycle the round trip of 15 miles but in winter took a bus from Wedmore to Glastonbury, then another to Ashcott. The two of them lived in a large bedroom in the farmhouse and cooked on a primus in the same room. Later they saved up enough to buy one of the first black and white television sets. They remember fifteen or so people piled into the bedroom watching the Coronation.

In August and September they went blackberry picking – the blackberries on Tealham were a month earlier than elsewhere. They fetched 2d a pound at Mrs Harvey's at the Mill Shop in Heath House and were then packed up in barrels and taken to Wedmore for resale. One day John picked nearly a hundredweight, earning over £2 – more than a week's wages. When the price rose to 6d, everyone in the neighbourhood started picking and spoiled their business, so they stopped. Doreen always loved the time of picking.

John talked about some of the other characters to be found out on the moors. Albie Watts, who I remember as an old man, used to work for John's father at one stage. But he also spent a considerable amount of his own time out on the moors. Albie was mad about eels, and about fishing in general. This was not some casual hobby, but part of his living and way of life. His great joy was 'pecking' and 'ray-balling' for eels.

Ray-balling was a local way of catching eels in the rhynes. A yard of wool was threaded with worms an inch apart, using a bristle taken from a broom. The wool was lightly gathered up with a piece of thread and attached to a 10 foot pole by a bit of bicycle mudguard stay to give spring. The ray-ball was then dropped into the water and jiggled up and down. Eels would grab the worms and hang onto the wool, which helped by snagging their teeth. They were hauled up and hung over a bucket or basin into which they fell when they let go. Sometimes two or three would grab at once. A good evening might see 12 – 14 pounds of eels; at other times it might be only one or two. Sometimes a pike would grab the eels or even bite off the ray-ball.

Pecking used a flat-bladed, pronged spear to catch eels in the river or

45

rhyne. This was done in daylight, as they needed to see the holes where the eels lay, and demanded still, clear water and good eyesight. They looked for the hole where the eels went into the bottom, then they stabbed down. It needed skill and knowledge, for the eels went in at an angle and they had to judge where they lay. The actual blow would be a couple of feet away from the hole. But it was a cruel method, for the peck cut and squeezed the eels' sides without killing them, and eventually it was outlawed.

The eels were rubbed in ashes to enable them to be held, for they were covered in slime, while the skins were used as virtually unbreakable boot-laces. Another method of fishing, used for catching pike as well as eels, was to cut the end off a Wellington boot and cap the end with a pocket of netting. This was then placed in a fast-flowing piece of water. If you were lucky a pike would swim into the tube but be unable to reverse because of the direction of its fins.

People pay hundreds of pounds now for special equipment but a man like Albie Watts would catch as much as he wanted with home-made bits which cost nothing. As John observed, "It makes you think about how we have progressed!"

Wildfowling was another important part of moorland life. During winter floods, people used to get their boats out, tie blackthorn bushes over them to act as camouflage, and go out after ducks and geese. Nobody had proper gun-punts and fixed guns were not used as they were on the Fens, but 8- and 10-bores abounded and were wielded with enthusiasm. Although John knew of no one who was a full-time professional wildfowler, it was undoubtedly an important part of many families' livelihood. Some sold part of their bag, others fed on the resulting birds which formed an important part of their diet.

Twice a year people used to come in for a day's snipe shooting across the moors. In those days snipe were present in large numbers, but were still extremely difficult to shoot. Experts developed a technique of shooting within yards of the birds taking off. To be successful it was necessary to hit the bird while it was flying straight and level, before it started jinking. This demanded amazing reflexes and keen eyesight and only a few people developed this skill. Experienced snipe-shooters were recognised by the feathers in their hats.

After marrying, the boys developed a second career in addition to their farm work. They would be out milking at 5.30 am and then would move on to ditching at 7.30. Their day would often extend over twenty hours and this is how they built up their business. Within a few years they were ditching for people over most of the moors, handling 3,500 ropes of ditches by the end (a rope was 7 yards and was the official method of measuring this type of work). This led on to a much bigger contracting business which they ran together after the death of their father, continuing for eleven years. They even contracted to keep the lanes clear of snow from Watchfield Inn to Cheddar, which could involve working all night, huddled under a sack on an open tractor. At one stage they bought an old Morris Cowley, converted to carry five churns on the back, and used it to go down to milking. It had special wheels with bolt-on lugs and was used also for chain-harrowing. Eventually brother Bill took over his father-in-law's farm and John ran Landsend. At its peak this farm had 70 acres of owned land and rented another 70 or so.

The war brought changes and excitements. There were two army camps up on Great Hill (the farm name for a part of Keyton Hill) and the men used to go up to the shop at Heath House for cigarettes and other purchases. Towards the end of the war German prisoners used to be brought over to clean out the ditches and cut the verges. They had big orange or blue patches on their uniforms, and were accompanied by two or three guards with fixed

Wildfowling was another important part of moorland life in past times. Mallard drake tearing past at top speed.

47

bayonets. However the greatest excitement came the day that Bristol was badly bombed. A German bomber was shot down and crashed on Sweet's peat ground. (The full story of this bomber and its crew is told later in this chapter by Stanley Tucker, who took custody of one of the airmen.) Another vivid memory of these times was that all the fields were covered with reflective strips which the planes dropped to try and fool the radar.

During the war the farm milked between twenty and twenty-five cows, with a horse and cart to provide transport. When John was at school his father bought him an ancient bicycle for £1, so that he could get back faster from school and milk earlier. Unfortunately for his father this did not work out – John used to give rides to the girls and gradually became later and later.

The Ducketts bought their first tractor in 1949 – a grey petrol Ferguson, lightweight, without protection from the weather. The year before that they bought their first milking bail for use out on the moors. This was a mobile, sled-mounted, engine-driven milking machine. Prior to that all milking was by hand. After that first venture, the Duckett brothers were at the forefront in the use of machinery on moor and farm, being among the first to own a digger.

One hardy family lived near the deserted village, by Sand Drove out on Tadham Moor. There were eight or nine of them who were rowed in to the Latcham's tie-up point each day in the winter and then ran in over the hill to Blackford School. They never missed a day. Theirs were always the first signatures in the book and neither rain nor snow put them off. Other children at Blackford would be absent for one reason or another, but not the Fears. Their father generally spent the day in the area or at Wedmore working for local farmers, the Isgars. He would row the children back again in the evening.

In earlier times, before John was born, others also rowed themselves across the moors, but for quite different reasons. Some came all the way from Burtle, under the shadow of the Poldens, to visit the Grouse and Pheasant in Heath House. According to legend, they rowed back by lantern-light, drunk, weaving their way across the dark waters and singing.

The shop at the mill lasted well into his time while his brother and he demolished the windmill itself around 1960, when the structure became dangerous. The mill was still working when he was a lad, but a bungalow stands now where the sails used to creak and groan. A Mr Mutters used to drive a steam lorry over from Cheddar, full of corn and cake for crushing. He would pull the whistle lanyard as the machine left Wedmore so that the mill would be ready for him. Grandfather Duckett ran the mill when John's father was young. One evening his father was riding back to Splott Farm in Blackford, with the takings from the mill, when he ran into a rope tied across the road, placed there by thieves to catch the unwary. He came off heavily but managed to evade the men in the darkness and ran into the farm. So all was not rural peace even in those days.

Icy periods brought extra perils. One man was killed when the ice broke while he was walking a rhyne. The moors were frozen over regularly but around 1963 there was over 18 inches of ice on the rhynes, as they found when

Tractor coming in off the moors on a wild day.

they broke it with a digger. On another occasion John watched three otters swimming along a lightly frozen ditch, coming up every so often by the bank and breaking through to breathe. He told me he had seen quite a few otters out in the fields in his time, but not in recent years. There used to be more kingfishers than now – he was pleased to hear that I had just seen one on the North Drain. Apparently there had once been a little waterfall at the bottom of Great Hill which often held two or three kingfishers; they liked the moving water.

I asked if there were any stories of ghosts or witches in the area.

"Stanley Puddy always said that the ground by Yellow Batches was haunted," said John, "We laughed at this, perhaps unwisely. There was a mound in the field, said to be the remains of a shed, and I was down there with Richard one day when it came up a real storm. A whirlwind blew up all of a sudden all round us and our hair stood on end. It was a most extraordinary feeling. The cows stampeded and rushed round the field and the dog started howling. Suddenly we were chilled to the bone and felt most strange. It all stopped when the sky cleared again and the whole atmosphere changed. We lost our sense of horror. When we talked to Stanley Puddy about this, he told us that an old man was supposed to have committed suicide on that spot. All I can say was that it impressed us and still does to this day."

This led on to the subject of other deaths and strange happenings. In 1968, during the great summer floods, an old man, Ernest Duckett (no relation though all Ducketts are said to have started from Norman origins in the eleventh century), was drowned upstairs in his bedroom at Blackford.

"Who could imagine how deep that water was, looking at Blackford today," said John. "It was way over the top of the signpost on the corner below Sexeys pub. It's a funny thing but after those floods there have never been the fish out on the moors that were there before."

Doreen told me about the gypsies who visited the moors, and an Indian who used to come and sell ties and other things door to door, and who would come in specially for a glass of 'your nice cool milk'. Six or seven gypsy caravans used to arrive every year and park by Westham on the edge of the

Our three girls at the time of the 1968 great summer floods, showing where the water had come, right up to the edge of the moor.

moors. The gypsies made pegs from the wood in the hedges and copses of the area and pushed hard to sell the results.

"One year the Indian arrived and kept on pressing me to buy something. I could not see anything I wanted and we had not much spare money, so I said no. He continued on at me, saying it would be good luck if I bought something. I said no again, so he left, saying that my luck would not be good. Shortly after that a gypsy arrived and much the same happened. I did not want any of her clothes pegs. She was quite blunt and said that I would have bad luck if I did not buy. She also left, but called out that my luck would be bad. Shortly after, my mother died and my father a month later. I have always wondered after that."

51

Some years ago the pressures of running a milking herd on their own became too great for John and Doreen. They had not had a holiday in all their married life and were completely tied to milking. They sold most of the implements and let out the grass as keep. This has been an extremely happy move and they have developed a new life round it. John has just retired after working for years on one of the local peat works, driving a machine for someone else. One of their boys has taken after his father and drives his own digger, as a contractor. The other two have started a successful nursery raising plants under polythene tunnels on the farm land. Hard work is a way of life for the whole family.

Christopher Duckett – farmer and cheesemaker

We have noticed changes over the years, but it is best left to a farmer to describe how these changes have affected him. Christopher Duckett's family has farmed the area for generations. He and his brother – no direct relation to John and Doreen, although they are probably connected somewhere back in history – own nearly 200 acres and rent other fields. As with many farms, most of it is hill ground, but they also farm 70 acres on the moors, and it is an important part of their enterprise. Their way of life is bound up with cattle, permanent pasture and the soft surface of the peat. Their speciality is cheese – not Cheddar as you might expect, but Caerphilly. Apparently this cheese was first produced in this area for the miners of South Wales. It is a very mild white cheese which was said to be particularly kind to the dust-ravaged throats of the miners and it is delicious with fresh bread. Another variety, known as Wedmore cheese, consists of Caerphilly with a layer of chives in the middle. This subtle flavour moves throughout the cheese. The Ducketts supply the majority of their product to wholesalers and much of it goes to pubs and hotels.

The process of cheesemaking is a fascinating and laborious one, demanding constant attention and much hard labour. On a number of occasions I watched fascinated as the product emerged from the milk and ended up as perfect, round cheese. Perhaps the most startling points about the process are the sheer intensity of it, the number of people involved and the amount of washing up and cleaning that takes place. One of the people who work for Christopher told his family he did more washing up in a morning than they did in a week. The whole process is extremely vigorous and hard work, with long periods bent over a deep tank stirring and cutting, but it looks a happy place to work – perhaps that is what makes the cheese so good!

It all starts with 100 gallons of milk being kept overnight in a gleaming stainless steel vat, which is then heated in the morning. A starter is added at this point – a culture which is bought freeze-dried and then used from batch to batch for about four to six months. This mixture is left for an hour until the new day's milk comes in and two hundred gallons of this is added to the mixture and it is all heated to 90 °F. Various tests are then carried out to check acidity and other factors before vegetable rennet is added to form the curd, which eventually becomes the cheese.

The mixture is left for 45 minutes, then cut in three directions with a special knife with angled blades. Then comes the hard

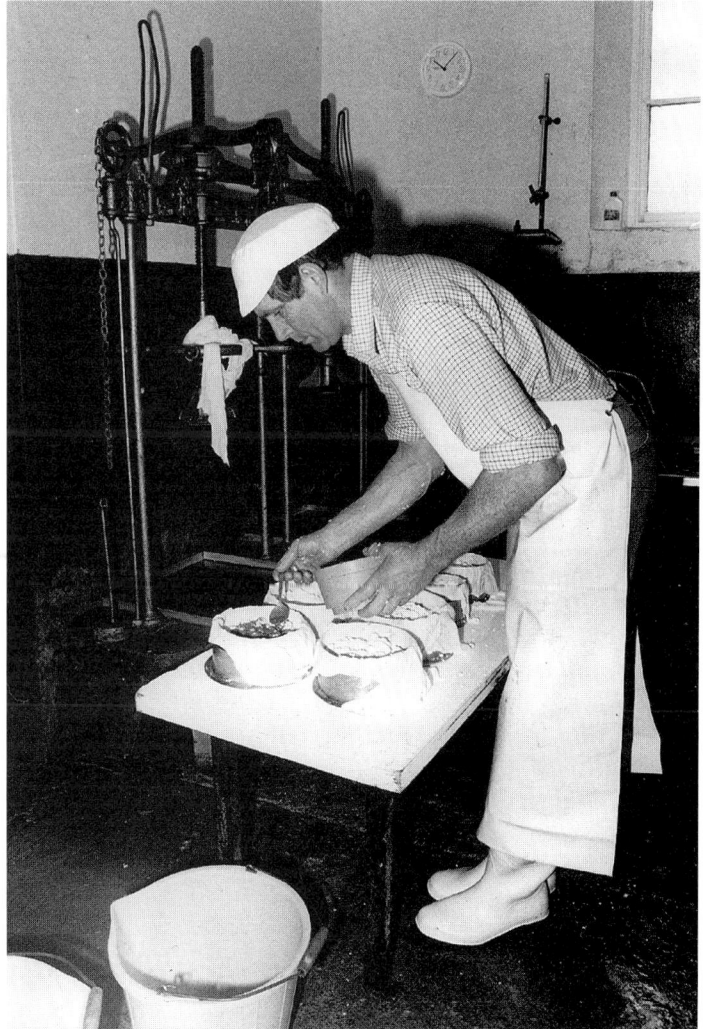

Christopher Duckett in the dairy, cheese-making.

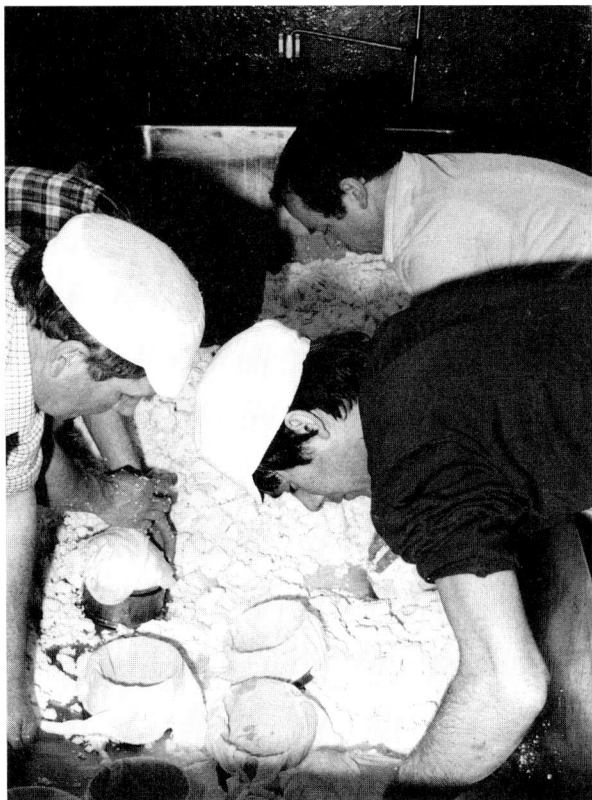

Christopher and Phillip Duckett and helpers at the most frantic stage of the business of cheese-making, filling the moulds — all hands to work!

part: the mixture is stirred by hand continuously for 45 minutes to an hour, until the curd snaps cleanly when bent. The Ducketts believe that this hand-stirring produces a particular quality in their cheese. The whey is drawn off at this stage, a lengthy process, before the curd is cut and moved, then cut in two directions again and stacked on end. The 1 inch cubes which are left after all this are then spread over the surface of the vat and salt is mixed in, after which the mixture is put in moulds with a cloth lining and lightly pressed for half an hour. The cheese is removed from the mould and the cloth and salted again, before being replaced, inverted, in the mould for eighteen hours of further pressing. Finally, the cheese, which is still soft, is placed in a bath of brine for a further twenty-four hours, emerging hardened and in its final form.

There is not much respite in this process and it is necessary to have a regular routine to ensure that each stage is carried through fully and that people do not continually bump into each other in the crowded room.

The Ducketts also run a Caravan Club site for up to five tourers behind the farmyard. I was told that this was used principally by people breaking their journey to Devon or Cornwall; few people appreciate the diversity and charm of Somerset as a holiday destination in its own right. One of the great features of this campsite is waking up to see a llama and her calf peering down from their long necks! Christopher has kept a few of these animals for many years now. Their wool is used in sweaters, but they are principally family pets.

One of Christopher's main concerns is the continually changing pattern of farming. The introduction of milk quotas had produced one set of problems, while by 1991 there were clear signs that the sheep business was on the decline and there were considerable problems in the cattle trade resulting from the outbreak of BSE, the so-called 'mad cow disease'.

Another concern arises from the noticeable drying of the moors. Christopher attended a meeting called by the Ministry of Agriculture, Food and Fisheries (MAFF), at which a scientist explained the chemical changes which took place in peat once it had dried out completely. It was suggested that it could prove impossible to reactivate it if this happened. This made him think much more deeply about conditions on the moor. In 1990 they had been close to a catastrophic drying out. The Brue was higher than the water in the North Drain and it was generally believed that the ditches were only a matter of weeks away from losing all their water. What will happen in the longer term? This is not only of specific interest to him as a local farmer on the moor but also in his capacity as an active member of the Lower Brue Drainage Board.

These remarks are particularly significant as they show that the drying out of the moors is being acknowledged by people other than conservationists. It becomes a serious matter when prominent farmers acknowledge their worries on this score. Though Christopher, and his father before him, have always been fascinated by the wildlife of the area. I remember having a cup of coffee with them and watching an orphaned badger strolling round the sitting-room. On a later occasion Christopher reared some barn owls which had been brought to him for help. They lived in the barn for some time before departing.

I asked Christopher how farming and life on the moors in general had altered in the many years he had known it. He paused for a moment, then said:

"There have been many changes over the last twenty or thirty years, but in essence the moors remain the same. When I left school and started on the farm some twenty-five years ago, we milked 50 or so Friesians. Now we have 120 milkers. The main difference is that two and a half families are now being supported by the land, where previously there was only one. Our total holding has increased through buying neighbouring fields, and also by renting some hill ground."

Like many local farms, his land is split up considerably. Few farms have a ring fence round them. Moor ground used to be considered a good insurance for a dry summer, although the season was short. It was cheap land but had to be bought as it came up, a bit at a time, for the pressures of inheritance have divided and split the farms over the years. Some fields are owned by sons, daughters and descendants of farmers and are considered sound investments, providing income and security for their old age.

"Twenty-five years ago we had 50 Friesians, now we milk 120".

56

"Does your land fit the same pattern?"

"Oh yes, our own land is considerably split, though we have a decent sized block out on the moors. The distance between the blocks, combined with our concentration on cheese, means that we farm the land a little differently from some of our fellow farmers. We retain the bail milking system during the summer. Few others remain on the open moor."

"When I was a boy," he said, "I stood on Tealham and counted twenty-two milking bails. The most I have seen this summer are four – and much of the time it is two or three."

The passing of the churn signalled the end of the bail for many people in the area. When the time came for milk to be collected in tankers, farmers invested in expensive equipment, tanks, specially designed modern parlours and modern sterilisation techniques, and it made sense to rationalise their farming methods accordingly.

"I suppose it depends where the majority of your ground lies and what sort of enterprises you run?"

"Yes, most farms round here have both hill and moor ground. The hill ground is used mainly for milk production now, while moorland is devoted to rearing beef cattle and for hay – quite different from the old days, when little hay was made out on the moor. Silage tends to be taken on the edges of the moor, or on the hill ground, where haulage to the farm and parlour is minimised. These changes coincided with improvements in prices for beef and a move to intensify production generally by cross-breeding from the milking herd. Friesian heifers were bred with beef bulls to produce beef as a by-product of the main milk herd and increase the overall return from the enterprise. Beef cross calves are worth more. It started with the Hereford cross which produced a calf that was particularly attractive in the market place."

I commented on the changes in the colours of the cattle.

"They always used to be black and white, but now I see a variety of colours."

"Certainly, the colours of the cattle have changed over the years," agreed Christopher. "The black and white cows are Friesians, still favourites for milking. But continental breeds have come into their own and are used as the principal crosses, although Hereford bulls are still to be seen. Here the majority are Simenthal, but Charolais and Limosan are used also. They give heavy, rapid-growing beef animals which are more profitable than the older, traditional crosses in this style of farming."

Because he is a cheesemaker, Christopher has a different outlook from other farmers. In his business it is important that he produces a constant supply of milk to keep his processing going. He needs to milk out on the moor, so as to utilise his resources fully, and that is why he still uses a bail. His 70 acres on Tealham is in a single block and the system works well. It would take a considerable time if he had to walk the cattle up on to the hill twice a day.

"Milk quotas have helped change the nature of farming – they are one of the reasons for the reduction in the number of bails. The objective of the quota system is to cut milk production in the EC, but it is a complex and extraordinary process. Take how it affected us. The quota was based on existing production at a certain date and, because of circumstances at that time, was not very fair in these parts. The key year for production against which the cuts would be set was 1983. Unfortunately this was a poor year on the moors. If you were able to prove that there had been a 15 per cent reduction over normal years, this could have been taken into account in the assessments. It turned out that most people had suffered a 10 to 12 per cent reduction in that base year, not enough to be counted officially. So they ended up with a 10 per cent cut on a yield which was already 10 per cent or so below normal."

"I remember there was considerable worry at the time."

"There certainly was, but it has all settled down now. Some people decided to accept payment to get out of milk, and sold their quotas. Those who were left increased their quotas by buying these, so they still had reasonable herds. In fact people are now producing less, but doing so more efficiently. Instead of feeding for increased yield to produce increased marginal profits, they are adjusting their extra feeding to give the lowest cost per litre. In many ways this has been a good thing and farming is better for it."

"Has this affected the standard of living of those in milk?"

"No, not really. People were making a good living out of milk before the introduction of quotas. Now that the quotas have become concentrated in fewer hands, dairy farmers are doing well again. Prices have risen over the years and are good."

I asked about the price of land.

He paused a moment to think, before replying, "No, the price of land does not appear to have suffered as a result, although it is bound to affect some of the outlying fields with no milk quota attached. Otherwise land has held up well here compared with some other parts of the country. Indeed, quota is a highly saleable commodity. Many changes of ownership have taken place as a result of the value of the milk quota and the incentives offered by the Government to get out of milk production. A number of middle-aged farmers, or those nearing retirement, have taken the opportunity to sell up and retire, or invest elsewhere, with a nice amount of capital realised from it all. Clearly this is a problem for those with families following on, but it has been a godsend to some who do not have this problem of succession."

"Apart from milk, the whole of agriculture seems to be in a state of some disarray at the moment. Is this really so?"

"It is pretty uncertain still. You have to keep your wits about you. Grain and pure beef production both appear to have a poor outlook, but sheep compensate in many areas. There are many more sheep on the moors now, although indications are that sheep farmers are beginning to feel the squeeze. There seems to be no way in which the EC can stop things swinging from shortage to surplus."

"What do you think will happen here? Are other enterprises the answer – trees for instance?"

"I am worried that moorland will no longer be in demand. If yields can be raised elsewhere by improved methods, will anyone want the moorland, where farmers are restricted to the old methods? It's not that I want to see major changes. Many people like the traditional methods of farming here.

Golden plover feeding on one of the Duckett moorland fields one winter. In their time these fields have supported breeding snipe, lapwings and curlew, as well as many small birds.

Perhaps government payments will hold the area together. I don't know.

"I wouldn't like to see conifers grown here. They wouldn't seem right. If trees are to be grown they should be the traditional kinds – broadleaved. However, I don't know whether anyone could make a living out of them. It needs special forms of incentive to grow a crop with such a long cycle as that – outside one man's lifetime."

"What about the new system of grants," I asked, "enabling many farmers to stick to the old ways of farming – the Environmentally Sensitive Area (ESA) and Site of Special Scientific Interest (SSSI) schemes?"

"It's not being your own master. It's not being sure whether the agreement will stay the same from year to year. Will the compensation remain the same, grow with inflation or be reduced by a later decree? But principally it is knowing that you cannot do what you want with your own fields, your own land. At the present it seems to be fair and ensures that you do not lose, but it is not the money; it is who controls the way we farm. I get depressed about it all at times. I wonder what is going to happen, what our task-masters will decide about pumping, about the number of cows we can keep and when they will be allowed onto the fields."

I left him putting on his boots for a last look at the cows, before the end of his long day.

Stanley Tucker – carpenter

Stanley Tucker was born in 1904 in the upstairs bedroom of the house in which he still lives. His grandfather farmed at Laurel Farm in Westham, but died young, and grandmother decided that they would leave farming and start a new life at the mill at Heath House, which she ran for many years. Stanley cannot remember it as a windmill, although the sails lay in the field for many years. The grindstones were operated by an oil engine which used to be started with a blowlamp under the sump. When his Uncle William decided to marry, his grandmother came to his father and said that she would buy the house in which Mr Tucker now lives, provided his father would come with her – "There's no room for two women in a house," she said.

When his grandmother died, his father took a housekeeper but this situation did not last long as the lady was forever off visiting a nearby farmer and his cider. He looked after himself then until he went over to Burtle one day and met Stanley's mother, who was visiting her sister. She agreed to come over as housekeeper and they later married.

When Stanley's grandmother first came to the mill, she started a shop, which continued in the same room until 1955, under a succession of owners. But the family sold the mill soon after grandmother died.

After two or three years of marriage, his mother went to the doctor and said, "There's something wrong with me. I don't feel right." The doctor examined her and then said, "There's nothing I can do for you. Don't you know what's wrong with you?"

"No Doctor, or I wouldn't be here bothering you," she replied tartly.

"Well, you'll be holding it in your arms soon!" he said.

She was somewhat astonished, as she was over 40 years old, but eventually Stanley was born, an only child.

He left school at twelve, with a certificate saying he had completed all the necessary attendances and was of good character. He started work with old Mr Edney at the forge by Landsend, opposite our house. Mr Edney's son,

61

Tom, was the blacksmith there and had learned his trade at Walls of Blackford. There were also carpenters, decorators and wheelwrights in the business, and it supplied a complete repair service for the local community.

For the first three years Stanley was paid nothing as an apprentice. He was supposed to be given dinner and tea but he was frequently away for the day and it was easier to stop off at home than to go on down to the forge and have to walk back. "I could have a bit of bread and jam at home as easily as back at Edney's." Before taking tea at the forge, he had to chop up a box of wood for lighting the fire in the morning, but was not allowed to do this before six o clock – after work. It was tough discipline, but he enjoyed learning the new trade and showed an aptitude for the work.

After that he was paid 2/6d a week, rising to 5/- and gradually progressing. At the end of nine years he was earning 30/- one fortnight and £2 the next – a rather peculiar arrangement. The hours were long, from eight to six on weekdays and eight to five on Saturdays, but he enjoyed the work. He stayed there for nine years, until he was twenty-one, then his mother died and he was left the house.

On the day he became twenty-one, they were out at Westham, doing a job for Bruton Estate. They had to take down an old ceiling, exposing the thatch up above, and pulled it all out onto the lawn, a dirty and dusty job. Young Stanley looked round, and said, "Well that's it. I'm going to ask for a raise." He told his co-worker, who made sure he was not going to be there at that time, for Mr Edney was a tough man who went at them like anything – though well-respected in the neighbourhood.

"Well, Mr Edney, what about it? I've got to look after myself now, are you going to raise my wages?"

"How much were you thinking about?"

"£1 a week."

"No, you boys are all the same. Just when I've taught you everything I know, you want more money. No."

"In that case I resign from Saturday." Stanley picked up his tools at the end of work and walked out, not looking back. The next day someone suggested that he ought to go and see William Parker in Wedmore. He was a carpenter and had married Stanley's Uncle William's widow. Mr Parker offered Stanley 30 shillings a week and his principal work, which he greatly enjoyed, was to be as a wheelwright.

Mr Parker found that Stanley had not been in wheelwright work before, so set to and showed him how this skilful work was done. He was a wonderful teacher who had developed accurate and time-saving methods to produce first-class work.

"I learned those final master-skills in the two years I was with Mr Parker. He had such well thought-out ways of doing jobs. I was particularly keen on the work involved in making cart-wheels. I was taught how to make the 'felloes' in such a way that, when the iron tyre was cooled to shrink it on the wheel rim, the joints tightened to a hair line. I have seen paint hide many a poor joint filled with putty in my time." Felloes are sections of the outer rim of the wheel, each of which contain two spokes, which set against each other under pressure from the tyre. The spokes had to be fitted precisely to these so that every alternate spoke was offset $\frac{3}{8}$ inch to provide structural strength against bending forces when cornering. Without this, the wheel would collapse like an umbrella in the wind, if the cart cornered fast.

Mr Parker's father had also started in timber, but in a different capacity. He had begun his working life at Harris's Sawmill at Blackford, where he was given the job of sawing planks. This involved supporting a trunk over a saw-pit and using a double-handled saw. One man stood above, while the youngster stood below in the pit and endured the sawdust falling on him, as well as the hard grind of wielding the saw for hours on end. The day started

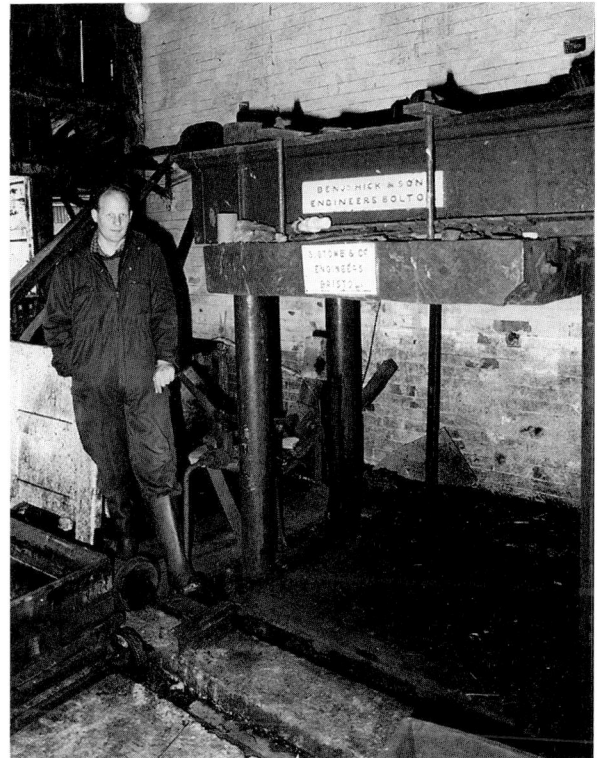

Stanley Tucker started work at the Forge next to our house and looked out over Old Rhyne and Tealham Moor.

63

at six o'clock and it must have been exceedingly tough for a young lad.

All the while, Mr Tucker was being asked to do more private jobs around Heath House. The hours were better at Parker's than at Edney's – from eight to five on weekdays and eight to one on Saturdays, so he was able to undertake this other work on Saturday afternoons. The volume built up as his reputation grew, until it became too much to manage. After two years, he went to his boss and said he was being pressed to set up on his own, and had decided to resign. He had learned a great deal from Mr Parker and they parted with mutual respect. He heard from another source that his boss had backed him against anyone, as being the best wheelwright in the district. He set up in his home workshop at the beginning of 1928 and was married by the end of the year. He has been self-employed ever since, although he has retired now.

I asked him how he moved himself and his materials around when he started up on his own. He began with a bicycle which lasted him for years. In those days firms would deliver materials direct to where they were to be used or in some cases the farmers would send a horse and cart over to fetch what was needed. Much of the work involved fitting cow stalls. Then in 1929 he bought a 1¾ horsepower Raleigh motorcycle for £6 from a departing Methodist minister and he rode a motorcycle for the rest of his working life. But he never had a sidecar. "My wife said you'd never catch her in one, so I thought it was wasn't worth it. I always had a solo."

The pub at Heath House, the Grouse and Pheasant, continued in existence until at least the end of the twenties. The first known landlord and landlady were Mr and Mrs Page, who later retired around 1913 to a cottage on the Westham road nearby. There is a splendid story about them. Mr Page was very keen on growing cider apples but his wife did not agree; she wanted him to plant more vegetables. However, Mr Page planted the trees, but one day his wife sent out two schoolboys with a hook each to take off the crowns. Her husband came back to see them at it and the boys fled before him, leaving just two rows of trees still whole; these remain to this day.

Mrs Stone, known locally as Silver Ginny, took over the pub from them and ran it until she remarried and retired in the early twenties. She sold cider in the main, much made on the premises, and also opened a small shop. When she retired the pub was sold to George Gooding. He and his wife had to learn everything from scratch, including how to make cider. When 'horsing' up the barrel, to fill it, they forgot to 'plim' it up with water to tighten the staves against each other. The cider poured out again onto the floor. Mrs Gooding's solution was to rub soap into the cracks. "I never did hear what it tasted like."

The moors were a strange place and the roads were terrible at times. Jack's Drove was not tarred until after the war; with all the animals and carts moving along it, it was a mass of dung and slime when it was wet and there were clouds of choking dust when it was dry. The Heath House road was tarred just after the First World War. In the days of horses and carts there would be a stream of them running up and down to the moor all day, fetching milk churns and taking farmers down. Heath House was always full of the noise of wheels and hoofs and a source of constant bustle.

I asked about life down on the heath when he was young.

"In those days it was wet the whole winter, sometimes deeper and worse than others. A lot of people lived down on the heath then, although their cottages have all gone now. For instance there were four cottages out on Allermoor Drove just before it crosses Sand Drove. On Church Drove there were three by the 'deserted' village and the Fears lived further back on the south side, where there is now a bramble-filled copse."

"Coming the other way down the Mark Road, going towards Blakeway, there were two cottages on the north side, then another moorland cottage, one further just before the present kennels and a chapel beyond. Opposite were three cottages, including the present site of the bungalow farmhouse. My wife's parents, Mr and Mrs Rogers, lived at another cottage next to the kennels, before they moved up to Heath House."

It was a hard life on the moors but there was plenty to do during the summer months. People who had land cut, dried and sold peat for fuel. If they did not have the land they would cut for others. Between them, they cleaned out all the ditches for the Drainage Board during the summer, cut spars for thatching the ricks, and helped farmers at hay-making. They also looked after barren or dry stock on the moors. Sheep were a particular problem and Stanley remembers having a headache on Saturdays when it was time to move them, although his father never allowed him to get away with it.

Life on the moors may have been hard, but it had its compensations and humour. Two bakers, Drake, and Moggs, delivered round the area, including the heath. Moggs's man was known as Bonar Law, for he always talked politics. Tommy Binning was the roundsman for Drake and the person with whom the family normally dealt. Apparently he was rather bulky. One winter, Mr and Mrs Dick King, who lived in the cottage between Yellow Batches and Jack's Drove, saw a cart coming down the drove and round the corner towards them. It missed its way and plunged into the rhyne, bread floating all round it and the horse struggling.

"It's that girt fat fellow, he'll be drowned," they said. "Hurry let's get un out." When they reached the spot they found the cart was not that of Mr Binning but the one from Moggs and there was no one with it. The horse had set off on its own and knew the way so well it had come all the way down from Wedmore before going off the edge!

The Rogers family milked some cows and used to carry it in churn to Peacock Farm, beyond Turnpike Cottage, on the road across Westhay and Godney Moors. They dropped the milk and brought fresh water back from the farm in the churn. A number of farmers had combined to pipe drinking water down from a spring at Mudgley, which was used for drinking, while all washing and household jobs were done with water from the ditch. In winter the cottage was usually flooded on the ground floor and they laid boards to walk on and raised them as the water level rose. On rare occasions they had to decamp completely.

All families out on the heath kept a boat tied up for winter. Indeed Stanley used to build boats at Edney's, dragging them down through the orchard to

launch them on Little Rhyne. In her youth, his wife used to walk four miles to school at Bagley, on top of the ridge to the east of Mudgley. In winter, Blakeway normally stayed above the floods and quite often her parents would drive little Miss Rogers to Blakeway in the cart, so that she could walk up to Bagley. Sometimes Blakeway flooded and a cousin of theirs drowned when his horse took fright in the floods and plunged off the road into the rhyne.

The coming of electricity to Heath House just after the Second World War was an important event. People were asked what their likely consumption of electricity might be.

Stanley replied, "We've never had anything to do with electricity. How can we know what we might use?" The first survey showed that the hamlet would not use enough to justify connection, so the second time everyone

Bleak Farm, on the southern edge of Tadham Moor, off Blakeway, remote and cut off in the old days of long winter flooding.

made sure that they estimated enough. Wedmore had electric earlier when a few richer private individuals clubbed together and bought a power station of their own in Billings Hill.

I asked about the Second World War and how it had affected them. Apparently there was a raid on Bristol in about 1942, and the bombers had such a rough time trying to reach the city that many turned round and dumped their loads in the surrounding countryside. Stanley was a special constable at the time, and on the night of the Bristol raid he was off duty and talking to a few friends outside his home when a plane went over, its engine sounding hesitant. Then the noise of the engines stopped. Not long after they heard someone walking up the road, followed by a little white dog.

"It's Farmer Hole," someone said, for he had a dog just like that. The man walked on, holding his hands in the air.

"I German airman," he said.

"You'd better come in along with me," said Stanley. "Have you got a gun?" The man took out a little revolver and gave it to him. They went into the kitchen and phoned the sergeant, who came and took the German to Burnham Police Station for the night. Before he went they questioned him, but his knowledge of English was sketchy.

"Water?"

"No."

"Hedges?"

"Yes."

"Cows?"

"No."

"How many people?"

"Four."

He would not answer any other questions. He was very young and frightened of what might happen to him as the airmen had been fed stories of how badly they would be treated. The sergeant came along and he and one or two others went off looking around the moors in the darkness, in case there were any more Germans walking around the area. They found nothing and eventually came back to Heath House, but not before the moors had done their worst. Another special constable, from Cheddar, was warned against the ditches but thought he could jump one. The moorlanders tried to warn him but he would not listen. Instead of having a long run and taking off well before the bank he lumbered up to the very edge, which was very soft, failed to take off when his feet became enmired in the peat, and fell flat on his face in the middle. Stanley lent him a pair of trousers and a shirt to get him home again but reckoned "he didn't try that ever again".

The next morning they went off with the sergeant looking for more traces. The door of the plane was found in the Hall grounds near Wedmore. The sergeant and his party started at Castle Farm and walked on towards Sand Drove but before they reached it found a dead airman in the field. His parachute had not opened properly, or else had fouled something on the plane. He had fallen so hard that his body made a perfect impression in the peat. On looking closer it could be seen that he had been strangled by the cord of his parachute. They discovered that his name was Hendrik, and that he was eighteen years old. A nearby farmer had a pick-up truck, the only thing which could get near the spot.

"But its only licensed for farm-work," he said.

"Never mind the licensing, you bring it out," said the sergeant and so he was moved to a table in Stanley's workshop for the night. On the way down from Sand, they were stopped by a lady living in a nearby big house, who asked if she could look at the German. After she persisted she was allowed to look.

"That's how I like to see them – dead," she said and walked back up the road.

Two other airmen were picked up in Watchfield, to the west of the moors. They found the Heinkel itself among some trees on the south-east of Tadham Moor. It is a long way down beneath the peat now; people have looked for it, but without success.

Alan Banwell – farmer and district councillor

Finally, may I present someone who is involved both in farming and more widely in local politics; he is able to step outside the constrained world of a small area and see it in a wider context. Alan Banwell is a man of many parts and interests as well as having farmed from his boyhood on the same farm, of which about 20 per cent has always been on the moors, although the farm has greatly increased in size over the years.

Alan started milking when he was nine. He retired not long ago and handed over the business to his two sons, although he still owns the land. He is busier than ever, being a very active Sedgemoor District Councillor with a

Councillor Alan Banwell is still fascinated with the farming life, though he has now handed over to his sons.

special interest in the countryside and he represents the National Farmers' Union (NFU) on a committee with English Nature, which meets periodically, as well as being involved in the Countryside Forum. He is also a member of the Peat Reclamation Board which looks at the use of land following peat-digging.

When he first started on his father's farm it earned half its income from cider-making and the remainder from milk. The farm was around 100 acres in total, of which 20 were out on the moors. A herd of twenty-five Shorthorns were milked by hand. In those days it was reckoned that one person could milk up to eight cows.

Most of the cattle out on the moor were part of a milking herd, but there were some beef, Shorthorn cross Hereford. At that time there were no sheep on the wet part – fluke was too much of a problem. The milk would be taken to the factory in Wedmore – later converted into a scent factory and now part of a shopping mall. A great queue of carts would be lined up through the village after milking. Farms produced small quantities in those days; three to four churns was considered a reasonable output. In 1940 this system was changed and the Milk Marketing Board (MMB) arranged for Herb Wall at Blackford to collect the local milk and take it to the United Dairies Creamery at Rooksbridge on a lorry. The milk was in churns and every farm had a platform at the closest point to the road, on which they were left. A few years ago this system was replaced by tanker collections direct from the farm, involving a further extensive reorganisation as well as a considerable investment.

In the 1950s the Banwells bought their first milking bail, a Simplex, after their first tractor, a Ferguson, was purchased in 1947. The farm is now 250 acres, with some 50 acres out on the moor.

Around 1976 they gave up cider-making because of the pressures on markets from the big cider firms. They have always kept some cider orchards, however, and are currently planting new ones, but now sell the apples direct to the cider-makers. The apples are picked by machine when they fall, with three picks at different times. It is labour intensive but each time they shake the branches and pick the fallen fruit, the remaining crop gains in bulk.

The farm milked 108 Friesians at its peak, but the milk quota reduced this to 90. Then in 1987 they sold their quota and went into beef and sheep. The farm has changed its enterprises considerably since those early days and particularly so in the last few years. Now they have some 80 cattle on the farm, 30 suckling cows and followers, and a flock of over 500 breeding ewes. Alan's sons are particularly keen on sheep and specialise in them. Alan believes that farmers must specialise to be successful now. They breed sheep, as well as fattening for sale. They hired rams for a couple of years but have recently bought five pedigree Texels and three pedigree Blue Demains.

In the old days Tealham was a place for summer farming only. Alan's father used to take the cattle out in mid-May and they would be brought back to the hill land in November. Alan's own precept has always been that "when the birds come in, the cattle should come out". He looked for the arrival of the first flocks of peewits in the autumn and would then bring the cattle back up the hill.

The wet part of the moor was never used for making hay but the higher fields on the edge were. A field below Keyton Hill used to be farmed by his uncle and Alan would help with the hay-making, which was always late in the year. Huge cocks were made and left as late as possible, then they would be brought in on the wagon and put into a stack near the farm, for winter feeding, close to where the cattle overwintered.

Before pumping, the land was very rough indeed, with great straps of iris and rushes up to 4 feet high over much of it. People spent a lot of time cutting these 'useless' growths by hand. There were two kinds of people working out on the moors in those days. The regular farm staff did the milking and tended the animals, and also did some cutting. Others, who lived out on the moors, were either casual workers or had a couple of paddocks of, say, 20 acres on the moor on which they milked a few cows, devoting the rest of their time to casual work. This included ditching, cutting weeds, counting or looking after dry cattle, digging peat, cutting thatching spars and any other casual jobs there were. All these were done manually and took up a lot of time, so such people were needed. One family, the Fears, who lived out on Chine Drove, were well known for this type of work and their house was only abandoned after the war.

Most of the moor has been dug for peat at one time or another, much of it privately for fuel, although it is rarely used as such these days. The modern diggings on Allermoor Drove lie outside the official Designated Peat Area. Apparently they were started originally by levelling 'the humps and bumps' and it continued from that. An entrepreneurial member of the family which now runs this digging started his career by milking a few cows on the drove – a habit not really approved of by the owners of the land on either side, who actually own it. The droves were higher than the fields and dried out first, so they became passable earlier. This should have enabled the owners to reach the

furthest fields but it was not possible when milking took place and mired up the access. It was consequently a continual source of dissension. Another well-known farmer, who has now moved away from the area, also started his progress by milking cows on the droves, moving from one to the other as he was driven off. Eventually he bought a farm and ran a regular herd like everyone else. It would not be possible to build up a farm in this way today.

"In those days what was needed was ingenuity, access to some land and hard labour; now one needs capital more than anything else."

Pounding often made it impossible to reach some fields out on the moor. Others were unusable most years because they were covered in stagnant water even at the height of summer. One of the reasons that cattle

The hay would be put into a stack for the winter.

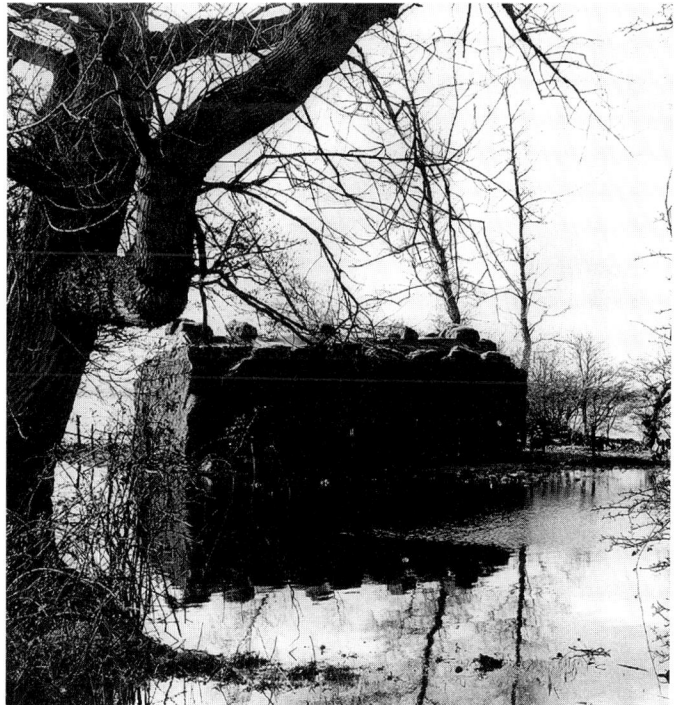

could not go out on the moors until at least mid-May, even in favourable fields, was that the standing water left a scum on the surface, which the cows would not touch. This stagnant deposit had to be allowed to disperse naturally.

"The fields were a riot of colour in those days. Those by Bounds Rhyne were yellow all over with kingcups; others were pink with orchids."

Then in the late 1950s came the pumps. New Rhyne was widened to make the North Drain and the North Drain Pumping Station was built. This immediately made the moors usable in a more predictable manner. The pumps were originally installed to control flooding. Then it was realised that the water-table could be controlled quite precisely for much of the time and a more severe pumping regime took over, finally the pumps were automated. This has had the effect of drying out the moors much more severely.

From a personal perspective Alan believes winter pumping levels are too low. It is important that some depth of water is kept in the ditches. When they are low the ground dries out too much, while the ditch often has a brown deposit on the bottom which is a form of pollution.

The Banwells were amongst the first to try to discover whether cultivation would be of value on the moors. It was an effort to improve the grassland rather than grow arable crops, so they cultivated an experimental plot of 6 acres. They did not attempt to underdrain the ground and used a cultivator rather than a plough to prepare the ground. It was then generally believed that ploughing would lead to so much damage that the machinery might well sink below the surface. They took advice from ADAS, the government advisory service, and even tried liming the field at the same time. Other experiments were conducted with fertilisers. None of them was a success and the ground has long gone back to its original state. It was a failure, but worth doing to prove a point. The advice eventually given was to put the money into better land rather than trying to 'improve' the moor grounds. Indications were that, while arable crops might have done well, improved grassland was not as good as the native untouched sward.

Alan believes that flood-silting is of value provided the water does not lie too long. The ground is as fertile now as it was, but it needs the right treatment. It will not grow anything when the surface gets down to the bare peat, for instance if it is scraped. They clear their stock houses out and build a manure heap in the yard. It heats up and composts, helped sometimes by a load of slurry, and goes out in the autumn. This suits the moors ideally. No artificial fertiliser is used on the moor, although it is used on higher grounds to bulk out the silage. In his opinion it is not necessary on the fields, which are used for grazing and hay-making only.

I asked why people have taken further advantage of the lower water table by underdraining the fields.

"It means that they can get farm implements out throughout the year; it is said they can obtain earlier bites of grass to increase milk yields; the fields can be reseeded with grasses thought to be better suited to drier conditions; and they can plant roots and other arable crops. While the demonstration farm on Tealham has proved that excellent arable crops can be produced, the claims for improved grass have not stood up to testing."

Alan Banwell summed up the current position as he sees it.

"The old idea of 'them and us' is vanishing and it is seen that there have to be changes in attitude. Some people may not like it, but farm income could now be seen to be made up, in this area at least, of a mixture of grants received to preserve a form of farming, plus the earnings from milk, beef or sheep. The farm then becomes viable as an enterprise, and this seems to be the way for the future."

The Banwells have much of their land covered either by ESA payments or as an SSSI. All their land on Tealham is an SSSI, subject to a management agreement with English Nature. They see this as an acceptable part of modern farming which should lead to a continuing life on the land and the preservation of a wonderful landscape, together with its associated wildlife.

HISTORY AND DRAINAGE

Tealham and Tadham Moors are seen traditionally as being attached to Wedmore, their closest village. For much of the history of the moors, they have been places where the hill people worked, or made a part of their living, rather than where many people lived. Indeed Tealham has remained empty of people for all its history, although Tadham supported a small population after drainage.

The River Axe was navigable past Wedmore to Bleadney, half way between Wells and Wedmore, in the eighth century. Thus it was an important link between the towns and villages on the edge of the moors and the outside world, through its nearby jetties. Wedmore undoubtedly benefited from this.

The story of these moors and their people, is inextricably bound up with the great events, the history and the drainage of the Levels as a whole. For many thousands of years the area of the Parrett and Axe estuaries, between Brean Down and Bridgwater, has been the entrance to an area of lowland stretching into the heart of Somerset. Over the years the water level has risen and fallen and then finally settled broadly at what it is now. Originally it was

half-land, half-water, marshy, dank, shut in. Now it has been drained, but remains a land divided by water and kept from flooding by massive sea-walls. Its bounds have largely remained the same, determined by the skeleton of rocks and clay which surround it. The low line of the Polden hills, stretching from Street to Puriton, divides the Levels into two arms – the Brue Valley running up to Glastonbury and the course of the River Parrett on its way to Langport and Ilchester, some 20 miles inland. To this day these more than 170,000 acres remain separate from surrounding countryside, with an air of mystery which can be felt rather than defined.

Until the first flood defences were built by the great abbeys after the Norman Conquest, the sea rolled in and out of the marshes as the tide rose and fell, sometimes inundating far inland as the winds piled up the waters of the Bristol Channel. Sea-levels rose and fell over the millennia, raising and then drowning ground. The formation of the peat moors goes back a long way. Vegetation grew and died, raising the level of the ground. Peat started to be composed in the area around 6000 BC. By 4500 BC, the present-day

Tealham has remained empty of houses and people for all its history.

77

peatlands were being laid down and the process was completed by 3500 BC, when many people lived in the area. Five hundred years later, much of the salt had been washed out by rain and the composition of the herbage had changed once more. Over the next few hundred years people built trackways across the peat and there was evidence of considerable activity. But raised bogs gradually formed, swamping the paths and eventually overwhelming man's efforts to keep the tracks above the surface.

The final change in sea-level took place around 250 AD. The marshes and bogs were again flooded with sea water and the growth of the raised bogs was halted. Rainfall was reduced and by 400 AD the bogs were dead. Further sea-floods took place at this time and more clay was deposited, leaving the composition of the soil and local geology as it is now.

After that man took over the shaping of the land, although there were many centuries of progress and regression, gain and loss, before the present landscape emerged. Even today, with the latest technology available, floods still gain the upper hand periodically, for much of the level of the land is below sea-level at some state of the tide. Should sea-levels rise with the predicted greenhouse effect, this will become even more of a problem, possibly leading to the permanent flooding of the area and a state approaching what it was thousands of years ago. At present Tealham Moor is a few feet above mean sea-level. As the tides at Weston-super-Mare range from 38 to 28 feet, depending on the state of the moon, with a mean height of 19 feet, it will be appreciated that, for much of the time the moors are actually beneath sea-level. Thus dryness and freedom from regular flooding is an artificial state, dependent on sea-defences, raised river banks and pumping stations.

How has this situation been reached? It is a fascinating story of continual endeavour, depending initially on the efforts of the great monasteries, which must be considered in relation to the history of the area as a whole.

Wedmore first came to prominence·in 878, when King Alfred defeated Guthrum the Dane at Ethandun. After the battle the King took the defeated Danes to Aller and they were baptised into the Church rather than being all killed, as was the normal practice in those days. The all-important ceremony of the loosening of the chrism – the baptismal robe – took place at Wedmore, together with the signing of an important peace-treaty, under which the Danes were confined to the north-east under the Danelagh, while the rest of England lay under the benevolent domination of Alfred. Although skirmishes continued for years, this Christianisation of the Danes and the great Treaty of Wedmore preserved the peace, giving a long period of stability, and set on course the development of modern-day England.

Who could look at Wedmore now – a prosperous but unimportant large village – and ever imagine that it could have played such a vital part in history? At that date there was even a royal palace there. It is recorded that a certain Eolderman Aethelnoth of Wedmore helped Alfred make the peace.

In the late nineteenth century, a vicar of Wedmore, S.H. Harvey, who went on to publish the Wedmore Chronicle, excavated the supposed site of Alfred's palace on Mudgley Hill by Wedmore and found a medieval building dating to the start of the twelfth century. An old man in the parish told the Reverend Harvey that it had once belonged to a man who was 'not a king but just like a king' – a perfect description of the Lord Protector, the Duke of Somerset, who took over Mudgley from the Lord Dean of Wells in 1547. Was this built over the original palace site, or is this still waiting to be discovered elsewhere in the village?

Two other vitally important places in the history of the moors and their people were the great bishopric of Wells, separated from Sherbourne in 909, and the holy place of Glastonbury. Just before the Peace of Wedmore, Glastonbury fell briefly into the hands of the Danes, who utterly destroyed and pillaged the settlement and its ancient church so that, for some time, it was no longer of any importance. However St Dunstan was born at Glastonbury in 925 and raised it to new glory when he became abbot in 942, before going on to become Archbishop of Canterbury. Glastonbury was so important during his life that three kings were buried there: Edmund, Edgar and Edmund Ironside.

It is recorded that another king, Edwy, gave part of his Manor of Wedmore

Glastonbury Abbey, where three kings were buried and much of the drainage of the Levels originated. Centre of learning, cradle of Christianity and the place where Arthur and Guinevere were said to be buried – 'that holy place'.

to Glastonbury Abbey, while in 1030 King Canute came to Glastonbury to declare his respect for the privileges and rights of the Abbey after he had welded the Danes and the Saxons into the new nation of England. Somerset indeed played its place in English politics at that time.

The Bishop and Deans of Wells owned the Manor of Wedmore for some 500 years from the middle of the eleventh century. The church holdings were split up at the dissolution of the monasteries and the manor, consisting of some 70 acres of land and another 100 acres of heath, woods and orchards, was sold into private hands in 1577.

The next great event for the area came in 1085, after William had conquered the country with his Normans. He required a record of what he had taken and so asked for the great book of Domesday to be prepared. Although it did not cover the whole country, it was a very precise description of that part it did record. Every piece of land was measured and described, with the stock it held and crops grown.

In the Domesday Book there is a description of the Manor of Wedmore, which was held by the Bishop of Wells at that time. Of the taxable land, there were 4,320 acres of arable, 50 acres of woodland, 70 acres of meadow and 120 acres of pasture. Over 12,000 acres was classed as useless and unproductive on the manor holdings – the moors came under this category. There were 10 hides of land in the manor, consisting of 36 ploughlands, 6 wild marshes and 2 fisheries. The total holding was 16,620 acres, of similar bounds to the 1880 parishes of Wedmore, Mark and Theale, less Clewer. Interestingly, nearby Panborough was recorded as having a vineyard – a number have opened up again in the area in the last few years.

In that great survey of 1085, 179,000 acres of land were unaccounted for in Somerset, being the total of the unproductive marshland and wastes (estimated at 140,000 acres in the 1981 Somerset County Council report on the Somerset moors and Levels).

Basically 'moors and wastes' described that part of the land near sea-level, much of which was covered with peat. The meadow would be on the higher clay lands of the area. There has always been a distinction between the swampy peatlands and the more conventional clay valleys and hillsides which were easier to till or graze once the scrub and trees had been cleared. The Isle of Wedmore, nearby Nyland Hill and the various other hillocks rising above the Levels are but bumps on the surface – the Isle of Wedmore is only 150 feet at its highest point – but they do rise above the peat and formed the usable backbone of the country when water and marsh surrounded everything. This backbone was where settlements were built and farms were started, while cargo-carrying ships tied up along the lower edges.

The surrounding marshes and rivers provided food in the form of great numbers of wildfowl, which were hunted both directly and through decoy pools. Waterways were used in lieu of roads to transport people and goods to otherwise inaccessible settlements. Some surprising places were busy ports in their time: Rackley, below Crook Peak on the Mendips; Langport, miles inland at the edge of Sedgemoor; Little Scotland to the eastern side of Wedmore; Bleadney, near Wells; Pilton; and even Glastonbury itself. It is difficult to appreciate this now, as many of the former waterways are narrow ditches which end in nothing and there is little sign of their former importance.

The whole geography of Somerset has been turned upside down by the efforts of people over the centuries. The flow of rivers has been reversed, canals and drains dug and other great works abandoned. The only common element has been a struggle to use more effectively that which was covered in water for much of the year. What used to be a hollow county, with impassable bogs and marshes in the centre, only drying out for a couple of months a year, has been transformed into one of the great dairy lands of Europe. It is a heroic story which can only be fully appreciated by comparing ancient maps with those showing the modern countryside.

The whole geography of Somerset has been turned upside down by its people over the centuries. The flow of rivers has been reversed, canals and drains dug and the waters removed. The North Drain in summer.

Meare Pool, a great inland lake shown on old maps a few miles to the south-east of our moors, was of considerable significance until the Middle Ages. Then it was finally drained in the course of one of the many schemes for altering the water flow in the area which have preoccupied men in this part of the country. In Henry VIII's time Meare Pool was recorded as being $1\frac{1}{2}$ miles wide and 5 miles in circumference – a good size by any reckoning. It was an important carp-fishery for the monks of Glastonbury Abbey and the Abbot's Fish-House still exists in the village of Meare. The monks preserved fish and game inside its thick walls, using blocks of ice cut during the winter. It is an extraordinarily handsome building and well preserved, and looks particularly spectacular at dusk, reflected in sheets of water which lie in front after heavy rain.

A most important factor in the development of the local area was the opening up of a water-borne route to Mark from Glastonbury in 1235, which was then extended to join the River Axe by the end of the century. The Mark-Yeo River became the Pilrow Cut. In 1316 the whole route was completed and was said to be tidal from the Axe to the Brue by way of Mark, passing along Tealham and Tadham Moors. Meare Pool formed an important part of this waterway. In 1500 it was reported that this route enabled wooden seating to be sent from Bristol to Glastonbury for the Abbey. Part of this route is still in existence, but only as a narrow, deep, drainage ditch which runs along to join the North Drain on the edge of Tealham Moor. The only part which looks as though it could have been navigable is a short stretch which forms the heart of Mark village. From there a rhyne continues to run north from Mark corner towards Rooksbridge and the Old River Axe. Looking at the map today it is difficult to envisage the way man has altered the course of the natural waterways over the years and even more difficult to imagine that sea-borne traffic could pass through Tealham on its way to Glastonbury in the Middle Ages.

From the Iron Age until the early fourteenth century, the land of the Levels was considered marsh and was left well alone. The climate must have been enough to deter anyone, damp, with ague, crippling people with rheumatism

83

and wreaking havoc on their sinuses – all dreadful problems in days when remedies were not far advanced.

The main monasteries of Glastonbury, Athelney and Muchelney were responsible for much of the drainage work, with Wells also taking an interest through some of its lands. These great Abbeys were founded between 700 and 933 and started enclosing land within a hundred years. Much of the enclosure that took place at first was of land at the margins. There is a record in 1129 of the Abbot of Glastonbury inspecting enclosed land at Lympsham, 8 or 9 miles to the north-west of Tealham.

From 1200 onwards general land reclamation started to speed up. This was helped by the Statute of Merton in 1235, which recognised the rights of the lord of the manor to enclose waste or common ground, provided he made provision for sufficient pasture for his free tenants. River banks were raised to prevent flooding. Main drainage ditches – rhynes in local parlance – were dug across the open ground to speed the outflow of water. The boundary ditches also drained the land, while enclosing it and making it cattle-proof. In 1308, the Bishop of Wells enclosed Wedmore Lowgrounds, 600 acres of alluvial land to the east of Wedmore, plus Blackford Moor on the west. However, the raised bogs of the central Brue valley – including Tealham and Tadham – were still considered useless and not worth the effort, although there was mention of a stream on Tealham Moor (appearing under that name for the first time, it would seem) in 1327. Again, in 1340 there was mention of a swannery at Wedmore. However, the first reclamation of real moorland was to the east of Glastonbury.

By 1500, one third of the floodable land in Somerset had been reclaimed – 23,000 acres out of 70,000 said to have been at risk at that time. What remained were the great moorland wastes north and south of the Poldens. At that time only 12,000 acres of King's Sedgemoor was usable for two or three months in the year. In 1607 the power of the flood was again revealed. The Vale of Avalon was inundated to a depth of 12 feet when the sea-wall gave way at Burnham. It was reported that thirty villages were flooded and Glastonbury was completely surrounded by water, which must have been a remarkable sight.

In 1638 it was noted that 798 acres of Tealham and 1,802 acres of Tadham Moor were not yet reclaimed. This figure remained static until the enclosures at the very end of the eighteenth century. Our moors have therefore only existed in their present form for under 200 years – an astonishing thought when you looks out across the so-solid land which appears as though it has been there for ever. Some 30,000 acres of the Levels remained undrained in 1800 – just over 44 per cent of the present ESA of the Levels and Moors.

In 1685 one of the last battles to be fought on English soil took place by the Bussex Rhyne on Sedgemoor. The Duke of Monmouth was defeated by, amongst others, the future Duke of Marlborough, John Churchill. Monmouth fled, leaving his great peasant army to face the consequences, which were seen over much of Somerset, both at the time of the battle and afterwards, in the form of the Bloody Assizes of Judge Jeffries. Many people were slaughtered by the soldiers during or after the battle, while others were hanged in the principal villages of the area. Judge Jeffries Field in Wedmore is said to be one site where some were executed.

In 1770 work started on reclaiming the Brue Valley, the last of the real wildernesses. In 1775 a map showed farms and hamlets round Heath House and Westham, just above the heath, including a building on the site of our cottage, but nothing on the moors, except for one set of buildings in the very middle of Tadham, no doubt the site of the first drained land. The main settlements in the area were at Glastonbury, Wedmore, Blackford, Mark, Meare and Westhay. Mark causeway was joined to Wedmore and a road existed from Wedmore to Blakeway, where the North Drain now crosses it. Jack's Drove, which bisects the moors, was shown as a road over part of Tealham, but coming to a dead end.

One of the most traumatic events in the history of our moors took place in the late eighteenth century, with the great enclosures. In addition to altering the farming practices of the area, it brought great changes through the colonisation of part of the moors. Tealham remained largely unsettled but Tadham and Aller Moors altered considerably in the changeover from commoners' rights

In 1775 Jack's Drove was shown as a road over part of Tealham Moor, but coming to a dead end. A view looking up from the bridge to Heath House and our cottage on the hill.

to fenced-in single ownership of each field, with the concomitant drainage which made the higher spots habitable throughout the year. At that time people were allowed to claim title and build a house, provided they could manage to complete a certain procedure, during the course of twenty-four hours. A considerable number of houses were built in this manner on Tadham and were enlarged as the years passed. This was certainly the origin of our 'deserted' village.

Tealham Moor was enclosed in 1785 and Tadham in 1788. The way in which this was carried out and who occupied the various grounds after enclosure was described some years ago by a local farmer, Cuthbert Rose, in a fascinating book on the enclosures as they affected Wedmore. Tadham was covered in more detail than Tealham but it makes most interesting reading and helps us understand how the present moors have evolved.

Tealham Moor was enclosed in 1785, the boundaries made by digging ditches and rhynes.

The original grounds were commons or wastes, tracts of rough grazing which were only free of water for a short period each year. Although they were called commons, the rights to graze were strictly controlled by the lord of the manor, subject to some form of rental or work in lieu. The Enclosure Acts were designed to give rights to those same individuals and provide them with access to their own piece of ground. The problem was the cost of enclosure. Smaller owners were unable to meet this cost and sold out to those who could.

A plan of each enclosure was drawn up and complete details of drainage, boundaries and access roads were marked on it. Engineering works then proceeded from this. Droves were carriage-road widths of ground, left to provide access to every field in the area. Boundaries were marked by rhynes and ditches which led into the various rivers or streams in an interconnected network. Bridges were built over any waterways and then the whole working moor was handed over to its owners. The upkeep of ditches, droves and other works was thereafter the responsibility of the owners of the various plots. Droves were maintained by the field owners who required access. It was a complex and well-thought-out plan which many people now feel attempted to be as fair as possible to those involved.

A lot of information is available about that time because the cost had to be apportioned between those who benefited. John Billingsley wrote *A Survey of Agriculture of the County of Somerset in 1795*, just after the enclosures had taken place in the area. In it he recorded that contractors were paid 1/2d to 2/- per rope of 20 feet for ditching, which contrasted with a labourer's summer wages of 1/4d per day with cider, and rather less in winter. A farm cottage would attract a rent of between 30/- and 50/- per year at that time.

A further important change came about in 1801, with the passing of the Brue Drainage Act. This allowed the river to be straightened and a new clyse (sluice) constructed at Highbridge, with a lower sill. The North and South Drains were cut, with outlets into the Brue, although the fall was so small that they were not very effective. Nevertheless they brought a considerable change; during this period controlled flooding was introduced. The deposition of layers of silt provided an excellent natural fertiliser and promoted heavy growth of grass.

By 1822 Tadham was recorded as being well populated. Jack's Drove then joined up with Totney Drove, an east-west road also known now as Mark Road. But Blakeway still stopped short of Westhay, cut off by the river Brue. Even in 1822 it was still not possible to reach Cheddar by road from Wedmore, although tracks no doubt were open.

At the end of the eighteenth century Hannah More, the famous religious author and educationalist, opened a school at Wedmore, although it was not universally popular. The Dean of Wells appealed from the pulpit to have it closed but was fortunately not successful. It is not recorded why he was so against it. Hannah More was reported to have thought Wedmore 'depraved and shocking' at this time, which was the reason for starting her Sunday school there. At the same time the brothers Wall, from Wedmore, were champions of the backsword, becoming rich enough from this to build a house. They went on to field a complete cricket team from within the family.

In 1833 the Glastonbury canal opened and ran for a generation before succumbing to the costs of trying to keep it in working order. The canal linked Glastonbury to a tidal lock at Highbridge via the Brue Valley and the

Drainage moved ahead at a much greater rate in the 19th century. Tam standing on the edge of a rhyne, one of the 'viewed' ditches for which the Lower Brue Drainage Board is now responsible.

South Drain. Unfortunately it was rendered uncompetitive by its soil structure. The centre of the canal rose under pressure from the spoil on the banks and no solution to this problem was found at the time. It has remained something of a problem to all drainage specialists since, and nearly sank the opening of the Huntspill River in this century.

An overview of the village of Wedmore is given in the census of 1855, when it reached its peak population. Over 4,000 people were recorded as living in its bounds and there was a variety of shops and factories. These included a brickworks, a brewery, and a tannery. There was a cooperage, wheelwrights, blacksmiths, saddlers, a shoemaker and a clockmaker as well

89

as a barber and a tailor. Clearly it was a prosperous place, with a large general shop visited by people from many areas and still remembered in the village, together with a number of inns. By 1901 the population had diminished to under 3,000. The 1981 census showed a population of 2,757 although it has been growing fast since then, with the construction of new housing estates and much infilling.

In 1873 it was reported that ague (malaria) was commonplace in the Brue valley, though it was said to be a mild variety – and this only 120 years ago!

But the state of the marshes and peatland started to change with the introduction of steam pumps in the middle of the nineteenth century. Drainage could then move ahead at a much greater rate, with more chance of success, although the Levels often proved that they were as unpredictable as ever. The first pumps were introduced, on Westonzoyland Moor, in 1830. They were inadequate and costly but gradually gained in efficiency with the introduction of improved models. Between 1941 and 1950 many steam pumps were replaced by diesel units, with even greater gains in cost and operational efficiency.

In 1940 it was decided that a reliable supply of water was essential for the Puriton Munitions factory on the Poldens and this brought about the last and final stage of drainage on the Levels. A channel was dug between the Parrett Estuary and Gold Corner, just south of Tealham. The Huntspill River was constructed as a long thin reservoir with new sluices at each end. Originally it was planned to be 24 feet deep but the old trouble of spoil forcing up the centre of the channel again arose and eventually a depth of 16' feet was determined as feasible and practical for the needs of the factory, which required 3.5 million gallons a day. The new diesel pumps at Gold Corner Pumping Station were able to move 250 million gallons in 24 hours.

Water policy since 1958

By 1968, there were pumping stations in the Brue and Axe valleys at Gold Corner, North Drain and Clewer. There were clyses at Hobbs Boat and further down the Axe, at Highbridge, Cripp's Clyse (where the South Drain link joins

In 1987 a pump was converted to electric power and drainage levels were automated. The North Drain Pumping Station.

the North Drain) and Dunball. Only the Parrett and its tributaries were now open to the tide.

But a further considerable change took place on Tealham and Tadham in 1958, with the construction of the North Drain Pumping Station, at the same time as New Rhyne was widened to become the North Drain. This new regime was the most significant event in the history of these moors, bringing final control by man over the natural order of flooding.

The new machinery meant that it was possible to lift the waters off the land and into the Brue whatever the state of flood. Thereafter the only constraint lay in the state of wind and tide at the clyse at Highbridge. If the

91

water level was low the sluice would open automatically and dump the waters into the Bristol Channel. If winds had piled up the waters into the great bag of the Severn Estuary, the clyse could not be opened, for the outside water would be at a higher level than that inside. Then the ever-increasing waters would remain confined inland and no amount of pumping would have any effect, and waters pouring down from Mendip would brim the rivers and drains until they overflowed onto the surrounding countryside. This situation will continue as long as present land and sea-levels remain and will be further exacerbated under the greenhouse effect.

The ownership and control of this drainage system is complex. Ditches are the smallest feeders, surrounding the fields, and are put in by the individual farmers while rhynes are larger, officially maintained tributaries of the main drains. The Lower Brue Drainage Board is responsible 'for providing a system into which private land may drain'. Its policy document, *'The function of the Drainage Board'*, says:

> *This Board's function is to improve and maintain the rhyne system without which the whole of the area would be subject to flooding, the land generally being below high tide water mark. We also contribute towards the cost of the upkeep of the sea walls and of the rivers into which our rhynes flow...*
>
> *The National Rivers Authority – Wessex Region's responsibility, as far as watercourses are concerned, is limited to the main rivers. A Drainage Board looks after such channels (called viewing rhynes) as it deems necessary to maintain to provide a network for the connection to the main rivers of the ditches, which are only required for the drainage of particular fields or particular areas of land... Drainage Boards rely on voluntary, unpaid services of Drainage Board Members with intimate knowledge of the areas which they serve to select and maintain only the watercourses which are really necessary to provide the connecting function already mentioned. In addition to the basic function of drainage, the Board also has to exercise control over the flow of water in its main rhynes and ensure that there is adequate availability of water in all parts of the Board's area to maintain water levels appropriate for stock fence, stock drinking and nature conservation requirements.'*

It is interesting to note that the passage about nature conservation was put in by the Board before it became a part of their statutory duties under the 1989 Water Act. It betokens a practical realisation of their changing role in this new world.

The Lower Brue Drainage Board was set up under the Somersetshire Drainage Act of 1877 and is responsible for over 22,000 acres. The main rhynes were defined at that time, although they have been amended over the years. Before 1877, dyke-reeves used to ensure that ditches were maintained for the common good. The system was seen to be open to abuse, as only one person took a decision over each case, so the Boards were instituted with the idea of introducing a system free from possible corruption. The members would give joint decisions based on the experience of everyone involved. They were required to consider the overall welfare and well-being of the land. There are twenty IDBs in the Somerset and South Avon area.

Until recently, drainage rates were paid by both owner and occupier, but this changed on 1st April 1993, when new regulations came into effect, under which all land was revalued as of 1989, since when rates are paid only by occupiers..

The Board has twenty-one members elected annually by ratepayers according to a complicated sliding scale based on land-holding. Since 1993 the Board collects urban drainage rates (special levy), through the local council. The latter are entitled to put forward a further twenty-two members, but have only introduced two to date. Contributions pay for new drainage work together with administration and maintenance of existing works. Although elections are annual, in practice people tend to be elected for life or until they retire from farming, and it often proves difficult to fill vacancies. In the Lower Brue Drainage Board there is a part-time Clerk, together with full-time Engineer, and a Collector.

Although the Boards are elected, they are not always truly democratic. It is reported that a single family controlled one small Board with the exception of one member, the local vicar. Clearly the Government has taken note of this problem, under the 1993 regulations, with some Board members being appointed by local Councils.

The National Rivers Authority (NRA) is responsible for all water matters but local Drainage Boards do not report to it. Instead they head up the Ministry of Agriculture, Food and Fisheries. The NRA receives water from the rhynes into its main river system and is responsible for discharging it, as well as providing defences against the sea gaining access to the land again. It is a complicated relationship but has worked reasonably harmoniously over the years. Although there are rumblings from outside against the absolute power to drain exercised by the Internal Drainage Boards and the NRA.

Until the 1940s, pumping stations were operated by the IDBs, then they were assumed by the old Water Authorities (whose responsibilities have now been taken over by the NRA), who continued to operate them to the same policies. After SSSIs were declared in the 1980s, the IDBs believed that matters would continue as before, with them calling the tune, but the Water Authority no longer felt it could, for example, lower the water-table further at the request of a particular IDB. It understood that it had a duty under the SSSI to maintain the status quo. The pen – the pre-set level at which pumping will hold drain and rhyne levels – was reduced during the sixties and seventies, but no further reduction has occurred since 1980.

Until recently, the function of the IDBs, in country areas, was seen as looking after the interests of the farmers, to keep the land productive for as much of the year as possible. In recent years, however, an increasing representation has been received from those concerned with conservation and the environment, and the considerable changes brought about by the 1989 Water Act have placed a legal emphasis on the conservation of the environment and wildlife, as well as farming and traditional interests.

In times of drought the water-table is kept up by keeping the sluices closed for much of the time. Any water which still runs off the watershed is trapped in the Brue and the North and South Drains. The water-table rises and grass growth is promoted. When rain has been above average, or at the start of the summer, judicious adjustment to the sluices and controlled pumping ensures that the lower-lying areas are dried out. In this way a long growing season is combined with stable ground.

In the early days after installation of the pumps at the North Drain, levels were set manually. During the week the keepers of the great engines would watch markers and switch on the pumps when these levels were reached, though normally no-one was on duty at night. At weekends overtime would be involved and by Sunday evenings the water level would have risen appreciably in the North Drain and surrounding rhynes and ditches.

In 1987 one pump was converted to electric power and drainage levels were automated, the pumps switching on and off at preset levels, and the welcome respites at weekends and during the night have therefore ceased. Although the water levels were gradually lowered before 1980, there is no doubt that the real drying of the moors has occurred since automation was introduced; all local observation confirms this. The Water Authority (and later the NRA) has never regarded this as a change in regime, yet there has been a 300 per cent increase in pumping potential since 1987. Now the pumps cut in when levels rise to a predetermined point throughout the 168 hours of the week; whereas previously people were on duty for only 45 – 50 hours a week, unless there was a particular emergency. No wonder the moors have dried out so considerably over the last few years!

As I write, with rain falling heavily, the water in many ditches is just a curl in the bottom, a snake of silver between chocolate banks. The North Drain is running at great speed beneath the bridge on Jack's Drove, indicating that pumping is at full bore. Yet it is January, when the fields are empty of livestock, so it is difficult to reconcile this with any policy which makes sense in either farming or wildlife terms.

Now any over-flooding is removed rapidly, instead of thoroughly soaking the pores of the soil as it did when it stayed for days on end. The topsoil is not being allowed to waterlog at the beginning of winter, as it has in the past. By pumping more frequently the whole structure of the soil is being altered. Machine-cleaned rhynes, with slicker bank surfaces and little vegetation, let the water run without obstruction, contributing further to the powerful suction round the edges of the fields, without allowing any reserve for warmer months.

In his remarkable book, *The Draining of the Somerset Levels*, published in 1970, Professor Michael Williams was still writing about the days when all drainage was 'good'. It was the duty of the Water Authorities to encourage anything which would increase farming efficiency. The book contains no real references to ecology, wildlife or the quality of life. Nevertheless he does talk about the process of conversion from diesel to electric pumps and the effects which might be felt in terms of shrinkage of the soil. I cannot do better than quote the whole passage, for it sums up clearly the facts of what is now happening.

'Whenever electric pumps have been installed, a vast improvement(sic) *has resulted...A strict control of water-level is now possible and surface water can be cleared within hours of appearing...*

As a result of the recent increase in pumping and the general improvement in drainage, two difficulties may be expected. The first is that of peat shrinkage and wastage through improved drainage. Experience in the Fenland of eastern England has shown what enormous problems these could become. Nevertheless, it appears unlikely that the same changes would take place in the Levels where all conditions tend to keep the peat saturated. Foremost among these conditions is the regional pattern of farming, which is overwhelmingly pastoral in nature, being based on relatively high rainfall and therefore tolerating a high degree of soil moisture. Over 90 per cent of the farms are devoted to dairying and stock-rearing, and over 90 per cent, on average, of the area of a Levels parish is given over to permanent grass or rough grazing, cultivation being confined almost entirely to flood-free 'islands' and upland edges. A low water table is therefore not essential, and the peat is not allowed to dry out. The saturation of the peat is also consciously aided by the practice of 'wet-draining', whereby water is kept in the rhynes for fencing and irrigation purposes, and, it is averred by some farmers, to prevent the welling-up of the rhyne bottoms, which would occur if the weight of the water was absent. In addition to these factors there is still the controlled flooding of the moors for warping and pest control (although these practices are of declining importance), and there is the possibility of uncontrolled floods, both of which cause the saturation of the peat. In the experience of the River Board, peat shrinkage 'has not been measurable'; however, the possibility of the danger arising with improved farming techniques is recognised, and all pump inflows have been constructed so that a possible 4ft lowering of the surface could be accommodated in the future.

The second difficulty arising from the trend towards pumping is that it will increase the already high level of water in the main channels. This danger has been made more real by the continual construction of stronger and higher embankments, which make it more difficult for the swollen rivers to break through and dissipate their volume in the surrounding moors.

It is noticeable that the artificially-drained areas have sunk and are now the first to be flooded when such is allowed to happen. Pied wagtail on Tadham Moor.

97

Unfortunately, what was predicted in Professor Williams's book has occurred and the situation has changed. Arable land is no longer confined mainly to the 'flood-free islands and upland edges'; some 5,500 acres of the Levels were cultivated in 1991. Government action has now stopped this trend, but the very existence of this cultivated land determines the levels of water on the over 90 per cent of farm land not requiring a low water table.

There are further effects from this on farming and fertility. The moor peat is not naturally fertile, for it is an inert material. One only has to observe what happens when a ditch is cleared to appreciate this. Regrowth of grass or herbage on the bank-side scrapings is extremely slow and it may take years for the natural grass to return. This is the consequence of stopping natural fertilising of the ground by flood-silt – a feature of any undrained wetland or water-meadow.

The pumps are set to suck powerfully and immediately as soon as water levels rise. Variable-speed pumping means that the rate of discharge can be increased extremely quickly when required. Rhynes have been canalised and deepened and are cleared annually or twice-yearly, IDB sluices are open all winter, so there is no impediment to the water running immediately off the moors. This has had the effect, in recent years of low rainfall, of drying off the land at an alarming rate. In 1990 Tealham had floods in January but by early summer farmers were complaining of a lack of water. The physical evidence of change is quite clear: the land is sinking below the droves and roads, it no longer quakes when machinery or cattle pass along it and water rarely lies for long in the runnels in winter.

The very structure of the soil is changing, for it is no longer being kept moist a few inches below the surface. When peat dries out it does so more or less permanently, as it is a largely impervious substance once it has hardened after losing its normal moisture.

In the years up to the early 1980s all this mattered little to most people. The word from Government was to look after farming interests above all else. Only the crankiest conservationists raised their voices in protest and even they had little real evidence of any measurable problem – just a feeling of unease at the way our wilder countryside was disappearing.

Then in 1983 the Government completely reversed its policy in relation to farming and decided to offer payments in return for farmers looking after SSSIs. This was the start of a recognition that there was no longer any need to clear and drain land to provide the most 'efficient' means of growing yet more food at the expense of everything else. It was the time when Europe realised that there were other priorities and that the environment needed protecting from policies which had resulted in so much overproduction of food.

While politicians like to claim that it was a recognition of 'green' values which produced the U-turn, money was the real key, as it always is. Economics showed that it was cheaper to provide payments to protect a way of life, rather than paying higher subsidies to produce food that no-one wanted.

The SSSI scheme of payments for loss of profits, which arose from complying with restrictions applied under the Order, was followed in 1987 by a scheme inspired by the then European Community (now the European Union) whereby cash was made available as a right to people in certain selected Environmentally Sensitive Areas (ESAs), which included 68,000 acres of the Somerset Levels and the whole of Tealham and Tadham Moors. Under this scheme, farmers were encouraged to continue to farm traditionally in return for payments made by the Ministry of Agriculture, Food and Fisheries (MAFF). It was designed to provide a reasonable living, while preserving the characteristics of the countryside. But – and it was an extremely important 'but' – no mention was made about water levels. They did not even feature in the terms of the first ESA scheme, though this has finished and recently been replaced by another which recognises water as a key element. .

This need not have mattered if the Water Authorities, their successor the NRA, and the IDBs had acted strongly under the spirit of the regulations. But while action was taken by the Water Authority, in refusing to sanction further drainage after 1980 or, as they put it, maintaining the status quo, this was no more than turning a blind eye to the real situation. The moors have become

Nowadays many ditches are cleaned out at frequent intervals by more efficient mechanical diggers, so less herbage grows and the banks are steeper, providing difficult feeding access for young birds. A healthy summer ditch some years back.

drier year by year and many believe that they may have even reached the point of no return.

On Tealham and Tadham there has been an acceleration in the drainage process in the years since the area was declared an ESA. Pumping is more thorough; many ditches are cleaned out increasingly frequently by more efficient mechanical diggers, so that little or no herbage grows in them; and there is no respite in pumping. The higher summer pen ends promptly each year in early December, and brown sides appear on the rhynes as the water drops some six inches and stays there until the next spring. Twists of water run along the bottom of shallow ditches where water lapped the edge of the grass the day before, such is the power of the winter pumping. Why?

The reason is not obvious. Cattle no longer live on the moors in winter. Sheep have recently arrived, and while it is true that they feed off the late aftermath in early winter, they do not usually stay out on this ground, and the time when a 'lamb mountain' is announced cannot be far off. Of course farmers have to have somewhere to spread manure from the yards and some goes onto the moors, though not much; muck-spreading means that heavy machinery needs to get out onto what used to be soft ground during the winter months. But surely this cannot be the sole reason for the increased stringency of the drainage regime.

One reason which has been given is that it enables cattle to be taken out to the moor earlier than they otherwise would, so as to gain maximum advantage from the early grass. But it does not require a winter-long lowering of the water table to achieve this.

The NRA gives other technical reasons for lowering the water table in winter, but none seem important enough to justify such drastic effects on wildlife. They say that in peaty areas it is easier to dredge rhynes and ditches when the water is low; that if the fields are normally kept dry in the wet winter months, they are free to act as storage reservoirs when it does rain heavily, thus preventing early inundation; that wetland is cold land, which delays spring growth; and that waterlogging delays some agricultural operations.

I asked an NRA official why the pen was changed in early December? Why not set any lower pen – if there has to be one – in, say, February or even March? Such a change would certainly provide better conditions for wintering waders and waterfowl and keep the overall state of the wetlands closer to their former conditions, while still fulfilling the NRA requirements for such activities as ditch dredging and early growth of spring grass. After consideration, he said that such timing might be feasible. Even more telling was the remark that, "if there had been a conservation lobby twenty years ago, the winter pen would probably never have been set below that of summer".

Unfortunately antagonism seems to have built up between the Lower Brue Drainage Board on the one hand and some of the bodies representing conservation on Tealham and Tadham on the other; the latter also appear to have rather strained relations with some of the farmers in the area. It reflects a lack of understanding of people and how to deal with them.

"They conservationists want to stop us farming our own land. What do they know about milk or hay, or what tillage is needed?" is a remark that has been heard in the community.

But the other side of the argument is also voiced, "Don't they realise that ESA payments will stop if the original reason for them is lost, when wetland becomes dry pasture?" This could be a real threat to many who accept both the need for ESAs and the reality of living with subsidy.

Another opinion is that, "in a few years all this bloody conservation will be forgotten. All they mountains will be finished and they'll be wanting us to produce more again."

So what is happening to Tealham and Tadham Moors now that man has achieved his ambition and tamed the effects of the flood? Where are we going?

The last few years have seen two apparently anomalous situations fighting for precedence. First, there is the declaration of the area as an ESA, with many farmers receiving payments to maintain permanent pasture and improve wildlife habitat. At the same time the existence of SSSIs on so much land has enabled the National Conservancy Council to stop further ploughing and deep drainage. This ought to halt change and bring some benefits. However, in practice a more efficiently lowered water table has meant that the expected habitat improvement has not taken place. It looked as though the policy of doing nothing was winning.

Until recently it was believed that there was no outside authority which could overrule the IDBs and the local Water Authorities in their decisions on drainage matters. It appears this situation has been changed with the clarification of legislation arising from water privatisation. Now there are new responsibilities towards the environment and conservation built into the constitutions of the

The Water Act of 1989 placed equal emphasis on conservation. Redshank still breed on Tealham Moor.

Water Authorities' successor bodies. So at this stage it seemed important to put some questions to those ultimately responsible for implementing water policy in the area.

The NRA was set up in 1989, as a successor to the Water Authorities, with responsibility for water-regulating functions: flood defence, land drainage, water quality, pollution control, water resources conservation and management, fisheries, aquatic recreation, conservation of water and the environment. So I went to see their Wessex Region, which, amongst other areas, is responsible for Somerset Levels – as well as Tealham Moor.

It is clear that the relationship between the authorities and farming has altered considerably over the years. The old Water Authority's function was to ease and improve the farmers' lot in the quest for greater productivity. Gradually this has changed, and the NRA took over from Wessex Water under a new set of conditions set by the Water Act of 1989. This placed emphasis on farming and also led to special emphasis on wildlife, so that the NRA has to care for wildlife both while carrying out its traditional functions and as a special task in its own right. This is a dramatic change.

I asked why, in their opinion, Tealham Moor has dried out so much in the last few years. I was told that the very dry winters of 1989 and 1990, with their long summer droughts, undoubtedly exacerbated conditions. Moreover new variable speed pumps with automatic pumping levels have kept the water table much more even than previously, and farmers have taken advantage of the changing conditions and installed their own systems, which has increased the problem. There has also been a long, cumulative effect from the lowering of the winter pen.

I was not satisfied with this reply and probed further. My own and other peoples' observations had shown a definite increase in the speed of change recently. It was clear that the increased intensity of pumping since automation in 1987 had contributed to this effect but no one would admit to this. Indeed, no acknowledgement was made of any drying out of the moors in a letter I received at the time, which read: 'As we are maintaining the same level now as we were before the automation occurred, I do not understand your deduction that [the] area is drier.' The point was again made that water levels had not been changed at the main pumping stations since 1980. They stated that people had been available previously and would have undertaken overtime where it was necessary. Further it was implied that the operators would have overpumped to allow for rising water levels at night and over weekends.

My observations and those of others contradict these assertions. A frequent rise in levels was seen over weekends prior to 1987; while anyone familiar with the area will say how much more extreme the pumping is now when it rains hard. People who talk about the effects use similar words: 'the ditches are pumped dry to leave but a trickle of water in the bottom.'

However, the NRA told me that their officers had become concerned about the long-term changes which were taking place on the Levels and which were not consistent with their duty to conservation. The Somerset Flood Defence Committee is the statutory body which determines how flood defences will be executed by the NRA. In 1991 it formed a subcommittee to consider afresh the water policy on the Levels in the light of legislation which involves this responsibility for conservation. The subcommittee consisted of various members of the main Committee, together with the General Manager, Flood-Defence Manager and Conservation Manager of the NRA, and the Chief Executive of the Somerset Trust for Nature Conservation. Written evidence was taken from interested parties following three meetings at which various views were expressed. Meetings were held separately with the NFU and the IDB; with MAFF; and with conservationists. The results of this emerged in a report issued by the NRA and were extremely important in that they reflected an entirely new outlook. The report sought to raise water-levels in parts of the moor and stressed the need to consider conservation measures, wildlife and farming in planning for the future.

Some immediate action was taken in response to the reports of changes on Tealham and Tadham. NRA engineers took a closer look at the North Drain Pumping Station and its automation. The pump on and off levels had originally been set at a differential of nearly 18 inches and it was found that this caused great surges in the ditches as the power cut in for long periods and produced the trickles of water mentioned earlier. The differential was then cut to 6 inches after some experimentation. While it will take a long period to see the effect on residual water in the pores of the fields, there are some changes in water behaviour in the ditches and rhynes ditches – the final part of the network. The great surges do not occur under normal circumstances and it is an altogether gentler process. Only time will tell whether this is a significant long-term change.

Perhaps most importantly the point was made that everyone – farmers, the NRA and conservationists – were all pressing MAFF to make future ESA payments dependent on a premium for higher water tables. In 1993 a new ESA scheme came into force and Tier 3 of this did indeed take water-levels into account. Full details of this are given in Chapter 8, but special payments are now available for keeping blocks of land flooded throughout the winter and two such areas are now in operation on Tealham Moor.

These developments left me with a markedly more hopeful view of the future. Undoubtedly the NRA now takes its conservation responsibilities as seriously as their many other duties. I thought it would then be a good idea to take my investigations to the next rung in the ladder, the Lower Brue Drainage Board.

According to some conservationists that was the body that was obstructing change. It was said by some that they exacerbated the problems on the moors. Was this really so? Clearly it was important to discuss its responsibilities and where it stood in this debate. I spent a fascinating couple of hours hearing about this and having all my questions answered fully and openly.

I first asked how the water table or water levels were set. There are two distinct phases. In winter, from approximately December to May, all sluices in the rhynes are opened wide so as to get rid of the water as quickly as possible. During the summer, the practice is reversed – sluices are closed to conserve water in the ditches and rhynes. The sluices are then raised or lowered during the course of the summer to balance the water in the rhynes and ditches and ensure the land does not dry out. Localised problems of particular blocks can be dealt with by individual sluices. There is no other requirement. I was told that no pressure had been exerted on the Water Authority or the NRA to raise or lower the pens.

Tealham and Tadham remain mainly permanent pasture in 1991.

As far as conservation is concerned, the Board sees itself as sitting on the fence, although the point was made several times that they are conscious of the need to take SSSIs into account. The Board sees itself as having a duty both to conservation and to farming. A dozen or so years ago there was no talk of conservation. Then the first people approached them about their policy and gradually it has taken on greater importance. The Board works well with the Vincent Wildlife Trust and English Nature, though it has proved more difficult to achieve a meeting of minds with some other bodies. It was emphasised that, although individual members may have strong views about a specific matter, the Board as a body bends over backwards to consider all factors. It believes it takes a considered view before making any decision on policy.

Although I am sure that there will continue to be differences of opinion on the details of how to attain the aims of both conservationists and farmers, I believe that a slow but sure change is taking place. There is more awareness of the pressures on maintaining the countryside and the wildlife in it, although there will inevitably be some who will fight for their complete independence to the finish. The Lower Brue Drainage Board sits in the middle of this discussion and, if only from long practice, tends to reflect its farmer members' opinions. As these change, so will its views.

Tealham and Tadham remain mainly permanent pasture. Several farms have underdrained land and private pumping stations drone away in spring and autumn evenings. But most farms have not been allowed to re-seed this drained land, as they are on officially notified SSSIs and subject to official restraint. However a County Council demonstration farm on Tealham Moor has some drained and ploughed ground, with a diesel drainage pump and deep ditches round it, and practises various types of agriculture in order to study the effect of new methods on a moorland farm.

So, after following this progress, from the marshlands of thousands of years ago to present-day pastures, what does the moor consist of now and how is it affected by recent changes?

Of a total of around 2,750 acres, just over 2,400 acres remain untouched permanent pasture and 200 odd are deep-drained, with private pumping stations, while another 90 acres are gravity-drained. Of this drained ground 70 acres has been ploughed, while the total acreage dedicated to Tier 3 ESA payments, with light flooding occurring all winter on two blocks, is 118 acres – the start of a change of attitude which many hope will be permanent.

As this book goes to press the first thoughts have been put down on paper for possible future official schemes to control water-levels more precisely for the whole of Tealham and similar key areas of the moors. This would indeed be a victory for common sense and pragmatism.

MOORLAND BIRDLIFE

The moors strike people differently. For many, they are a haven for wildlife, full of unusual species in some numbers. Others may be disappointed, feeling that there is little wildlife around, particularly if they visit the area on a colourless, bleached out, over-hot day in late summer or one of those mysterious winter days when everything seems to have vanished. But at other times there is a surprising vigour. Great billowing clouds of lapwings fill the sky or clouds of dark starlings rise to an unknown fear, the rustle of their wings seeming to lie over all other sounds. Countless thousands of birds fill the sky at one moment and as suddenly leave them empty.

The size of the skyscape has something to do with it. Although it is not so vast as that of the Fenlands – there is a low rim of hills to pull it down to scale – it can be awesome. It reduces us humans and our comfortable depth of vision to a tiny portion of the whole.

There is a distinct pattern to the moorland year. The same creatures arrive at the same time, almost regardless of weather; flowers emerge through spring grass or late snow at much the same time each season. The calendar of nature runs true unless external forces corrupt it. It is only when you realise that something has not happened, some creature is late or has not arrived, that you begin to wonder why. But it is easier to register a new occurrence than a non-event.

This has been the case with the effects of drainage over recent years. They only gradually become apparent. We wondered vaguely why the pattern of wildlife seemed different. Then we realised that changes had been taking place insidiously for some years. The odd field had been mole drained; ditches

A family party of Bewick's swans. These swans have been shown to pair for life and the young stick with them even after their long flight from Siberia.

cleaned by mechanical digger more frequently and more thoroughly; a field had been ploughed and reseeded, another was being fed with artificial fertiliser in autumn and spring. The balance of flora built up through hundreds of years of traditional farming cannot be restored, once it has vanished following the introduction of new grasses and the use of artificial fertilisers.

Nevertheless change should not be condemned for its own sake. The moors have altered continually since they first started to emerge from the brackish floods and were first used to graze flocks. There have been continuing changes to the environment since the first ditches were dug in Norman times. The birds, mammals and insects have had to adapt and change to fit the new conditions, at times favourable and at others inimical. We become used to a certain set of circumstances, a special population of wildlife marking the passing of the seasons. Any change to this, resulting in the loss of a familiar bird, seems like the death of an old friend. We weep inside in silent protest, but some other creature may arrive to fill the vacuum.

This chapter and the next give an idea of the variety of wildlife found on the moors over the past twenty or so years but, if current practices continue, there is a real danger of a continuing loss of richness and variety which will diminish our life and that of our children.

Water birds

More than anything, the moors are a land of water; slow moving rhynes, little rills bubbling over as frost melts; and the long lines of gripes filling with water as the winter fields soak up the rains until they can hold no more. So it is the water birds which come to mind first when I am far from home. Perhaps the heron, that tall, lanky fisherman, is the true familiar of the moorland spirits.

At times our great open spaces are mysteriously empty of life. At others, particularly in the pre-spring period when the earth is coming to life once again, it is difficult to drive a few hundred yards without disturbing a gaunt skeletal figure from its fishing. The heron then flaps heavily into the air and cruises over the fields to find some new section of rhyne on which to concentrate. Roadside rhynes seem to hold the sweetest water, the largest and most easily caught fish and the most succulent frogs, judging by the number of birds which rise up mournfully on slow-beating, wide, high-lift wings, disturbed yet again by a passing car. The power of those apparently cumbersome wings should not be underestimated. One huge down-stroke can row them feet into the air where they twist and turn like a sparrowhawk.

These moorland herons breed in a mixed wood on the edge of Tadham. Their untidy nests are occupied early in the year, when winter winds blow hard and ice rimes the ditch edges. Rooks nest in the same trees, often on the same branches, and a permanent state of war exists between them while they are building their nests and in the early stages of sitting. The rooks appear to resent the herons and this boils over and causes great panic among the herons during windy weather. Each time a heron comes in to land on the topmost twigs of a tree, as is their practice, a rook will stoop, like some avenging fighter, right across its front. It quite deliberately tries to upset what is an extremely delicate manoeuvre for such a large but light bird, with its enormous wing area. Timing has to be precise if a heron is to gain its balance in the gusts, and on such a minute perch. Because of their size and extreme lightness of bone, they are vulnerable to unexpected gusts, and there are times when they blow like thistledown. I have watched fascinated as rooks interfere in this way with their landings, and the herons have to wheel round again before coming in for another try. This can happen three or four times.

When they are feeding their young they travel further afield than normal. Presumably the closer rhynes are fished out, as early families clamour for food. One of these flyways is right over our house. Sometimes, when it is warm and still, the herons float along, barely flapping, then circle two or three times before gliding on downhill. The thermals over Keyton Hill help them on their way. On these long spring flights they often give their presence away by a series of harsh calls, as if holding a shouted mid-air conversation. A heron slowly flapping across the moors at low level must be among the

Heron hunched up beside a rhyne. They look bulky but are extraordinarily light, with hollow bones and huge wingspan to give them surprisingly quick reactions.

113

Mallard are present all year and breed extensively in the area.

most evocative of sights. It gives the impression that it was here long before us and will be around long after we have gone. It has adapted from marshy swamp living to successful survival in a landscape of grassland and drainage ditches, so it should be able to cope with further changes as they occur in the future. Its main enemies are cold and ice covering its feeding grounds.

Water edged, water soaked, always within sight and sound of water, the area is a natural habitat for ducks. At certain times they are here in abundance, at others the place is mysteriously empty. A number of species are seen regularly; mallard and teal are present all the year. When mink first arrived, duck numbers diminished, but seem to have recovered. Mallard produce young over much of the year, seemingly unaffected by any except the worst of weather. Perhaps this is the main reason for their success as a species. I have seen ducklings on the rhyne at the end of February, sparkling and glowing like scraps of gold, swimming vigorously into a glorious golden sunset, while the icy air was honed like a razor.

The size, weight and pugnacity of the mallard must be another factor in its survival. In captivity, they are notorious for their ferocity towards drakes of other species. In the frenzy of spring courtship they have been known to drown shoveler and gadwall drakes. They are also keen on mating with other

species, and extremely rough in their methods. Should they take a fancy to a duck of a smaller species, they may almost drown then in their frenzy and fatalities are not uncommon while mating. Handsome the mallard drake may be, but under the finery lies the heart of a born bully.

Teal, by contrast, are small, lightly built birds. They are nervous in the extreme and always the first to jump at signs of danger. When disturbed, they are liable to circle longer than other duck before landing again in their favourite feeding place. They may appear delicate but they are actually tough little creatures, and are present the whole winter, however dreadful the weather, well adapted to our habitat. One winter I watched a pair picking their way across the frozen waters of the River Brue, finding a variety of things to eat as they went, for the cold does not seem to diminish their vitality, as it does so many other species. The ones I saw were alert and obviously making good use of conditions which had driven many other birds from the moors.

When I see a spring of teal – what an appropriate collective term – catapult up, rising 10 feet or so in an instant, the moment seems to contain the very essence of life. Sometimes eye and mind seem to change gear and the leap appears to take place in slow motion. The wings flex with the power of the strokes, almost meeting underneath, and the whole bird quivers with the effort. They leap, then dash off, flying low and fast, camouflaged against the dull winter background. They are familiar, a part of the scenery, yet completely wild and alien.

Teal do not often allow you to come near, being possessed of some super-sense to detect you even behind a bank. The cold may have dulled their normal sharp senses on this occasion.

Teal are among the most difficult birds to photograph in the wild. I have tried to stalk them on many occasions. I will see a little party through a gap in the bank, far away. Then comes the long stalk, worming my way through the dead ground between them and me, certain that I cannot be seen. But suddenly they will be up like rockets! How? Do they sense my presence? Do they have eyes on stalks?

Unlike wigeon and other surface-feeding ducks, they do not circle and return overhead. They are far more cautious. They scent danger and use the contours of the land effectively, flashing by at high speed for a first reconnaissance, only dropping down when they are certain that danger is past.

One spring I was driving across the moor and caught sight of what looked like a pair of teal on Old Rhyne. I stopped the car on the hump bridge and pulled out the binoculars. A fine pair of garganey or summer teal came into focus. The drake was unmistakable, with a fine line of white down the neck, although the female was indistinguishable from a teal. Were they passing through or stopping to breed in these so suitable surroundings? I never did find out, though I had my suspicions. Someone else reported later sightings, so perhaps they stayed after all.

Duck pour in in their hundreds and thousands when it has rained for a long time, followed by a day or two of hard freezing and then a quick thaw. February is the usual time for such an influx. The fields are then at their most delectable. They are pooled and runnelled with water, pale green in the sunlight. The edges may be rimed with ice, stained yellow from the peat-water below. Sometimes such conditions bring in absolutely nothing; at others, what appear to be the same conditions will bring in wave after wave of ducks and sometimes even some grey geese.

One year I spent Boxing Day in a canoe paddling over the centre of normally dry fields in the middle of Tealham Moor. For several hundred yards on either side of the North Drain, it was deep enough for canoeing. Later I managed to make my way down almost as far as the farms at the bottom of Westham village. It was a most extraordinary aftermath to Christmas. Glastonbury Tor looked as though it floated on a great sea and appeared to be wreathed in a continually moving cloud of insects, the outflyers of great clouds of wigeon circling restlessly in the clear light. This great concourse gradually settled, so that rafts of birds built up until they all but covered the shallow waters around the North Drain. The next day they were all gone – it was as if they had never been.

It turned out to be a memorable morning. My daughter Fiona was steering and paddling while I struggled to cope with a long and awkward camera lens in the confines of the narrow and unstable canoe. To compound our problems, a strong breeze was blowing and it proved exceedingly difficult to steer the craft with the paddler up front – a position which was dictated by my weight. However time and the excitement of the chase did not allow for a change.

Just as a group of birds came into range and I started to focus, the boat would begin to rotate, slowly at first and then with gathering speed. I would twist to keep up and then the birds would vanish from the viewfinder at that critical moment when they had at last come into focus.

"Surely you can keep it steady for a few seconds," I said crossly.

Duck pour in in their hundreds and thousands when conditions are just right. Wigeon by the North Drain.

"All right, you have a go. I'm doing my best!"

Nevertheless we enjoyed it and managed to take some memorable shots of those great hordes of birds on this temporary inland sea.

Wigeon are always the predominant species at these times. Sometimes they are the only ducks present. There is nothing they prefer more than short, wet, tender grass, which they graze as seriously as sheep. They give an impression of white as they take off, the prominent wing bars catching the eye. The birds call and chat most engagingly as they fly overhead. The males have a lovely liquid double whistle, which is heard most often while feeding. In flight the more predominant sound is the 'gurr, gurr' of the females. The birds circle endlessly when disturbed by a walker as though they are wary in the extreme, they seem determined always to land in the same special spot.

You can fool them by standing quite still and blending in with some prominent object. Even though the fields of Tealham are quite open, the gates stand out and I have found that I can trick the birds into returning simply by standing close up to a thick gatepost. Part of the secret is to wear a hat which shades the eyes and the white of the face. Nothing seems to give one's presence away more than a pale face moving in line with them as they pass over.

I have stood out in the middle of the moor on many a clear, frosty morning, dogs in to heel, and watched the wigeon circling over, slowly losing height with each circuit, their eyes fixed on their special bit of grazing. Their wings flex and straighten, incredibly smooth and powerful. Their bodies are streamlined, torpedo-shaped, yet strangely bulky. As they fly, their heads move and they look at each other as they chat. It seems a convivial affair.

On one memorable occasion, the crowd of birds on the banks of the North Drain turned out to be composed of equal numbers of teal and wigeon. This is the only time I have been able to identify obviously foreign flocks of the former, and it gave me a splendid opportunity to see the difference in temperament and character between these two species. They kept close together, but grouped quite separately. The wigeon grazed methodically down the lines of short grass, in a long rank, while the teal fed indiscriminately, darting here and there to pick up morsels. When a passer-by disturbed the flock, the teal shot straight up into the air, all together, but the wigeon rose in waves, so that the sky above the feeding point gradually filled with ducks, like aircraft gathering above an airfield before setting out on a wartime bombing raid. The teal were up and out of sight in seconds, hugging the contours and hiding themselves in the background. The wigeon seemed to fly as if in slow motion. Each wave was quite separate and each bird just a fraction behind the next. It was as if they were painted on a roll of cloth which was unfolding to show a widening scene.

The next day, the wigeon were still there, but there was no sign of the restless teal. Instead there were a number of shoveler drakes, unbelievably brilliant in the sunshine and the clear, frosty air. I settled down to watch them with considerable pleasure. They are among my favourite ducks, perhaps because their heavy bills give them a slight air of ungainliness, although this disappears in flight. Then they assume a classic angular shape which suits them well. They have great speed and dash. Although they fly with great power, they are extremely manoeuvrable. I have seen a pair leap out of the reeds exactly like a spring of teal, and then corkscrew away as if avoiding a hail of bullets.

Pintails are less frequent, though still regular, visitors. Incredibly elegant, graceful and quite unmistakable, the drake can be picked out immediately, whether in flight or feeding out on the fields. Both male and female have a sinuous grace, although the male takes this to the extreme, posing with careful indifference, like a Japanese watercolour. His neck stretches and arches with studied nonchalance, the elegance emphasised by the long white line stretching up the neck from the breast into the chocolate brown head. This line moves and changes shape as the bird feeds, while the delicate barring on the flanks ripples like the visible movement of muscles under the skin.

One winter I found myself splashing through a series of fields, in varying depths of water. It was one of those days when everything went just right. The air crisp and fresh. Only the faintest breeze ruffled the surface water into crisp patterns, and the sun was brilliant. The reflected sky looked almost Prussian blue against the startling pale green of the grass standing through the surface water. Someone was walking their dog along the far bank and I watched curiously as some tiny dots took off from the surface. Something was still around. The ducks vanished, flying hard and straight.

"There goes my chance," I muttered. The dogs continued to search the fields ahead. I leaned on the gate, whistling, just gazing round at that marvellous scene. Suddenly a little group of ducks came hurtling round from behind a clump of thorns. They were going like bullets, their pinions whistling shrilly as they came straight at me as if they had not seen me. Automatically I swung the camera, following through, and had an unexpectedly clear series of pictures; as sharp and crystalline as the moment itself. My mind seemed to have slipped into slow-motion and I had all the time in the world to focus and

Goosanders travelling fast. 'All were males, with dark heads and brilliant white breasts.

120

shoot – although the goosanders must have been travelling very fast indeed. What excitement! I had this clear impression of short, narrow wings and solid, streamlined bodies. All were males, with dark heads at the end of long necks and brilliant white breasts.

Every year we see these splendid ducks for a day or two. There does not appear to be any pattern to their arrival and departure, weather seems to be the key, not season. Wary of walkers, they swim like true diving ducks, part-submerged, streamlined, powerful. They are often accompanied by smew, which are dwarfed by their large companions. For a couple of years the accompanying smew has been a solitary red-headed female. She fed and flew with them as if attached by a piece of string.

Another day I was walking past Old Rhyne and, just for form's sake, called

Smew, seen occasionally on the North Drain, usually in company with goosanders.

121

the dogs to heel and kept in the dead ground where possible. It was just as well. The field beyond, which edged the North Drain, was full of birds. Most were waders: lapwing and golden plover with a smattering of dunlin. But in the far corner I saw a little bunch of ducks. The majority were pintails, sinuous and graceful, together with a pair or two of wigeon, altogether tubbier and well fed. But the most conspicuous were a pair of shelduck in full colour, feeding a little apart from the rest and looking very much larger. The dozing pintails were all drakes, with long necks curved elegantly over their shoulders and heads tucked into wing coverts. The line of white and chocolate was clearly visible in the pale sunlight. All at once they were off! The dogs must have disturbed them and they leapt into the air as if propelled by springs.

I waited, restraining the dogs, then decided to cross the gate as unobtrusively as possible, trying to keep down low and blend in with the line of the post. But I need not have bothered. The feeding birds in the far runnels were mainly dunlin. The lapwings in between made off in waves, but nothing seemed to disturb the dunlin. They just ran ahead of us as we approached and eventually one or two flopped where they were and slept. The dogs were intrigued. I could see their noses twitching as they fought their feelings valiantly to obey my muttered commands to stay at heel. It was clear that the whole flock of dunlin was absolutely exhausted. They must have just landed after a long flight and were quite unafraid of me or the dogs. This all pointed to a long journey from some place where there were few people.

Dunlin, exhausted after its great migratory flight.

Eventually, the whole flock lifted off and flew a few dozen yards off, leaving me alone with a pair which skittered about feeding only a few feet away. By this time the sun was extremely low in the sky and these little birds were bathed in a curious and very beautiful bronze light. At times they seemed almost mauve tinted. I have never seen colours like it and the photographs I took reflect part of this, although not with the freshness of reality itself. The dunlin ran around in front of us, dabbing here, burying their bills there, pausing a moment as if to listen before jabbing and pushing again. The immediate need for food was paramount, surmounting their fatigue and natural wariness.

It was fascinating watching them so closely. The field was awash, but little islands, tussocks of herbage or the remains of mole hills, emerged above the water. The dunlin swam from island to island with vigorous strokes, creating quite a bow wave. Eventually they stopped, put their heads under their wings and went to sleep. We crept away without disturbing them further and walked home in the coppery twilight.

Shelduck strike me as being our least typical moorland ducks. They are really inhabitants of the sea and saltmarsh and look totally alien when they visit us. They do so periodically, to no set pattern, arriving when the mood takes them and usually leaving within a day. The brilliant orange, green and white of their plumage looks exotic and out of place on our fields, but welcome for all that. They are very beautiful, but not of the moors. Bridgwater Bay lies about a quarter of an hour's flight away. It is a major haunt of shelduck and one of the few places in the world where they gather in their thousands during the flightless period of the moult.

On rare occasions geese arrive out on the moor. There are also a couple of pairs of resident greylags which live out on the fringes, raised by and attached to a small private nature reserve. I hope that they will breed and multiply but so far this has not happened and they keep away over by the Polden hills most of the time. Regular, but infrequent, visitors are Canada geese, huge and foreign-looking. Of the two, I think greylags are preferable; they fit in with

123

When it is really cold flights of grey geese drop into the fields. Greylag geese over Tealham Moor.

the scale of the landscape better. Canada geese are really too large.

When it is really cold we see great wavering formations of geese passing high overhead. Twice in recent years these have landed for a few hours and I have watched wild whitefronts grazing their way across some of the drier fields. More unusual was the bird which accompanied a flight of Bewick's swans for a couple of seasons. This turned out to be a bean goose, a rare stranger indeed. The goose stuck to the swans like glue, forming up in the

124

flight and always taking the same position – about two-thirds of the way down and flying with its wingtip within inches of that of its chosen companion. On the ground it joined the line of the others and cropped its way industriously across the field.

The Bewick's swans are the pride of our moors, although sadly their numbers have been reduced considerably over the years. Only time will tell whether this is just a fluctuation or a permanent state of affairs. One possible cause may be the huge feeding programme which takes place every winter at Slimbridge, and which has attracted considerable numbers of these beautiful birds from other habitats. Alternatively, new drainage methods and lower water tables may be altering moorland habitats, or weather factors may have caused a temporary change. At this stage we can only hope that it will correct itself in due course.

Whatever the cause, the flocks of Bewick's swans were at their peak some years ago – one day I counted 70 grazing their way across a wet field, and large parties frequently remained for weeks on end – but now we see perhaps one or two family parties and then only at the beginning or end of the season, obviously just stopping off on their long migration to or from Siberia.

On the other hand, flocks of mute swans have increased considerably over the same period. I have counted over a hundred of them on many occasions recently, particularly in spring and summer. This seems to indicate that the type and standard of the grass cannot be unattractive to the family as a whole. Although I am delighted to see this large collection of mutes, I must confess to a twinge of disappointment that they are not Bewicks.

There is something extremely romantic about the very presence of the Bewick's swans. They breed in the wilds of Siberia and it is easy to imagine them flying over miles of tundra, and then the great steppes of Russia, to reach us – from a wilderness to a very different world of orderly fields. I remember with great clarity the first time I saw these splendid birds here. We had only been living above the moors for a short while when I went out for a walk one cold and extremely windy winter day. For some reason I had mounted my long lens on a tripod and was walking across a field with this unwieldy contraption on my shoulder. I was right in the middle of a great flat open space, in full view and totally exposed. I don't know what made me look round – I may have heard something without realising it, or it may have been some 'sixth sense'. I turned and saw a long line of huge white birds coming towards me, only about 20 feet up. It still gives me a prickly feeling to think of the sheer excitement of that moment.

There must have been a dozen birds or more. I could not take it all in. My whole world seemed to be full of swans. The long necks wavered in that sinuous movement I came to know so well in the next few years. There was an impression of black and yellow in place of the normal red bill, of long wings hardly moving from the horizontal. Then they were on me, and over. I caught my foot in the tripod and fell heavily. As I did so there was a burst of ironic bugling from the flock – or so it seemed to me at the time. When I

The herd of Bewick's swans started to fly over our house every evening, on their way to roost on Cheddar Reservoir.

126

looked up they had gone. The moors were empty. It was as if I had dreamed it and they had never existed.

Over the next ten years the flights built up. Twenty birds staying for several days one year became 30 and 40 remaining for a week at a time and returning time and again during the winter. We were able to take visitors down between January and March with a fair chance that we would be able to show them the swans. A pattern developed. The first small family party would arrive at the end of October. It often consisted of two sets of adults and three young. This first family party still appears most years, although we cannot tell whether they are the same adults. But the party size remains similar. It is an event to which we look forward with great pleasure; they seem almost a part of our family.

Of particular interest is the bill colour of the young birds. In most bird recognition books – the Wildfowl Trust booklet being an exception – this is shown as a dirty grey; however, the real colours are red and black. Sometimes the whole family arrived with yellow staining on head and neck, something I have noticed elsewhere with whooper swans, coming from feeding in peat-stained water.

As the birds settled into a recognisable pattern of visits and their stays lengthened, we found out more about them. It was a fascinating period of familiarisation and learning. They started flying over our house every night just as it was growing dark. The flight would be heralded by the distant sound of bugling, faint at first and then growing in intensity. In flight the swans talk to each other much of the time, but much less so when on the ground. The first murmured notes would start just before take-off, when their heads are raised stiffly erect and they walk on tiptoes. As they turn into the wind, their bugling becomes more distinct and pours out at full volume. Then they paddle across the grass and up into the air. The bugling continues as they climb and start across the hill, though it becomes more conversational as they settle into their main flight pattern. To some ears, it sounds like the talking of distant geese; to others it has a special sweetness and intensity of its own. For me it is one of the most urgent and exciting sounds in the world:

wildness and wilderness personified, perhaps equalled only by the skirling, eerie calls of a diver on a remote Scottish loch.

These particular swans appeared to be based on Axbridge Reservoir at night and flew in to the moors early in the morning, leaving again as the light fell in the evening.

These evening flights could be exciting affairs. One day I was out on Keyton Hill, walking the dogs as dusk fell. With it came the mist, as so often happens in early winter. It is a splendid sight to see the vapours rising off the moorland rhynes after a sunny day. It forms a layer which creeps across the fields, swirling off the source lines of ditch and rhyne. It is incredibly beautiful and rather eerie, heavy with shades of Avalon and medieval ghosts. The mist lies below us as a layer, above which rise the tops of the willows and thorns. On this night the effect was more powerful and it rolled up the hill reducing visibility quickly to only a few feet. I knew the way well and was not worried about bumping into anything, but the mist lay around us like a thick blanket, making me feel as if I were totally cut off from the real world.

Far away and below, muffled by the mist but haunting and hypnotic, came a burst of familiar swan-music. I listened to it strengthening, growing louder and nearer. I thought I could hear the faint sound of the great wings beating: the clatter of pinions on the wind, not the singing music of mute swan wings. The mist disoriented everything. The music swelled and then grew fainter. The wings were heard, then there was silence. It was if the birds were passing through a series of sound baffles. Suddenly, frighteningly and unexpectedly, seven or eight great shapes erupted out of the mist, only feet above us. A great burst of calling came from them and I could almost feel the wings straining to push the huge bodies up. As they passed over, they went up like helicopters, as shaken by the encounter as I was. Even the dogs flattened themselves as these great shadows swept in on us, magnified by the fog. Time seemed to slow down. Every detail of the great swans is etched on my memory: the sound of the wind hissing through the pinions; the heads, with their long Grecian noses tipped with black and yellow, turning down to look

'A stalk of grass is caught in the nick in the bill of one bird.' Bewicks walking towards the camera as I wait.

at me as they passed over; long necks swaying and great bodies following, with legs tucked tightly in on either side of the belly. I remember the mist opening and swirling aside as they pushed their way out into the open, materialising as if from nothing. For a brief moment I felt a part of that flight.

Other memories crowd in when I think of the Bewicks, moments of freezing cold, glued to the camera viewfinder, hardly daring to breathe, as a line of them grazed their way towards the car from which I was watching. They came closer and closer. A stalk of grass was caught in a nick in the bill of one bird. A feather on its breast lifted as a catch of breeze touched it. I had never dreamed I could be so close.

"Look at the size of them!" I said to the dog, who was peering out beside me. They seemed indifferent to me. I could not believe that they did not know I was there. They must have seen me and my vast lens gazing at them like some blind, featureless eye. Were they indifferent or did they know they were safe? Normally they are wary of everything. They rouse themselves if they see a movement on the fields and gaze round with great intensity, heads held stiffly on rigid necks.

Usually they choose an open field with a clear view all round and graze across it in a line. One bird seems to act as sentry, every few seconds lifting its head up from grazing for a quick look round. The first sign of worry is a quiet burst of conversation, then they move their necks up and down rhythmically, with a deliberate pattern to it. They stretch on tiptoes, necks ramrod stiff, when they feel threatened. One may exercise its wings briefly. They are alert, aware and ready for action. There is a pause, then they are off. They run along the grass, wings flexing and flowing with the effort. Photographs show the wonderful curling shapes of the great white wings. Some of these images are quite surrealistic and repay printing to show the purity of shape unsullied by detail or shading.

The swans take off surprisingly quickly and are unexpectedly fast once in the air. They are so big that you feel that they must be cumbersome, but they rapidly vanish from view. They often curl round in a huge circle and sweep by high overhead, bugling softly as they pass over. You can see them peering down at the place they have just left hoping, perhaps, that the intruder has gone. The sight and sound of these splendid birds on a crackling cold winter day is something to savour and store in the memory.

One October, half-expecting that I might see the first of the Bewicks, I drove down to the North Drain, and stopped beside a field by Totney Bridge. I swept the cold and colourless land with my glasses. I was in luck. Two old birds and a grey-tinged youngster stood on the far side. How elegant they looked, straight-necked, flat-billed and yet extremely large! But the heads appeared a little strange.

Then everything clicked into place and I realised that I was looking at a family of whooper swans. The bill was much bigger, sharper and flatter; the neck taller and slightly kinked at the top, pushing the head forward. The black and yellow of the bill were in a different pattern.

A large black dog appeared in the far corner of the field and the swans stirred into action, wings working, legs paddling, until at last they were airborne. They took a long run before they left the earth completely and then looked their size. In the air they were bulkier, more angular and somehow less handsome than our familiar smaller yellow-billed swans. The angle of the head and the long bill were more characterful than beautiful. Although they are marvellous-looking birds by any standards, they somehow lack the gentleness of line shown by the lighter Bewick's swans.

Waders

The waterlogged fields of winter attract waders from afar and we are visited by a number of species more usually seen by the sea. I well remember my astonishment the first winter I was here. I walked out across this great bare expanse of grass, splashing through runnels of water which lay in the gripes running across the fields. Everything seemed so empty and depressing on that grey autumn day, then there was movement near the edge, just a feeling caught beyond the rim of my vision. A dark cloud blew up into the sky. There

131

There was a flash of pure light as the fast-flying flock of dunlin turned as one to show the pale undersides of belly and wings.

was a flash of pure light as the fast-flying flock turned as one to show the pale undersides of belly and wings, and we saw the cloud consisted of a large number of fast-flying waders – the sort of flight you would expect to see over a sea wall. They were dunlin, accompanied by two or three hysterical redshank.

That was a most extraordinary afternoon. The dunlin were determined to give me a real demonstration of their presence and their aerobatic ability. I was treated to a most marvellous flying display. I was at the very centre of the ring as the distant flock gathered themselves together, put their heads down, so to speak, and headed straight for me. They flew past at high speed and the sound of their wings was like the tearing of rolls of paper. They were

so close that the photographs I took showed some birds sharply but others badly out of focus, filling half the negative. They must have been within a few feet of the long lens. After that, they split into little parties and seemed to be playing a game. They whistled past in opposing groups. I would be following one group with the lens and the other would rush by from behind. The sound of their wings is intense at close quarters and builds up rapidly with the speed at which they fly. It can give an awful shock even if you are expecting it.

One bright winter day I walked along the waterlogged edges of Old Rhyne, with the dogs running wild, coursing from side to side and getting a week's exercise in one afternoon. Although it was brilliant with sunshine and the blue waters glinted ultramarine in the hollows, nothing moved. It seemed perfect weather to bring out a profusion of birds but all I could see was a distant, momentary, blowing cloud of lapwings before they too settled down on the far side of the North Drain.

I was standing there sniffing the cool air and thinking how good it was to be alive out here on a day such as this, when I was rudely awakened. There was a loud ripping sound, just like the tearing of cloth. I found myself looking along the tail feathers of a dozen or so incredibly fast-flying waders. The golden plover were knifing their way across the field only a couple of feet above the grass. It was all sharply focused. I was honed into a state of complete awareness of what was going on, with my mind concentrated, like rays of light inside a lens. The waders were magnified. I could see every feather and the muscular movement beneath them. The wings were sharply pointed, angled and trim, hissing through the air with the power of each stroke. I saw this quite clearly as they sped away from me, their movements in a form of slow motion. I had all the time in the world to observe the strength and the ease of their flight – then I found the world running again at normal speed. It was as if a gear had changed.

What an amazing ability waders have. They fly as one unit. When one banks to starboard, so do they all. Their wings seem to beat at the same speed and in the same phase. How else would all the white undersides show like

133

flashes of snow at the same moment, followed by darkness as they all roll over to show their upper sides? This flight of plover showed all the skills of the smaller waders, but at higher speed and with even greater power. The well streamlined, porpoise-shaped bodies were bulky and muscle-packed. The wings looked slender, with little surface area to support the bodies, but they made up for this by the rapid beats, akin to jet fighters, held aloft by power.

They played tag with me that afternoon. I cannot imagine that they were flying for any reason except the joy of it and, dare I say it, having fun at my expense. We are not supposed to anthropomorphise nowadays and every aspect of bird behaviour is supposed to have a good biological reason, but I query that. Why should we have the sole right to behave irrationally, have fun or just enjoy ourselves? I have watched too many creatures doing things just for the hell of it to believe that. Certainly these birds were not searching for food, nor were they disturbed by anyone other than me. They could have had their pick of places. Instead they chose to fly at and around me for all of half an hour.

I walked slowly on, savouring the day, basking in the winter sunshine. After that first encounter I thought that I had disturbed them for good and that they would be on their way. Not at all. They came hurtling over Old Rhyne, flashing by at what seemed like the speed of light. A few feet from us they banked and tore on. The noise of this manoeuvre ripped at my ears. I could not believe that mere flying could produce such a volume of sound.

But what excitement it engendered. It made me feel as if I were part of the flock as it powered its way on, twisting and banking. It was one creature with multiple wings. When they were close I could hear the different intensities of sound produced by rapid manoeuvring. As they banked and tore away again, the sound of the wing-beats rose in intensity and pitch and then levelled off.

I have surprised fast flying birds on a number of occasions. Once it was a trio of ducks, another time, a flock of 30 or 40 dunlin. Both changed direction extremely sharply, the ducks shooting almost vertically up and the dunlin almost turning on their backs as they banked and streaked off at right angles to their original direction. The shriek of tortured feathers rang in my ears.

A few dunlin stay for much of the winter, as long as the ground is soggy and easy to dig their bills into. When conditions are just right, the soil waterlogged and lines and streaks of water running across the fields, many more join them. Smoking clouds of dunlin erupt into the air every few minutes and circle frantically at high speed before settling. They are such busy little birds, constantly on the move, darting from islet to islet in the wet ground, running beneath the feet of the swans, plover and gulls which feed in steady lines.

Lapwings are the most obvious and numerous of our native and visiting birds. Out on the moors, most fields have one or two breeding pairs and many more engage in the spring courtship rituals. They are joined later, in the uniform and dull green months of midsummer, by large influxes of young birds from outside the area. These vanish as the summer goes on and are replaced in winter by huge flocks of continental birds which stay on and off for most of the cold weather. Sometimes I think they have left, but it is surprising how they can be lost in the acres of flat moorland. They are such free spirits and the sight of a great cloud of them blowing into the air and then separating out into individual birds as they fly over, is the very essence of this unique and fascinating piece of country.

One of the great joys and spectacles of a winter walk is this restless spirit. On those splendid sunny days when the wind is gusting sharply, and the air has a razor quality, they seem to put on particularly magnificent displays. The sky, which has been quite empty, will fill and darken with birds. Often two or three flocks will take off at once, streaming up into the sky like smoke, forming different layers as they cross or merge. Lapwings have a habit of all flying off in one direction and, as they do so, spreading out in the sky, the cloud of birds thinning out until you realise that there are only a few individuals left – then none. It is a strange performance, a vanishing trick designed to baffle the onlooker. From a distance, the columns look like pillars of smoke winding up from separate bonfires.

On any bright day after Christmas you can see the lapwings starting their

Lapwings in their spring courtship flights.

first tentative courtship flights. This is one of the most dashing and beautiful of all bird displays and provides enthralling entertainment. The moors offer wonderful opportunities for observing it, as the roads cut right through the fields and there is little traffic during the week. It is possible to pick a likely spot, park the car on the verge and settle back for an entrancing display.

The first intimation of the display may be a sound like ripping cloth and the sight of one or two birds zigzagging across the field with a sudden surge of acceleration. The wings seem to change shape as the birds twist and turn in flight. As they bank hard and drive up, the pinions make this characteristic tearing sound. The wing ends take on a rounded paddle shape, while the inner portion lengthens and narrows – ideal for tight manoeuvring.

The female often stays on the ground and looks totally unimpressed by the whole procedure, turning her back on the hard-working male, who tears over in an ecstasy of high-speed joy. Earlier in the year the flights take the form of competitions between males. Three or four will rush round, towering into the sky, diving until you think they will flatten themselves, only to rise up again, rolling and turning as they do. It is a wonderful performance, characterised by a display of quite precise flight control. The birds fly within a whisker of each other, at faster than usual speeds, twisting and turning, banking, rolling, reversing and diving in a matter of moments. Dazzling is an understatement for such a virtuoso display.

Later the displays become much more intimate. The female takes off periodically and flies round in a circle at slow speeds. Afterwards she stands and watches the male as he performs his aerial ballet. She has to keep a close watch on him, for he sometimes dives so close that the wind of his passing rocks her on her feet. He twists and weaves and gives the most marvellous of displays, dancing on the wind at times, at others sounding like a diving Stuka, the wind ripping and sizzling in the flight feathers. The male lapwing devotes every ounce of his skill to showing just what a master of flight he is. In the course of a few minutes, every possible combination of turn, bank, roll and loop is shown off. Part of the display will be in complete silence, wings

Lapwing eggs.

moving without effort or strain, then the bird seems to turn some key and the air is filled with the shriek of his feathers.

Lapwing nests are not easy to find, for they are just scrapes in among the grasses, and the eggs are wonderfully well camouflaged. I do not make it my business to go looking for nests, but just occasionally I stumble across one and, even more rarely, see the young with their mother. One year I saw the whole cycle when one of our dogs came across the nest, by mistake. We were out on a walk and Tam was suffering especially from the dive-bombing attacks of a pair of lapwings. In those days she still believed she might catch a bird if she ran hard enough. She rushed after the birds, well off the line of the walk and, in doing so, stumbled over the nest. She stood over it sniffing and I saw the eggs lying in a twist of grass close by her feet. How could we have missed them? They are so large and so exposed, yet step back a couple of feet and they vanish from view. Then it is a job to find them again.

But more was to be vouchsafed that year. I was driving down one of the droves on a rather miserable, drizzly afternoon a few weeks later when something caught the corner of my eye. I stopped the car and searched the field with my binoculars. I found myself looking at a lapwing crouched down, side on. Something moved beside her, the feathers in her flank bulged and a little head emerged, black and white, with a very short bill. Another and another pushed up. She was protecting her three youngsters from the drizzle and cold of that day. I managed to take a series of shots before leaving them to the peace they deserved. I was lucky, for most waders leave the nest and keep on the move shortly after hatching. The young are precocious, able to walk and feed extremely quickly. They rely on their cryptic colouring for protection, hiding from predators by freezing in one spot as soon as they sense danger.

I was lucky enough to catch another shy wader in the same situation a few years ago when I was shown a number of curlew chicks just as they were leaving their nest on Tealham Moor. Roland Duckett, who farmed one of the fields by the North Drain, had a milking bail by the water edge and had watched this particular bird as it courted, nested, laid eggs and incubated them. He had shown me the nest earlier, although we had been careful not to disturb the birds. The biggest danger must have been from the large herd of Friesians eating their way steadily across the field for those weeks, although I have

Lapwing and chicks out on the moors.

Curlew eggs

Curlew chick

Curlew

140

noticed that it is rare to find birds' nests trampled underfoot – cattle are gentle creatures and appear to try and avoid eggs and sitting birds. The strangest thing about the curlew chicks was that they had little stubby bills and would have been unrecognisable to someone used only to pictures of adult birds with their long, down-curved bills.

I have always thought that curlew are some of the most glorious birds to have around. Their wonderful, bubbling, joyous cries must be among the most beautiful sounds in nature. As I worked in the orchard on a still evening, I would hear the sounds rising up from down below, bubbling, trilling, liquid and unbelievably musical. In winter this was a particular bonus, a counterpoint to the curious squeaking, rusty sounds of the lapwings as they were disturbed by a passing walker. We would stand outside sometimes as night fell, listening to the last sounds of the chorus of lapwings, golden plover and other creatures. As a faint undertone we would catch the far-off liquid notes of the curlew. Then the calls would rise in intensity, note following note faster and faster, until they blended into that final melancholy beauty before dying.

In spring the sounds would be everywhere. Three or four birds would fly around in a little group, moving from field to field, as if searching for the perfect spot. Their evocative cries would ascend up into the heavens with the birds as they flew around in most untypical fashion. At times they fluttered, then planed down, stiff-winged and wooden. They never stayed still. As one landed and advanced stiff-legged on the other, it would in turn take off, calling loudly. As the season advanced, the pairs separated out and chose their nesting field. Here they kept well apart, only one pair choosing a particular field. It ended up with pairs sufficiently far apart not to disturb each other, although that did not prevent them becoming highly upset at other intruders. Waders seem to have a particularly difficult time in the breeding season. Many species drive themselves almost mad at this time and the curlew is no exception. The male rises silently up from a corner of a field as someone walks by, then starts to call loudly and rather less musically than usual. Clearly he is totally put out by their proximity and tries to distract them with his antics. He circles widely, sometimes dropping down for a closer look, but never coming within gun-shot range. The parents behave less conspicuously as the young hatch.

One of my saddest realisations in recent years has been a gradual awareness that curlews are no longer regular visitors, let alone residents. Spring is a poorer season without their beautiful, bubbling calls; winter less joyous. As far as I know none have bred in the immediate area in the last few years though there is no obvious reason for this. I can only hope that the absence of the curlews is due to one of those mysterious phases which affect some species for a period, and not because of man-made changes.

A few years ago I would have bet that redshanks had left Tealham for good. Each year saw fewer pairs, until there were none in our particular area, but these last few years have brought a revival in their fortunes. The fields resound with their alarm calls in the spring and a number of young have been raised successfully, which goes to show that assessments should not be made over too short a period. Bird populations fluctuate naturally round a long cycle. It is too easy to think that permanent catastrophe has overtaken them when natural change is working its own way.

Redshanks are strange creatures. They seem to live on their nerves and must find life an awful strain at times. Redshanks have a particularly wearing time when nesting and make a noise quite disproportionate to their size. Last year I was fortunate to find one of their guard posts on a drove. The surface was firm enough for me to drive the car up and park nearby, where I had several lengthy sessions watching and listening to everything which went on. It was fascinating, but I came away wondering whether the birds would survive a few more days like this.

Most of the time the male sat on the gatepost, continually looking around, bobbing and twisting, head moving this way and that. He behaved just like some restless child, bored after a few moments on its own. If a crow, or even a bird as small as a starling, appeared beyond the boundary, he leapt into action flying over and circling near the intruder, crying all the time. It is a lovely call but, after a dozen repetitions, can become too much. When the imagined danger evaporates he flies over towards the nest and descend like a fluttering butterfly. The last you see is that moment when he pauses on the ground, on tiptoe, wings raised. A while later he will appear again on the post, bobbing and weaving, elegant with pencilled feathers, deep red beak and long, mobile legs.

One year I was lucky enough to see one of the young. One of the parents drew attention to itself by circling round, venturing ever closer, with stiff down-pointing wings. The other bird was flying in the same wooden fashion, but much further off. It was an extraordinary performance. Then one bird landed and walked forward slowly, obviously ushering something in front of it. A pair of tiny chicks emerged from the verge and trotted across the hard road and into the grass on the other side. I let them move on and then drove off. It didn't seem fair to intrude further.

Ruffs have been regular visitors in winter and late autumn. Sometimes the odd bird stayed into spring and I have hoped that there might have been a pattern emerging, leading to eventual breeding but I fear that this is only wishful thinking, though ruff breed in Holland in very similar country.

During the winter they are very different from the exotic powdered and bewigged creatures of spring.

Ruff are regular winter visitors to the moors.

Their shape is quite distinct from that of other waders. Perhaps plainness and anonymity of dress best describe the difference. They are plumper than redshanks, shorter of bill and with plainly coloured legs. The most unusual feature is one which I have yet to see illustrated in a bird guide. The feathers immediately behind the bill are pale and the effect is of a ring of white separating head from bill.

Although they are plain, like others of that clan they have an intrinsic beauty of form and in the tiny details of feather colouring. There is a particular time of great beauty out on the moors, when the fields are flooded, it is blowing hard and the sun shines through against the dark background of a gathering storm. At such times and at certain angles, with the sun catching and highlighting their backs, ruffs sparkle like jewels. You see the diamond pattern of individual wing coverts, with their dark centre and pale edges. As the birds dip and feed their way along the shallow flashes of water, these feathers catch the eye for a moment, dissolve into dull brown and then become almost iridescent in a ray of sunlight. Periodically they half stretch a wing and a leg, presenting them to the watcher like some precious, delicate carving.

Before coming here I had thought of the green sandpiper as a rarity. Although at the present time they may not be seen as often as previously, they are by no means uncommon out on the moors. They are as unexpected in their colour and appearance as in being here at all. On a grey winter day the bird appears black and white, especially in flight. My first sight of one zigzagging away from a rhyne like a snipe did not lead me to an instant identification.

Green sandpipers sometimes overwinter on the moors, although many are passage migrants arriving in late summer. They like to feed in shallow pools or shallow, gently running water. From observation, their perfect environment is a worked out peat cutting with a film of water along one edge. I watched half a dozen birds working their way down such a place on nearby Westhay Moor one day, pecking and feeding all the while. Then they all flew over to a little islet and went to sleep, heads tucked under wings. However one sandpiper always kept just sufficiently awake, for they are among the wariest

Green sandpipers on a peat digging. They arrive in late summer, and sometimes stay for the winter.

of birds. My wife accompanied me on one such visit and we watched entranced as the little row of sleeping sandpipers, so severely black and white, was joined by the iridescent fire of a kingfisher.

Sometimes the rhynes are pumped to such an extent that a section may just have a snake of moisture winding up the middle. Green sandpipers appear to like these conditions. For a day or so every suitable ditch will hold one or two of these pretty birds. Then they all vanish and no sign will be found for weeks on end.

The green sandpiper is not as frenetic as its common cousin but it still has the noticeable swaying bob characteristic of this family. If you are lucky in

145

spring it is possible to meet up also with the common sandpiper. On a couple of occasions I have come across one working its way down the banks of the North Drain. I was in a canoe the first time and was able to follow it as it fed its way down stream. The bobbing and swaying motion, not unlike that of a wagtail, was what first attracted my attention. It paid little attention to me or my drifting canoe, not even when I had to raise the paddle and make a stroke to correct the direction. It fed along the little coves and shallows, picking creatures from the mud and insects from among the grass. Every so often it would raise its sharp wings, stretch and then fly a few feet. The flight was weak and uncertain, with none of the dash of the green sandpiper. They are amiable and trusting little birds and always a welcome sight in the area.

I have left to last one of my favourite waders, a bird you cannot fail to see or hear on Tealham at most times of the year – snipe. They are residents and breed out on the open moor. Sometimes they are present in winter in considerable numbers. When I first came here, one of the most surprising discoveries was that some of the larger wader flocks consisted of hundreds of snipe. I had always previously thought of them as occurring in twos and threes, or as solitary creatures.

They continue to be part of the very fabric and weave of life on the moors although there are far fewer now. One of the most evocative and exciting sounds is that of snipe drumming in the spring and early summer. The noise, similar to the bleating of lambs, but with a definite rhythm and length, is made by the rush of air through rigidly extended outer tail feathers. The snipe draws a large ellipse in the air as it flies round its chosen nesting territory. Every so often it swoops down at an angle of about 45°, spreads its tail and produces the familiar sound. You can see the process quite easily with binoculars. The outer pair of feathers stick out at right angles to the body and quite separate from the rest of the tail. After the dive the bird climbs steeply up before levelling and then diving again. As each descent takes place, there is a slight pause before the sound is heard, as if speed has to be gathered before the feathers are let out to provide the right volume and pitch of sound.

On a balmy summer evening, with the light lowering over meadows brilliant with buttercups, several snipe may be heard drumming over the various fields. The sound of their display weaves in and out of the consciousness like the soporific murmuring of bees. Leaning on a gate becomes an occupation in its own right and many a supper has been left in the oven at this time.

As spring turns into summer, snipe start to nest, one or two pairs to a field. Then the males may be seen guarding nearby sitting mates. They perch on a strategic post, where they are able to see intruders threatening the nest. For much of the time they doze the day away, often with one leg tucked up under their feathers, but maintain a continuing state of vigilance. Curiously, however, they are far tamer than at any other time of the year. I presume that they are worried only by people or creatures approaching the nest itself. They often seem quite unconcerned about those who have a more direct interest in the birds themselves. Some years, the post may be beside the road. At times I have been able to drive up, stop the car about fifteen feet away, produce the long-lensed camera and start photographing, without any sign of interest from the bird. Sometimes the bird appears somnolent, hardly moving at all, silent and inwardly brooding, on other occasions he sits there ticking like a

Snipe – the male guarding his mate sitting nearby.

147

small time-bomb. The vigour of the sound is shown in the great explosion of energy which shakes his body with each utterance. The sound is made with a part-open beak and it is most distinctive, not loud, but carrying a long distance.

On a perfect summer evening, a wonderful patchwork quilt of sound is built up round the drumming of snipe in the four quarters of the sky and the quiet ticking of the guardians coming from two or three widely dispersed fence-posts. A burst of musical indignation comes from a far off pair of redshanks, disturbed by some totally harmless bird such as a passing wood pigeon. The bubbling trilling of curlew illuminates the distance, while the wild excitement of a pair of lapwings in late display round it off. At times like this I wonder how I can bear to spend even an evening away from the moors.

In winter, snipe are a quite different proposition. Indeed it is difficult to imagine that they are the same species. Most of the birds are of the common variety, although a few are the smaller jack snipe, distinguishable by their habit of flying off when disturbed but almost at once dropping down into cover again. The common snipe behaves quite differently. He shoots off like a bullet, with a curious squeaking cry. But he doesn't fly in a straight line. He jinks and twists for some considerable distance, before circling and rising steeply into the air. Like teal, snipe often keep circling high in the air and are not persuaded to land except when the danger, in their estimation, is firmly past.

Although I do not shoot, I can well imagine that hitting a snipe is a mark of considerable skill. Photographing them in flight is all but impossible – success is a matter of luck and persistence.

I walk down Old Rhyne, camera in hand, everything as set as can be. Brock ranges ahead and, inevitably, snipe start to shoot off in ones and twos, at times up to a dozen or so, in a ragged volley of rising birds. The camera follows them, butt into the shoulder, eye seeing the bird but failing to hold it in the viewfinder until it is too far away. Even if it is held, there is focusing to consider. I possess a miracle of engineering, the Novoflex squeeze-focus lens, but I still cannot react quickly enough. But there are times when my eye slows the bird down and the feathers on back and wing are seen as individual designs, though even then the bird usually manages to jink sideways just as my finger is squeezing the button.

They are at their most picturesque on frosty mornings, when the grass is rimed white and the stalks emerge from hard-frozen flashes lying on the surface of the waterlogged ground. Early sunlight makes everything sparkle and glisten like jewellery and the faint warmth in the rays bring little curls of vapour which catch the light. It is a time of sheer magic for us but, I suspect, it is a time of increasing misery for the snipe. They feed deep under the surface of the earth or mud, with their long, stout, but flexible bills, the tips of which are well-endowed with nerve ends to feel the movements of the worm. But this miraculous system is of little use if the bill is unable to penetrate the iron-hard surface. On such a morning, the birds are on the move the whole time, looking for the first patches of softer mud, to enable them to probe the depths. If they cannot find any, they must move on.

This occurs when there is a long spell of frosts and wind and the ground hardens and chills to some depth. However, the margins of some fields have water moving gently the whole time, flowing in the crumb of the soil and this keeps moist long after others. Even so, the birds can have a hard time of it in bad conditions. On such a morning, with the moors sparkling and delicately white on top of the pale green, snipe fly round in twos and threes, landing hopelessly on sheets of ice where they had imagined runnels and grass. Some crouch, weakened, and try and force a way through the surface crust. Others huddle under the lee of a tussock, too weary to rise. After a few days of really hard weather, gaunt corpses are found, stiff and frozen in the open fields.

Twice, when there has been heavy snow combined with hard frosts out on the moors, snipe have visited the house. Somehow they must know that there are permanently moist springs under the hedge and fly into an alien environment to take their last desperate chance. I have photographed both snipe and woodcock in such circumstances from the

149

downstairs bathroom window. The woodcock which visited us is the only one I have seen in the immediate area, although they are regular visitors to the woods at Shapwick Heath, a few miles away.

For much of the winter, the moors are a paradise for snipe. There are miles of ditches, soft verges where cows have trampled their way to drink in summer and masses of dung which has been spread in the autumn and early winter. The soft peat is easy going, with its many molehills, while the dung brings earthworms and other grubs to the surface.

Small birds

In spring the area is alive with movement; there are crowds of small birds everywhere. They erupt from the verges as cars brush by and dart and poke in every clump of thistles or brushwood.

Tealham is noted specially for its breeding population of yellow wagtails,

Tealham is noted for its breeding population of yellow wagtails.

colourful and exotic as any tropical species. Every third or fourth gatepost will have one of these beautiful creatures bobbing and dipping on it, and life will seem a lot more cheerful as you drive by. They hop down occasionally to pick up an insect or to quarrel with another glowing, brilliant male in a haze of fast-moving wings and fanning tails.

These golden-bright creatures are special to many people. They count them jealously each year and judge the state of the land by their numbers. Their brightness surprises people and they are of considerable interest, even to casual dog-walkers who usually look only at the most obvious wildlife as an adjunct to their other activities. The tropical yellow brightens up the most miserable spring day and cannot fail to catch the eye. Visitors tell us they saw a "canary sitting on a gatepost today" and we smile

Pipits also love to sit on gateposts, using them as vantage points for their fluttering forays into the grass after insects. Together with skylarks, they form the most obvious element of small-bird life on the moors. Most are the meadow variety, but sometimes it may be a tree pipit, which is subtly different, although it is difficult to see why. Both are richly striated and patched with brown and black. Both have a fine shape, with slender, beautifully shaped beak. The main difference lies in their voice. However, I have noticed that some tree pipits have quite amazing hind claws – long and curved. These seem so delicate and sharp that one can imagine them snagging on every tangle of twisted grass – most impractical.

Whinchats appear in spring, although their close relatives, stonechats, are seen at their most obvious in autumn or winter. Stonechat colouring is perfect for the rich autumnal season, matching the golden grasses and dying reds of the leaves. The bird hangs from a slender stem flaunting its tail and 'check-check-checking' like a tiny time-bomb. They really are most appealing but are also among the most infuriating of all creatures to photograph. They have a maddening habit of always being one step ahead. They seem to encourage you to follow then, when the camera is poised for that 'once in a lifetime' shot, they move on, to pause again in a perfect pose a little later. I have numerous pictures of the end of a tail or part of a spread wing.

Pairs of reed buntings often frequent the same area at this time of year – the young alders on the edges of drainage ditches and the fringes of reeds along the banks. In winter, the cock is a fascinating blend of streaks and blobs of chestnut on white, while in spring he assumes a brilliant black bib surrounded by white. Then he looks as if he has been washed and burnished. Sadly, reed buntings seem less common on the moors at present, though this may be a passing phase.

Little flocks of linnets are seen most often in spring and autumn. This is the time when they feed together on roadside clumps or among the remains of old thistles. In spring, they are so brilliantly flushed with colour that they seem quite different creatures from the dull autumn youngsters. They outshine their portraits in most bird guides – no-one seems to be able to paint that flush, which looks like the fire of inner health.

Of all the many small birds, the lark is the most poignant and everlasting in the memory of most of us. Its song has inspired poets through the centuries and it has lost none of its verve or vigour over this time. It starts into song as soon as winter sunshine begins to warm the atmosphere, in that period before spring is even a faint scent in the air. It rises up, endlessly reeling out its cascade of notes, seeming not to draw breath at all, climbing upon vibrating wings until it vanishes from view completely. Yet it remains as clearly heard as ever.

On a warm spring day, the moors are covered with a blanket of lark song. It is over everything and in every corner, all-pervading and sweet, without being cloying to the palate. Occasionally the bird is caught out and starts singing in the very depths of winter, when the air is sparkling and the sunshine brilliant, yet everything is stiff with cold. Even

Of all the small birds, the most everlasting in my memory is the lark, with its wonderful song.

so I cannot but believe it is a taste of warmer days to come. I have the same feeling when a snipe starts drumming over the fields in icy February, seemingly caught out in the same way. Once I heard the two at the same time – snipe drumming and lark singing on its ascending path. Life bubbled over and the January air sparkled like iced champagne, catching in the throat like the sear of the Arctic.

Owls and birds of prey

A large, flat area such as Tealham Moor is perfect for birds of prey and a considerable variety has been seen in recent years. Perhaps the most exotic and unusual for this type of habitat was a hawk which floated over some years ago. The telephone rang one morning. A friend's voice came over the line, urgent and incisive, "Quick, look outside. You'll see a red kite over your roof, unless the wind has changed. Hurry!"

I could not resist this, dropped the phone and my pen and dashed outside. Miracle of miracles, there it was. It drifted on downwind as it circled, with angled wings and deeply forked tail prominent in the bright July sunshine. A small crowd of swallows and swifts mobbed it, but it paid no attention, continuing its wide circles as the wind carried it away and across the moors. The only other times I had seen kites had been over the rugged hills of mid-Wales, a completely different type of landscape. It was amazing that I had seen it at all. My house is a couple of miles from that of my friend, and it was sheer luck that it was still there.

But not everything is so exotic. The commonest hawk is the kestrel, although in recent years it appears to have diminished in numbers somewhat. Probably this is connected with levels of vole populations and is just a part of the great natural cycle. I cannot see any other obvious reason. A few years ago it was quite usual to see three or four of these pretty birds hovering over the great, flat expanse of the moors, as if they were holding up the four corners of a blue tablecloth.

They maintain an exact position in the sky, relative to the ground, even in

153

The commonest hawk is still the kestrel, though somewhat reduced in numbers in the last few years. A series of pictures of hovering kestrels showed that the eye remains in a constant position, regardless of the behaviour of other parts.

high and gusty winds. This ability is well illustrated in some pictures I took a few years ago. I was parked on the top of a raised dyke in Holland and the bird was level with me and quite close. The wind was gusting quite severely at the time. The series of pictures show that while the wings, tail and body may be at varying angles to each other, the eye remains in the same spatial position. Its vision is several times as acute as ours and, by looking down intently from a fixed position, it is able to pick up and home in on the slightest movement.

The female is larger than the male, with brown and black barring on the

154

back; solid and efficient looking. The male is much brighter in colour, and slender. His brilliance and delicacy of colour are really only appreciated through a truly close view. He has a strongly marked moustachial line coming out of a beautiful blue crown, a red back, a long blue tail with a black band and white tip, and a powerful pair of shoulders.

Kestrels specialise in small prey, such as mice and voles, as is shown by the light bill – although notched like that of a true falcon. I must confess to a particular fondness for this commonest of birds of prey. If they were rare they would appear far more exotic to our normally uncaring eye.

Surprisingly, the next commonest hawk is the buzzard. This is not typical buzzard country by any stretch of the imagination. I think of them as soaring over the steep, thickly wooded hills of Devon, not tree-bare, sea-level moorland. However there is one part of the moors, out at the eastern end, with a smattering of oaks. It is a closer, softer country, lusher than the rest, enclosed, secret, and less often visited. This is the centre of their area, leading up to the well-wooded slopes around Wells.

At first I thought they were casual passers-by. They seemed out of character, temporary. Then one spring a pair was seen soaring over the house. They moved on to the open spaces of Tealham for several weeks on end, then they were gone again. Although we looked everywhere and strained our ears for that wonderful, wild mewing call, there was no sign. I had been right, or so I thought – they were just passing through; there was nothing here to attract them. What a disappointment!

The next year, and the next, they were heard again, and occasionally seen, lumbering heavily from oak to oak in that eastern part. At last we heard that

Buzzard populations have spread more widely in recent years and they are common on the Levels and the moors.

they had nested, secretly and unobtrusively, somewhere out in the quieter, more hidden parts of the moor. And so they have come to stay.

Buzzards have spread more widely throughout Britain but I am not sure that there are the same concentrations as there used to be. When I was a lad, living near Honiton, in the heart of Devon, I lay on the edge of a Stone Age fort on the very top of a hill, and looked down at a dozen buzzards circling below me. I have not seen such numbers since.

Buzzards have rounded wings like eagles and soar effortlessly. They often circle up in a thermal until they are lost to sight. The sound of their mewing cry filtering down through a canopy of leaves is wildly beautiful – spine-tinglingly so at times. Sometimes, when the wind is right, we hear it blowing up from the moors. This last summer we heard those wild cries and looked up at four buzzard circling high up above the house.

Occasionally we see a sparrowhawk hunting over the moors and twice one has visited the garden. I cannot understand why they appear to be such unusual birds in this area. While the open fields may not suit them best, there are plenty of hedges around and no gamekeepers to control their numbers. Elsewhere they seem to be on the increase, but not here.

Hedges are the staff of life to sparrowhawks. They offer the perfect setting for their method of hunting, with very little effort involved. The secret is surprise.

The sparrowhawk, blessed with long tail and broad, rounded wings, is highly manoeuvrable, able to turn on the proverbial sixpence. It flies along a hedge, below the crown and out of sight from the other side, then flips over the top and down, hoping to catch small birds feeding under the hedge. It is often a highly successful ploy. One day I was watching some linnets sunning themselves by a hedge when a sparrowhawk hurtled over the top and into their midst like a flying bomb. I had nearly as much of a fright as the birds, though I did not suffer the fate of one of them! The sheer speed and dash of the manoeuvre was breathtaking. The hawk hit one of the linnets a tremendous blow and was up and away with hardly a pause, clutching the limp body – leaving a puff of feathers floating away in the turbulence.

I have this intense vision of a staring yellow eye, barred breast and dark back, the whole bird rolling over the top of the hedge, seeming to fill the sky for a moment, then a scatter of birds, a drift of feathers, followed by silence.

Although stealth and cunning are the methods used for normal hunting, there are times when hawks behave quite out of character. When this happens they are remarkably difficult to identify. One spring I was out in the orchard and happened to look up. A pair of birds came drifting into view, circling with the wind. Wide-spread tails and longish wings made me think immediately of kestrels. A closer look through binoculars showed the barred breast of the sparrowhawk. How curious that those blunt wings should look so kestrel-like when soaring. They seemed to have lengthened and showed a quite definite point. However, there was one difference which showed up after further observation. The kestrel has a small head which seems to spring directly from the wing roots while the sparrowhawk has a more normal, balanced shape with a well-emphasised head, although the tail is as long as that of the falcon. The only other bird which may be confused with these two is the cuckoo. The general shape is similar – long, pointed wings, a long tail and similar size – but it looks as if it has no head at all. In flight the wings are on the extreme front of the body.

One dull autumn day I drove down to Jack's Drove Bridge and stopped the car to look at the North Drain, motionless under its burden of waterweed. My eye was caught by a commotion of birds circling over the nearby field. Most were gulls but one looked familiar, yet different. It was a sparrowhawk, circling slowly, deliberately, lost in itself, paying no attention at all to the mob of gulls. It seemed completely self-contained, moving in a world of its own, ignoring the rest. The long tail was the only part I saw move, twisting and flexing like that of a black kite. The barring on the tail was the only detail visible against the colour-absorbent sky. She – for the bird was so large it could only have been a female – slowly drifted across in the light breeze, working higher and higher into the sky. Still the frenzied gulls followed her until the whole circus passed out of sight.

Sometimes hobbies are seen as they pass over the moors. These slender, incredibly fast little falcons regularly hunt for dragonflies further over on Westhay Moor, where worked out peat diggings have left near-wilderness conditions. Huge areas of shallow water have been colonised by reeds, with shallow pools left here and there. These places abound with insects and many species of dragonflies are to be found in profusion. Here several hobbies may be seen hunting together in early spring. They are said to be the only birds of prey which are fast enough to catch swifts in level flight. They also catch dragonflies while flying and eat them without landing. They hold them in one foot and bend their heads down to feed as they skim by at undiminished speed – a remarkable sight.

Over Tealham, I see them soaring and circling, drifting with the wind, high overhead, alone. They are difficult to distinguish from the swifts and may even be after the same prey. They look the same – sickle-winged, dull-dark, absorbing all light. Then you notice that one pair is more dashing, perhaps larger, although it is difficult to be sure when the swifts are flying at several levels and the effect of perspective is lost. Gradually you notice that they are different in shape and mode of flight, although this too may not be obvious. They are fuller-bodied, wider-winged, altogether larger, especially the female. The pale undersides become visible for a moment, perhaps even a moustachial stripe or dark cap. All at once they are clearly visible and you wonder how you could have confused them with the machine-like swifts.

This sighting of a hobby always seems a special event, more of a privilege than the sight of almost any other bird, however rare. They are sky gipsies, wandering, secretive, exotic, foreign, dashing and totally their own creature. It is as if we are being given a glimpse into the world of royalty, not an everyday meeting with a stranger.

One February I saw a small, dark and dashing falcon fly low across a field to pitch on a post on Allermoor Drove. I managed to get reasonably close and saw that it had a dark head, a dark body and a paler collar when seen from behind. This jack merlin, small but compact and looking every inch a predator, moved his head slowly round searching the area in front and to the side. It gave a sense of calmness and great authority, although I do not know why I gained that impression. He seemed to be contained within himself, a complete contrast to the bobbing, fizzing impatience of the highly strung sparrowhawk I watched on that same post on another occasion. I had not really expected to see a merlin down on the moors, for they always seem to me to be birds of the open uplands. My most vivid memory of this falcon is of one racing down a bracken-covered Brecon mountain slope in the summer. In that setting it seemed completely appropriate.

Only once have I seen a peregrine over Tealham, and once over the house, although they are known to visit regularly each winter. However I suspect that I may have seen the effects of their presence on a number of occasions – with some of those sudden 'frights', when thousands of birds lift off from all over the moors in an inexplicable panic.

Some people consider the peregrine superior to all other birds. It is so perfectly constructed, so splendidly marked and coloured, such a master of flight – and of death. The speed of its stoop increases each time the tale is told. A terminal velocity of up to 180 miles per hour or more is reported by some observers. My own observations confirm that it is a master of this form of attack – a dive from altitude, wings nearly closed – and it hits with a tremendous blow, but I doubt whether that speed is reached. The peregrine must have a difficult job finding a target, however, for the far-off shadow of the falcon is enough to set every bird diving for cover or milling round near ground-level in a great mass to confuse it.

Factors other than season may determine the types

Little owl, one of the most successful owls, with a stable population. Often seen and heard around the moors.

Tawny owls suffered a huge reduction in population when the elms came down, but have recovered in recent years.

of bird present each year: drought or flooding in overseas territories, a shortage of specialist prey, or drastic hunting on their migration routes, may reduce populations considerably for a number of years. Then a couple of really successful breeding seasons will change the picture completely. Birds of prey are often affected in this way. On Tealham, for instance, little owls have one of the most stable populations, while the numbers of short-eared owls increase and decrease sharply according to the vole population.

The disappearance of the tawny owl was even more dramatic. In 1973 we lost most of the mature elms in the area. Indeed I do not know of any large trees which survived more than a year or so after the first major attack of Dutch elm disease. Saplings shoot each year and one or two are growing quite well around the house but little bursts of the disease also reappear with regularity. When the men arrived with their chain saws and cut down the huge trees along one of our boundaries and around the next door field, we felt naked, windswept and undefended.

But for the tawny owls it was far worse. In one year most of their traditional nesting sites disappeared. A large and thriving population vanished completely in the space of a few months. Since most of Somerset and the neighbouring counties were affected in the same way at the same time it is difficult to know where they went. Birds are mobile and can move until they find somewhere which suits them, but there must have been disputes over territory and no doubt many failed to breed for a year or so.

160

By 1987 there were welcome signs that the population was starting to recover – although we heard only the occasional night music – and I am glad to say that their revival has continued.

There are few sounds more exciting than a pair of tawny owls hooting at each other, then relapsing into the more conversational "wheet, wheet", or the even more intimate "keewhit". We came to know these sounds well when we looked after a couple of young injured owls until they were well enough to be released into the wild. They lived outside the kitchen in a big, specially constructed aviary. In those days there were plenty of wild tawny owls around and, as they grew older, other birds would join them in the evening. They flew in from the elms and sat on the roof of the aviary. Three wild birds visited at a time and the five birds would hold long and noisy conversations, but we were so pleased to see them that we never worried about that.

Little owls are much less musical – indeed it would not be unfair to call them discordant at times. They have a habit of sitting some considerable distance apart and calling monotonously and continually to each other for much of an afternoon. Nevertheless they are welcome residents, full of character. They appear extremely fierce, with their great staring yellow eyes, although they seem convivial enough when observed in company with others.

Few nest on the Levels, most preferring ancient apple trees in the old cider orchards on the edging hill-ground. Many of these trees still remain, I am glad to say, for they are a part of traditional Somerset. There is a revival in the fortune of the orchards, now that farmhouse cider is becoming so popular and farmers are starting their presses up again. New trees are being planted, but they are of the more modern varieties, on smaller root stocks, and it is unlikely that they will provide nesting places for many years to come. In the meantime there seem to be enough old trees for the needs of the owls and they continue to flourish.

A pair of little owls has nested for years in an orchard belonging to a neighbour. We enjoy their cacophony in a strange sort of way even though I feel like shouting at them to shut up when they are at their most boring and repetitive. The sounds signal the arrival of spring as effectively as the call of the cuckoo or the cooing of wood pigeons. The male bird sits for hours on an electric line in the next door field where, in the heady days of early summer, he is mobbed by swallows and martins. Later, young swallows sit in rows on that same wire, beside him.

We are fortunate that barn owls still live out on the moors. There are parts of England where they are no longer found. When we moved here, a pair of these splendid owls lived in a barn a couple of hundred yards from the house but this site has long been deserted, although that has nothing to do with the actions of the farmer, who did everything to ensure that they were undisturbed. They vanished one year and I have seen none up here on the raised ground

A barn owl flew along by the car and I was able to watch the flexing wings and twisting feathers as it hunted the ditches alongside.

since, although we occasionally hear the blood-curdling scream and long snoring calls which signify their presence. The sounds are sufficient to convince anyone not used to the country that someone is being murdered nearby.

One pair of barn owls is usually found near a covered haystack in a particularly remote and unvisited spot. Another lives in the more open western part of the moors, although it appears to be less well suited for nesting or roosting. Normally we see little of them. They hunt in the safety and anonymity of darkness. All we are likely to see for most of the year is the occasional glimpse of a white shadowy creature slipping out of the headlamp beam. However, they hunt in daylight in the early spring, when the female is sitting, then they appear as happy to hunt in bright light as at night. Most springs we watch them floating and wavering across the fields. They concentrate wonderfully during those flights and have little fear of man.

One day I was driving down Jack's Drove. It was grey, but there was sufficient light to provide clear visibility. One moment I was driving slowly along and the next a great white apparition appeared just to one side of the car and a few feet ahead of the windscreen. It was fascinating to see it as if through a telescope: the way its wings twisted and flexed, the detail of its feathers and how they moved relative to each other. Its head faced down and it flew an irregular wavering course, rolling a little, like a sailor ashore after a long voyage. I slowed to match its speed and we moved in concert for 60 yards or so, before it peeled off and followed the course of a rhyne. Every so often it would hover, searching the grasses beneath it with great care. I had not realised before what a long-winged bird the owl is. In normal flight, its wings appear rounded, short and broad; here they were seen to be long and tapering as it hovered with great precision. Its progress was slow, as it stopped over some particular spot every few yards. Suddenly it dropped. There was a struggle. It subsided and flattened into the hollow of the ditch before flying over to a post and settling down for quarter of an hour, no doubt to digest.

Barn owls are strange-looking creatures, quite unlike the softly-rounded tawny owls. They are handsome, pale, slender, sharp-featured and elegantly smooth. Seen in close-up they are almost reptilian. When we were looking after injured birds of both species, most people wanted to hold or get closer to the tawny, but said of the barn owl, "What a beautiful creature, but how cruel it looks!" In flight, barn owls are superb: not a hint of a sound from their feathers, pale as ghosts in the gloaming, vanishing into darkness without trace. They are supreme rat-catchers and most of the old farm buildings round here have openings into the lofts to encourage them to nest.

The short-eared owl is another bird which hovers frequently and hunts in daylight. Unfortunately it is neither resident nor a frequent visitor, although it is most welcome when it does come. In the twenty-seven odd years I have lived here, I have only seen them three times.

It is difficult to miss short-eared owls when they are present. They are large birds and have a habit of following a promising ditch line regardless of who is around and draw attention to themselves by stopping to hover every so often, usually only a few feet off the ground. During one remarkable winter, when three were present from October through to early spring, I had many opportunities to watch them on Tealham. What a winter that was, not just for the owls but also for ruffs, golden plover and great hordes of duck.

I first saw the owls when I was strolling over the top with the dogs, on our favourite walk over Keyton Hill and down to the moors. The dogs rushed ahead, eager and excited after a couple of days cooped up at home. They were as affected by the winter sun as any heifer out on spring grass. Everything felt fresh and it was great to be alive after days stuck in the office.

Then a large brown bird, nicely marked in autumnal colours, swung round the corner of the hedge and flew steadily towards me.

"Glory be! A short-eared owl. Quite unmistakable. It must be," I found myself shouting at the uncaring dogs. Tam looked puzzled and ran back towards me, while Brock rushed on and the owl flew nearer.

That was the year when the Bewick's swans came early – not long after the owl – and rain fell and fell at just the right times, so that we had light flooding out on the fields in December and for that vital period in late

Seen through a long lens, the great yellow orbs of the short-eared owl bore into the observer like headlights.

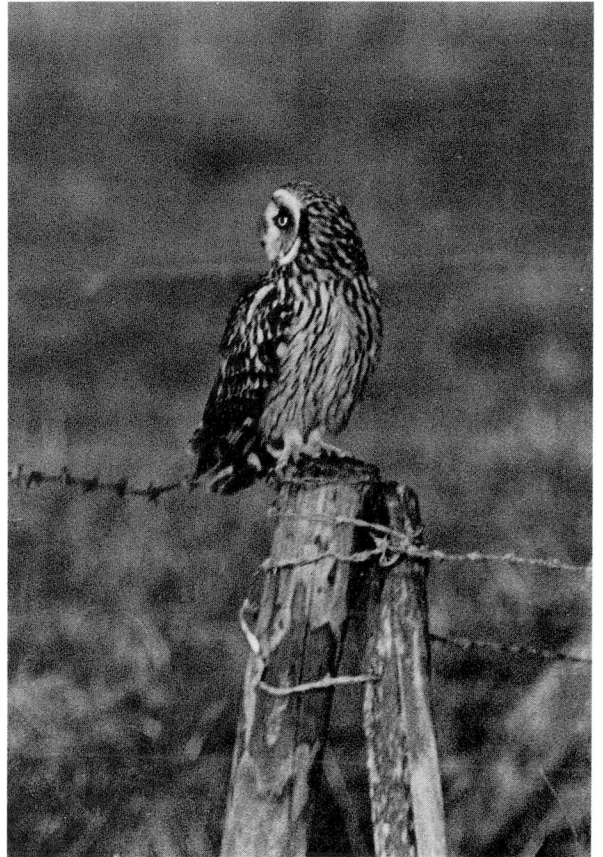

January and into early February. It was the year of years, when there were simply not enough daylight hours to see what was around – and it all started with the coming of the owl.

After that first encounter, I met it frequently, quartering the flat area below. Within three weeks it was joined by two others and they could be seen hunting the various sides of the same field, separated by a hedge or ditch length, but always in sight of each other. At times they passed within feet of me as they concentrated on their hunting flights. No whisper could be heard from their feathers, which is uncanny in such a large bird. At the same distance, a wader makes a sound like tearing cloth. Some ducks are even noisier: the pinions of a goldeneye whistle loudly as they slice through the air.

At a distance, short-eared owls seem more like harriers than owls. They have the same slender look and airy, buoyant flight. They pause and hover in the same way, slow-winged, wavering, but light as a feather. The birds which stayed that winter varied in colour from a patterned grey to an altogether richer hue, sandy with a touch of bracken. Within these quite distinct colours they were decorated and patterned like a woodcock, blending in perfectly with the rough background at rest and difficult to pick out when flying. In flight, the most distinctive feature is a wing pattern like an RAF roundel, but in beige, black and white. Its eyes are the most conspicuous features at rest. Seen through a long telephoto lens of high magnification, they are the focus of the very soul of the bird; your whole person is drawn into the blazing yellow orbs. They seem to penetrate the glass and bore into your eyes with piercing concentration, made the more intense by their unblinking stare. It is the same fierce staring quality as the sparrowhawk's, but without the latter's manic tinge.

Short-eared owl populations are said to follow those of voles. When vole numbers build up to a peak, through favourable weather and good local growing conditions, the owls increase the size of their clutches and most young are reared to maturity. As their feeding starts to have an effect on the vole population, there are problems in finding enough to eat, and the next broods are reduced accordingly. I have not noticed high vole populations on the Levels but those that matter are in the great breeding grounds of the owls: the Scottish border forests and the great open moors of the north.

A young green woodpecker feeding on the soft ground after a shower of rain. Numbers round here were greatly reduced when the elms came down.

Woodpeckers

The woodpecker is a bird with which most people are familiar, whether by way of childhood books, cider bottles or television cartoons. Sadly, they are not seen as often round here as they used to be, although it is good to report that their population is now recovering from an earlier low. They are not strictly birds of the moors but of the fringes, where orchards edge the low hills, or where thicker woods are found. However they suffered the same fate as the tawny owls. At one time there were many tall elms in the hedgerows and woodpeckers were common. Their loud laughing calls

A great-spotted woodpecker seen at close range, dazzling in its scarlet and black plumage.

and deep looping flight could be seen and heard on most bright summer days. Then came the terrible scourge of Dutch elm disease and all this changed in a matter of months.

It is difficult now to recall the size and number of the elms. Photographs taken before the disease struck show a completely different landscape, to a different scale. Huge trees sheltered and softened the hills and hedgerows. The surrounds to the moors were traditional pastoral England but every full-sized elm either fell down or was removed within a year of the disease striking, changing the landscape overnight. It is altogether harsher and more windswept now, although we have become used to it. Unfortunately little effort has been made to replace the elms with new plantings of other varieties, or by allowing ash saplings to regenerate naturally.

All three common British woodpeckers are found here. The most noticeable, because of its size and distinctive laugh, is the yaffle or green woodpecker. After the trees were cut down round the house, no woodpeckers were seen for a year or so. Then they took to breeding in surrounding orchards and the place brightened up again. The highlight of our woodpecker-year is midsummer. Families arrive on the lawn after a shower of rain and search for ants and other insects. The green and scarlet of the adults is quite brilliant, while the young look well fed and pampered.

The great spotted woodpecker is probably more common, although less

often noticed. It is spread more widely on moor as well as orchard and woodland. The older pollarded willow trees are favourite hunting grounds. Although they are brilliant birds – black and white and scarlet – they are remarkably well camouflaged in the light, shade and high contrast of a multitude of sharp pointed willow leaves. I have occasionally been lucky enough to see one close to. Once I was sitting in a hide, photographing fieldfares feeding on rotting apples, when a flash of colour caught the corner of my eye and I turned to see a splendid cock woodpecker digging away at an apple branch. He was only half-serious about the feeding, pausing to look round and then remaining still for a while. My main impression was of the brightness and clarity of the marking – so sharp and clean – the weight of the bill and the clear, bright eye. He was more birdlike, less reptilian, than the green woodpecker I had watched feeding among autumn leaves only days earlier.

The smallest of this family, the lesser spotted woodpecker, is much less well known. Whether this is a true reflection of its numbers, or a feature of its small size and habit of living in the canopies of the trees, is difficult to say. Only once have I had a really good look at one. A movement caught my eye on the trunk of a large and venerable elm. A small unobtrusive bird, about the size of a sparrow, was clinging to the rough trunk in typical woodpecker manner. It was a well-rounded, cosy-looking bird. Then it started shinning up the trunk, pecking away at the crevices in familiar manner. The colours of the bird were muted, until the light caught it at a particular angle, which brought the scarlet patch and vivid black and white patterns startlingly to life. For most of the time it was camouflaged, easily missed and mouselike.

The most exciting member of this family was seen under strange circumstances. I was sitting in my study, which looks across a small lawn sheltered by a spreading walnut tree. It was a beautiful June day but I was on the

The smallest of our woodpeckers, the sparrow-sized and elusive lesser-spotted seen on a now-vanished elm on the moor edge.

phone, talking to someone I know on the staff of the RSPB about some photographs he wanted, when a movement caught my eye and I found my attention wandering from the subject.

"Hold on a moment, Chris", I said. "There's something most extraordinary out here. Is a wryneck a strange-shaped bird, coloured like a woodcock and about the size of a starling?"

"Yes, why?

"There's one sitting on the branch outside the window!"

With that the bird ran rapidly along the branch onto the trunk, spiralled its way up into the canopy and out of sight. That one sighting was all I was to have. What a strange coincidence that I should have been on the phone to an expert as this happened. Wrynecks are unusual birds nowadays. Twenty or more years ago they were much less rare.

Some bird rarities

I must confess that rare birds mean less to me than perhaps they should. I do not have that deep-down thrill of discovery which undoubtedly affects many other people. Not that I object to those who do. It is as well that we all have different goals. Perhaps part of my wariness lies in discovering that one person's rarity is someone else's common bird. For example, we are desperate to persuade black-tailed godwits to nest here in Britain, while in Holland they breed beside the motorways and in the fields in large numbers, and are counted a common species.

For all my indifference, I have come across a number of rarities. Here on Tealham we have had our fair share of them over the years. So many more people are now bird-watching, and they are armed with reliable, easy to understand field guides, that they are bound to spot creatures which would have been missed by the casual watcher of the past.

A place such as Tealham, with its variety of habitats, rhynes, wide drains and old peat workings, with conditions which range from dryness in summer to prolonged flooding and waterlogging in winter, has as good a chance of attracting unusual birds as anywhere, and it has done so – although some have rather dubious origins. The strangest of all was a Sarus crane, a huge bird nearly as high as a person, which hails from India and Thailand. It arrived outside one of the houses at Mudgley one day and finally disappeared some months later. In between collecting food from local people, it would fly round the moors and be seen, gaunt and skeletal, out in the open fields, foreign-looking and far larger than our own herons. It must have escaped from some collection, but no one came looking for it. Then one day it simply spread its wings and flew, having survived the cold weather over the winter.

One spring, someone rang up to ask if I had seen a purple heron on my wanderings around the moors. A watcher thought he had spotted one and wanted confirmation. As it happens I had just returned from Holland where I had been watching one of these birds in country similar to ours. I was familiar with the angular shape and strange colouring and decided to go and have a

Purple heron flying over the moors, a rare visitor from the continent.

look for it. I knew where it had been seen and made off towards the far end of Tadham, where it butts on to Aller Moor. Here there are some wilder parts hidden from the road, little copses of brushwood and sallow, small closed-in fields, ponds and marshes and the remnants of peat workings. Herons fish this area, confident of little disturbance. Swans nest among the reeds, moorhen and teal fringe the open waters. I stopped the car part way along a drove which bisects the area.

"This is where it should be," I thought, 'but surely it will have moved on by now." At that moment I saw a very dark, strangely marked heron fly over, pause for a moment in flight, twist its neck for a look and then plane down to land no more than 50 yards away. It was quite unmistakable, a beautiful specimen of purple heron, in as clean and fine a plumage as the one I had seen in Holland. The wings and back have a strange purple sheen which is akin to the iridescence found on feathers of the pheasant family. The rest of the bird is of a warm colour, almost cinnamon in hue, while the line running from the head down the breast to the legs is prominent both in flight and at rest. Although this heron is smaller and darker than our grey heron, the most tell-tale point of identification is its strange angular shape.

An abiding memory of Holland in spring is of godwits rising up on fluttering wings, like huge butterflies, all along the low water-edged fields. Much of that country is remarkably like ours, drained by pumps, bounded by drainage ditches and with much permanent grass, while the gateways, Friesian cows and unmade droves are similar to those in Somerset. The distinctive 'grutto, grutto,' notes of the godwits were everywhere, mixing with the frenzy of redshanks disturbed.

After seeing this profusion, it is strange to think of the black-tailed godwit as a bird which needs protection and encouragement. But in England it is a rarity as a breeding bird and is extremely beautiful and distinctive in breeding plumage: cinnamon-red of head and breast, with a clean-cut black and white tail. So one can see the attraction of having it as a resident.

One year a pair stayed for a number of weeks in the spring, displaying on

A fine black-tailed godwit in breeding plumage. They tried to breed on Tealham Moor one spring.

a field which edged the North Drain. They called frantically whenever cars or people passed down the road and the cock bird towered up into the sky and fluttered slowly down, just as I had seen them doing in Holland. The sound and the fury became so insistent that I felt sure that they were breeding, then one morning they were gone. Before they left I had been certain that the female had been sitting, with the male perching on a nearby post, long-legged and brightly coloured. But silage making is noisy and someone was cutting in the next field when the birds disappeared, so perhaps this disturbed them.

In early October 1984, I was having tea with a bird-watching friend when someone else we knew roared up the drive and asked if he could borrow binoculars or a telescope. We all drove off to the fields below the house, where a strange-looking plover had been seen. Was it a normal golden plover with unusual plumage or the visitor from America which we suspected? The bird seemed different from the others in the field. It was difficult to see what that difference was. Bird watchers call this factor 'jizz', an indefinable something about size, shape or relative proportions which makes two similar birds quite different. It also describes the 'signature' of a particular bird, the special characteristic of attitude or behaviour which makes you confident that you have distinguished one small brown, anonymous bird from another.

'Our' bird looked fractionally smaller and less bulky than the crowds of its cousins round it. The legs were longer, making up for the lack of bulk, but I did not see it fly or lift its wings in the characteristic wader gesture, although one of our party did. This clinched the identification, for the underwings were grey, not white. We were looking at a lesser golden plover, a genuine rarity from America. I must confess to feeling no more than curiosity that this undistinguished bird had travelled so far out of its way to visit Somerset – as well as admiration for those who had picked it out from hundreds of its more common relatives.

One recent winter an osprey arrived on the moor. I saw it, but only briefly in the distance, huge and bulky in the gathering gloom. It was gone the next morning, but since then the marsh harrier, another large hawk, has become an altogether more familiar visitor.

For some years these fine birds have bred on a nearby reed-bed and the male is seen sometimes hunting over the moors during the summer, feeding his ever-hungry chicks. With wide, finger-ended wings, the cock bird wavers his way across the fields and along the ditches, often only feet high, like some giant butterfly. He pauses to hover for a moment, then drops down with wings pointing upwards, to rise again and fly off with something dangling from long legs. Marsh harriers are one of the gains from the great reed-beds left after peat extraction and well worth watching as they hunt the moors, where they look so much at home.

Since that first time marsh harriers have become regular visitors in the summer, hovering ponderously over rougher ground and diving down to come up with some small mammal in its talons.

OF HARES, DRAGONFLIES, AND OTHER CREATURES

Although birds are the most obvious forms of wildlife, there are a great deal of other creatures which make their living from the moors, whether within the ditches, hidden in the grass or among the trees and copses which go to make up this varied habitat. For much of the time it may not be realised that this world exists, then a sprinkling of snow brings a multitude of tracks crossing areas where you have seen nothing before.

The smallest creatures often make their presence known by lumps and bumps appearing on arms where they have bitten or sucked the blood. The moors are famous for their insect life, holding many rare or notable species, but they require the watcher to get out a glass to reveal their delicacy and shape.

Mammals
Undoubtedly the most exciting mammal of the area is the otter. I must start by confessing that I have never seen one here and I am unlikely to do so in the future. I do not keep the hours at which they are most likely to be seen. Nevertheless I have a thrill of anticipation every time I look out across the

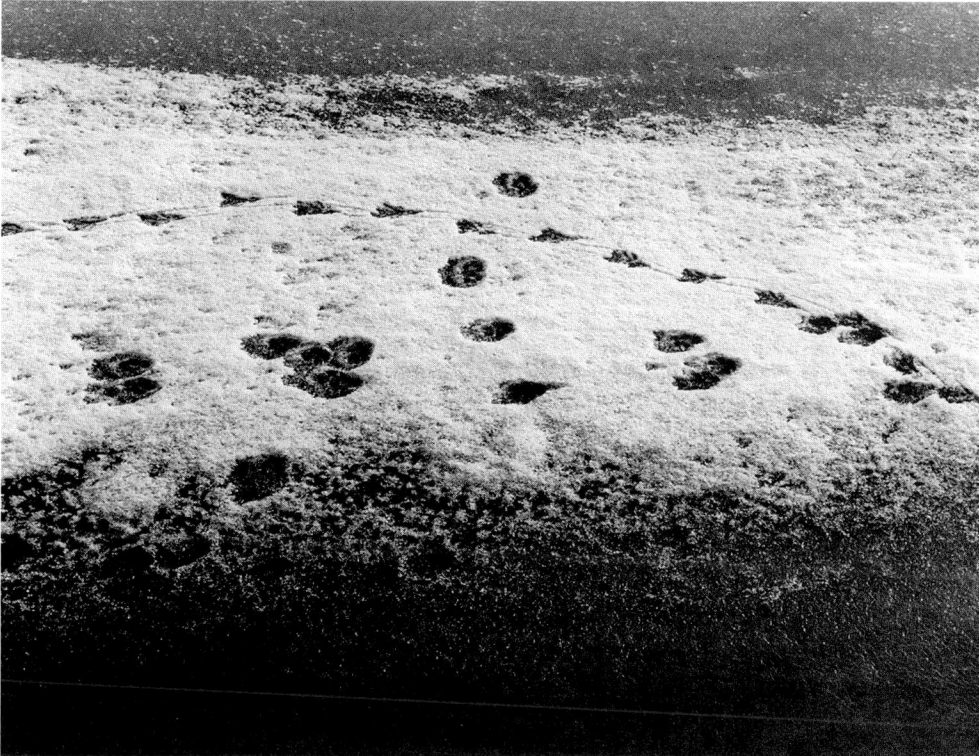

Otter and other tracks in the snow on Old Rhyne one winter.

North Drain in the dark, for it has been proved that they live here. I once saw an otter in Holland and was left with an impression of sinuous grace as it swam across between two patches of reed. I can only hope that one day I may be given a glimpse here.

That is not to say that I have not become aware of their presence on the moors. I have found their spraints' under Jack's Drove Bridge and photographed footprints in the snow lying on the frozen surface of Old Rhyne one winter. A long vee of thinner ice showed where the animal had burst through the surface and then walked along a powdering of snow, leaving clearly-marked footsteps. A few feet further on a moorhen had also walked across and then

175

departed in a hurry. The footsteps of the two creatures were muddled up and blurred at that point.

A local farmer tells the story of a visit out to his milking bail near the North Drain one early summer morning, long before most of us were stirring. He saw something move as the cows started to walk in for milking. To his astonishment he found himself looking at two part-grown otters playing and wrestling in the meadow, well away from the water. They paid little attention to the bustle around them and stayed for quite a while before disappearing, while the farmer busied himself with the milking.

One of the problems otters face results from the modern passion for tidying river banks. Their holts are usually situated in the hollows and roots of ancient trees – willows make especially good sites. Most river and drainage authorities appear to believe that no trees should be allowed on river banks and that watercourses need regular and frequent cleaning, as well as straightening. This has led to the disappearance of most traditional sites for otter holts. Some years ago the Somerset Trust for Nature Conservation started buying land on Tealham and Tadham Moors for reserves. It took advice and installed an artificial holt made from bricks and concrete pipes. The holt itself was buried in a pile of earth, and scrub has been allowed to grow on top. The pipes lead out just under the water's surface, exactly the way otters like it.

We had high hopes. Then, just before burying it in soil, the holt was opened up for a final check. There was no doubt that mink had been using it! A wing of a moorhen was found, together with a variety of bones, and there were mink footprints in the mud at the edge. Whether otter or mink finally use it, no one will know unless they watch continually through the dead of the night. But at least something is being done.

When mink were first seen in the area, it was feared that it would mean the end of the otter. Luckily this has not proved to be the case. Both appear to exist without affecting the other. Mink first became an obvious menace at the end of the 1970's. The first person to notice their spread and destructive powers was someone who had laid out a bit of land as a private nature reserve on the moors just below Chilton Polden. He had bought some wildfowl and had a number of varieties of ducks and geese nesting on an island in old peat workings. It was a most delightful place, nicely planted out with native trees such as willow, alder and birch, and with a thick under-storey of bushes. The birds flourished, then they started disappearing and nests were found cold and empty.

Finally the culprit was caught in the act. A chocolate-coloured mink was seen swimming over to the island. It was disturbed in the very act of killing, yet paid no attention to the human. Books were consulted, traps were bought and a vigorous regime of continuous warfare started. Because of their tameness and confidence, mink are easy to catch alive in traps set in pipes and tunnels round a fence. A great many were captured that first year and for the following season, then catches tailed off.

This tied in with observations in the wild. At first, mink new to an area go mad. They seem to have a form of blood-lust brought on, perhaps, by the easy hunting they find. Mallard and moorhens, formerly common on the moors, practically vanished and it became a rarity to see a brood of ducklings on the rhynes. One year I did not see a single moorhen. People all over the country became worried by the apparent threat posed by these all-conquering killers released into an unprepared countryside. Most were escapes from mink farms. Their only predator in Britain is man. They are smaller than otters, but the largest adults are powerful, muscular animals. They are of the weasel family and a good-sized mink can weigh well over 2 pounds, with a length from head to tail of over 2 feet. The problems come when a number of animals reach a new part where numbers of wildlife are comparatively high. The animals set out on an orgy of killing. Their prey are not prepared for this onslaught and some species are all but wiped out.

The sheer lunacy of those who deliberately sabotage mink farms and let the creatures out into the wild is beyond comprehension. They betray an extreme ignorance about nature and the facts of life. We saw this whole process at work on the moors and were extremely worried. The creatures showed no fear and seemed to be taking over. A friend of ours lives in a lonely house right in the middle of the moors. When floods come, the house is cut off except by road; it stands above the waters like an island. She keeps a flock of large white ducks which enjoy the grazing on these flood-prone fields. One day she went down to feed them and saw something dark on a duck's back. Without thinking she ran up, seized the mink and threw it as far as she could. The mink picked itself up and just looked at her. She was shaken to see what it was, but the duck recovered.

She used to see mink regularly, but there had not been any for some years when I last spoke to her about it. It appears that the mink killed all easily available prey and then moved on. They live like lords for a while, with plenty of prey for all, but this cannot continue. For any creature to breed successfully there has to be a ready supply of food. Overkill reduces the supply and animals fail to rear their young but a balance has to be reached eventually. Mink are as much a part of this process as any other animal. There are still mink in the area, of that there is no doubt – I see them periodically. But the remaining individuals are now a part of the chain of predation in these parts. The area will only support a small population and this is what remains.

One particular encounter with a mink is especially memorable. Tam, Brock and I were walking down to Old Rhyne by way of Keyton Hill one Christmas Eve. This is often a rather dead time of year and I was enjoying the crisp evening rather than expecting to see anything in particular. Indeed I was not even carrying a camera. The dogs rushed ahead, savouring every subtle aroma and scent in the long grass which edges the field. They were well ahead of me and I arrived at the ditch at the other end to find them sniffing busily, almost hungrily, at a hole in the largest of the three oak trees which stand alone at that point.

Although they are not particularly large, the trees are pocked with hollows and deeper holes where the trunks join the ground. Two of these holes seemed to be fascinating the dogs. They snuffled away noisily, tails wagging furiously. Brock was mystified and soon lost interest but Tam, with twelve years of experience behind her, became more and more excited. She pushed her nose down, little muffled barks escaping and her tail going faster. 'A rabbit,' I thought. Suddenly a dark head with shining button eyes appeared at the mouth of the second hole. The mink snarled and made a spitting noise, then vanished underground again. I called the dogs to heel and we sat and watched. The head came up several times. But it was not going to make a bolt for it and by this time it was getting dark.

"Let's hope the mink is still there." She peered out of the hole in the tree root as I arrived back with the camera.

179

I decided to fetch my camera, hoping the creature would still be there when I returned. It was a longish way, perhaps a mile there and back. I ran most of the way, heavy with boots and cold-weather gear, and collected the camera, the flash gun and a small telephoto lens. I would worry about the problems of focusing when I got there. A torch would surely frighten the creature off, but it seemed the only solution.

I had one camera body loaded with black and white film, the other with colour slide. I was as ready as I ever would be. Miracle of miracles, the mink was still there. Tam rushed over, thrust her nose into the black of the hole and sniffed loudly. A muffled spitting confirmed the presence of the mink. By this time it was all but dark and it was extremely difficult to see, let alone focus. I had noticed before that the mink seemed to prefer to look out of one particular hole, so used the torch to focus on the point where I judged it might come out, then waited in the dark. A series of photographs showed that the theory worked for about 50 per cent of the time. The mink was a beautiful creature, with almost black fur and a gorget of white under the chin. In the colour picture I took, the eyes reflect a shade of purple-green. The animal seemed uninterested in coming out completely, or in leaving the vicinity, although it could have done so with ease.

It was not until 1990 that I saw my first weasel on the moors. Perhaps the area is so open that these creatures keep away from humans. Even stoats are seen only infrequently. I must say I enjoy seeing all the members of this family; they are such intrepid and fearless hunters. They give the impression of being on their own, solitaries, battling for their families against a world which has its face set against them.

Stoats and weasels, like their larger cousin, the mink, share a lack of fear for man. They give the appearance of just not caring about us. If a car drives a stoat off a roadside kill, it will usually return for another look. Stop the car and wait, and soon you will see a small head bobbing up and down in the longer grass, trying to see more clearly. In a short while the animal will walk out into the road for a longer, harder look.

Once I saw a hunt and its ending; it was an extraordinary affair. I was driving along when I saw a rabbit shoot out of a field, along a farm track and onto the verge of the road. It was pursued by the sinuous, looping shape of a stoat. The rabbit had blood dripping from its shoulder and the stoat had red on its beautiful white gorget. The pair shot past the car, which still had its engine running. Neither paid any attention – the rabbit by reason of self-preservation and the stoat because it was totally engrossed in the chase. The rabbit turned and faced the stoat, paws up like a boxer. The stoat hit it with a wallop. There was a brief flurry. A few pieces of fluff flew off into the road. The two shapes separated and the rabbit suddenly took off into the grass. The stoat seemed dazed. It stood there a moment or two before sliding slowly and deliberately into the same field. It was in no hurry and seemed to have given up the chase.

There was another occasion when a stoat came off worst. A friend kept a few hens at the time – large birds, thickset and bulky. They lived outside in

Stoat under a stone. They are fearless little creatures and he paid little attention to me or the dog.

the orchard and laid their eggs and slept in a small shed near the house. She came down to let them out one morning, but when she opened the door the hens did not rush outside in their normal way, but gathered in a group in the centre. When she looked inside the circle, she found a dead stoat curled up in the straw, apparently unmarked. Had the hens killed it, or had it died in that spot in a natural fashion?

The absence of another creature has surprised me. I have seen water voles on varying types of stream and ditch in this country, but never here. I cannot understand why, unless the voles do not like the constantly varying levels in the rhynes and ditches.

The smaller voles, bank and field, have a dreadful time of it when the floods sweep over the moors. The worst affected are field voles, which prefer the wetter meadows. But scrub may also be invaded by the rising waters, and this catches some bank voles. The landscape is incredibly spectacular at times of flood, especially if the sun comes out from behind the grey rain clouds. We love to go for a walk then, but usually confine ourselves to the tarmac, because the droves are so unpredictable – it is easy to step into a dip and find water pouring over the top of your Wellingtons. That day my daughter saw something small swimming across a field and decided to have a closer look. This minute blob of a creature was swimming vigorously but did not seem to know how to get out. It looked thoroughly disorientated, swimming in and out on a series of ellipses, pausing only momentarily before battling out again, like some toy motor-cruiser.

Eventually he found a spot which suited him and hoisted out, coat soaked and matted to his body. He looked nearly done in and I wondered whether he would dry out or die of cold and exhaustion. But he just melted into the grass, disappearing in an instant. Thousands of these little creatures must be killed by such inundations, although animals seem to be better at predicting disaster than we are. Grebes, for instance, are known for their habit of raising the height of their nest hours or even days before flooding brings rising water levels.

Rabbits come and go, as they do in much of the country now. Myxomatosis appeared to have wiped them out completely for some years. Then the first small ones were seen out in the higher fields, or where the woods fringe the moors. They multiply quickly and it can seem as if the rabbit population is about to become a problem again; then, like lightning, the awful disease strikes again. The animals wander round in a daze, although they do not appear to be in pain. Their heads swell up and their eyes and nose weep continually until, eventually, their eyes seem as if they will burst out of their head. It looks like the wrath of God is descending on their population. Some time later you realise that none have been seen for ages.

Rabbits are attractive little creatures but they can do the most enormous amount of damage to crops. I don't think anyone is able say the same about hares. It would take large numbers to compete with sheep or cattle for grass and, by their nature, they do not band together. They live a solitary existence out in the open field, relying for protection on camouflage and stillness, rather than numbers. They are most delightful and entertaining animals – beautiful, lively and secretive. Unfortunately they also appear to be in decline on the moors. There does not seem to be any real reason why this should be: some of the fields may have changed, but the majority remain the same as they have always been – permanent grass with little fertiliser added, other than slurry. The only other change is the overall increase in pumping. None of this seems to add up to a less desirable environment for the hares. The other possibility is that the increasingly early cuts for silage affect the animals in their breeding, as it has undoubtedly in the case of a variety of bird-species.

I will never be able to understand how anyone can hunt hares. I can see both sides of the fox-hunting debate, but I see no justification whatsoever for hare-hunting. They are such gentle, inoffensive creatures. They cause no problems to farmers and are a joy to watch. Why, then, should the harriers come over every year and drag the fields, hoping to set the hounds on the unfortunate hare? At times like these, when the hare population is low and apparently not increasing, I resent the arrival of the hunt even more. I know that there are a great many people around who pray that they make no catch.

My wife and I hold hares in particular affection. For some considerable time we looked after two orphans. The first leveret arrived one weekend, looking minute in the hands of our next door neighbour's son. He had been out rolling one of the fields when he had spotted the leveret crouched in its form and managed to stop his tractor and rescued it before carrying on. We agreed to look after it, but then wondered how we were to do so. In particular, how were we to get milk into its tiny mouth? Then my wife had a brainwave. She rang Mike, our local chemist, and explained the problem. He said that what we needed was a pipette, and he had some in the shop. Nothing would dissuade him from fetching one and bringing it over – real country service!

Our first sight of Willy, a few days old, brought in from the moors by our neighbour after saving him from his roller.

So now we had the means. Would our willpower overcome the natural fear of the leveret? We judged that it could be no more than a day or so old. We learned that warm cows milk was suitable for a leveret and battle was joined. For such a minute creature he was remarkably tough and resisted our efforts with great success. After an hour we had a soaking wet leveret, drenched in milk outside but with hardly a drop inside. He would not suck, so we tried squirting the sticky milk in. He spat it out, rolling his eyes and looking extremely upset.

Clearly we could not carry on like this so we retired to lick our wounds, so to speak. First we installed the wet and matted little creature in a box of hay tucked up against a storage heater. In another hour he was dry and much happier and livelier. He was a different character completely, but he still would not suck, although he no longer spat out the milk. Finally he accepted the pipette being put into a corner of his mouth and started gulping. By the end of the evening we thought we had won the battle. Willy, as we had named him, should survive. The next morning he was lively and clean, his fur fluffed out and dry.

From then on Willy was fed regularly and started to get the idea of sucking, although not for long at any one time. Feeding took as long as it did with a human baby, and the whole household was regulated by the hare and its meals. After a few days he became totally wedded to the pipette, sucking and

Wild hare out in the fields, wary and speedy when disturbed.

185

grinding at it so hard that we feared he might bite off the end. For the first few days he lived quietly in a box against the heater. Then one morning he was missing but eventually he was traced to a dark corner behind the television set. He liked to snuggle up in such dark corners and would retire to one when he wanted a little peace from our over-affectionate children. In the evenings he liked to sit at our feet, apparently watching the television with great intensity.

He was far too active and lively, not to say athletic, to confine, so he had the run of the house. If one of us was reading he would creep up and vanish up inside our sweater where he would snuggle in tightly. My wife had a particularly soft sweater which was his absolute passion. Within a few days he assumed a definite character, and he was growing almost visibly. His ears betrayed his alertness even when he appeared to be resting. They would move the whole time, turning and twisting and testing the surroundings. He was soft and warm for the longer guard hairs of the outer coat concealed an inner fur which never became damp even in the heaviest rain. He had some endearing tricks, apart from the slightly disconcerting one of vanishing up a visitor's jersey. If you put your face down towards him he would lean forward and snuff you ever so gently. We felt extraordinarily privileged that this wild creature should be so trusting.

Soon it was clear that the time had come for him to have solid food and he was gradually weaned, although he continued to love a dish of milk in later life. He had learned to lick drops off our fingers at an early stage, so we began by putting breadcrumbs on our fingers, mixed with the milk. He loved this. Then he ate pieces of bread soaked with milk. Soon he was nibbling away at a mixture of warm milk, bread and porridge oats, and grew apace. I would not have believed such a frail creature could expand and thrive so fast. Within two weeks he had doubled in size – and in strength.

This strength was amazing. With his agility, and a skin which seemed to move quite independently of his body, he became a real problem to catch and hold. A wriggling child was an absolute amateur compared with our leveret, although the biggest problem was finding and catching him. This involved a game of hide and seek which ranged all over the ground floor of the cottage. His favourite place was behind the television set but even knowing that, he was still difficult to find at times – even in that unlikely setting his camouflage seemed to be outstanding. At that time our three girls were between 3 and 7 years old. The hare was a subject of unending fascination to them and the two younger ones just could not stop following him around, constantly petting and touching him. I think he hid to try and get away from them. In the evenings, after the children's bed time, he came to life and wandered round the house exploring everything. He was fascinated with the flickering television screen and would go up to it for an exploratory sniff every so often. For the rest of the time he would watch through curious, goggling, prominent eyes. He had one strange and totally unexpected habit. He would stand like a dog, on all fours, his legs extended. It looked strange to people who had been brought up on pictures of rabbits and hares squatting down on their haunches.

His propensity to hide himself, combined with the fact that we had to go out for much of the day, meant that we soon had to find him a change of habitation. Besides, we felt that he ought to be out in the fresh air. At that time we kept a collection of ornamental wildfowl – wigeon, pintails, barnacle geese and many others – behind the house. About half an acre was wired in at that time. In the middle of this enclosure we had an aviary which we had built for an injured wild bird. Now it was occupied by a silky hen which was sitting on a clutch of ducks' eggs. She was immovable, glued to her eggs, but the hare seemed to find it congenial, since the day was his main time for sleeping. In the evening he would be brought in for his feed and then spend the night exploring the house. His hay box was always empty in the morning.

One evening there was great excitement. My wife was so used to the routine of fetching him in that she no longer held him as tightly as before. On this evening he gave a twitch and was gone! He shot off uphill, but ran headlong into the pond. Romey swears that she saw it all in slow motion – legs paddling frantically in mid-air, before he plunged into the water. She felt sure he would sink like a stone but he dog-paddled buoyantly back to the bank and was as enthusiastic about the reunion as she was. The only problem was that he smelt terrible for a while and spent even longer than usual cleaning himself.

Perhaps the most exciting and important time was the day we came down to find that he had finished off the bowl of food we had left him overnight. Before that, everything had had to stop for feeding – a laborious and messy business. Now he was able to cope on his own and life no longer stopped for half an hour. He grew fast and we realised one day that he was becoming large and heavy and should spend his whole time outside. With much trepidation we left the door of his aviary open one evening and put his food outside. From that time on he led a completely integrated life as part of the community within the duck enclosure. At feeding time Romey would call him, and he would come lolloping out of the shadows to wait beside a queue of ducks and geese as the feeding troughs were filled. He seemed to like mixed corn and chicken pellets equally and fed alongside pinkfeet and mandarins, shoveler and Cape teal without worry. To the end he remained tame and easily approachable. He would always come to my wife's call. Jenny was wilder by far, but she too would always come to a call for feeding.

Jenny, our second leveret, was brought to us by a small boy who had acquired her in similar circumstances. The family found her difficult to look after and had no real facilities outside. They heard about us and Jenny joined the family, though she was wilder by far than Willy, although she too would come when called for feeding. She was partly weaned and we never achieved the intimacy with her that we had with Willy. Nevertheless she was a character in her own right and fitted into the community just as well, in her own way. She was shyer, remaining near cover whenever possible. One of the larger and more belligerent snow geese could easily scare her away from the food whereas Willy would pay no attention and just continue munching stolidly whatever was going on.

Young visitors were totally fascinated by the sight of a couple of hares feeding in a press of ducks just a few feet away from the kitchen. My wife

One of the more bizarre sights was a couple of hares feeding with the ducks just outside the kitchen window.

would open the window so that they could look out, before she went up to the pen with a bowl of food. She would call as she went in and an entourage of brightly coloured ducks and geese would follow her down. Then she would call Willy and Jenny down and they would lollop up to wait as eagerly as the rest for the ceremonial pouring into troughs. Heads down and bottoms up, they were indeed an unusual sight.

We had not thought of letting them out. They seemed so content and we wondered how they would cope with a world where dogs and men were no longer friends. They had over half an acre enclosed and food was provided. How would they survive in the outside world? We never really found the answer to that. One day, years after Willy was brought to us, a gate was left open and Willy went missing and never reappeared. After a few days we felt that Jenny was pining. She seemed different. Perhaps she would fetch him back? The gate was left open again, this time on purpose, and that was that. We never saw them again. It was the end of a chapter in our lives.

The amazing sense of intimacy with a wild creature like a hare has to be experienced to be believed. Perhaps my most vivid memory was when Willy still lived inside but was almost full-grown. I went into a room and found him gazing out of the window at the garden. I put my hand on his back in a spirit of friendliness, as one might with a dog. He just twitched his whiskers and continued to gaze out at the sunlight.

Foxes abound round here. I remember talking to someone who had seen the records of the Wedmore Preserving Club in a recent year. They had shot between 40 and 50 foxes during their regular drives through the moor. In recent years this has risen to double that figure without, apparently, affecting the foxes' numbers. The moors are too wet and dangerous for hunting so the club, together with irate smallholders who have lost chickens and ducks, are the sole enemies of the fox. They live round the edges, on the slopes of the hills, or even right at the bottom, at the lowest contour. The moors provide good hunting for foxes: the ground prey is easily stalked at night and the wind direction remains constant, not deflected by woods or banks.

Portrait of a fox. A handsome creature by any standards.

The foxes keep clear of man and his creatures for most of the year. The attacks on chickens and ducks occur only when food becomes vital in large quantities, when the vixen is feeding her cubs. We have noticed – and suffered from – this over the years. Our ducks laid out in the orchard, behind tall wire netting fences. Normally the birds were not troubled, but they are at their most vulnerable while sitting. Before hatching they remain glued to their eggs whatever the commotion. Foxes will do anything to get at them. They dig beneath the netting, jump over it by way of overhanging apple trees, or find a weak spot, then a trail of feathers shows where another unfortunate duck has been dragged off. We are able to prevent it if we know where the bird is sitting, but some manage to vanish completely into the undergrowth while nesting. Only their death trail shows where they were so well hidden from us.

Foxes have had to change their habits over the years. In the old days hens, ducks and geese were much more a part of the local economy. Every farmhouse had some hens scratching round the yard and a few ducks out in the open fields. Each cottage kept a few hens as well as, perhaps, a pig and some geese to fatten for Christmas. The poultry would have been free-range – shut in at night, but normally roaming where their will took them. As people have become better off, and with the ever-increasing costs of corn and other feeds, these small enterprises have tended to disappear. So the foxes have had to look elsewhere for their living. Being extremely versatile creatures, omnivores who eat everything from earthworms to chickens and dig up roots and take berries from the hedgerows, they have found no difficulty in meeting and living with modern country life. Dustbins put out overnight are sometimes found with lids off with a trail of tins and paper bags stretching into the middle of a nearby field.

Sometimes the rank smell of fox hangs over the damp morning hedge like a cloak, and periodically we see one sauntering past the window, for there is a vast den at the bottom of a slope which leads down to the moors, which has been a traditional haunt of both badger and fox. Some of these setts are supposed to have been occupied for as far back as people can remember –

centuries in all probability. This particular sett has seen its ups and downs over the years. Once our neighbour found a whole family of young badgers laid out, stone dead and cold, around the multiple entrances. Nobody knows for sure what had happened to them. After that the holes were filled in as being dangerous for people and machines, but in a few years they were all in use again, and the area is now a honeycomb of tunnels.

One late summer we came to know the badgers rather better. I had been out walking the dogs one evening just as the light was fading and for some reason we had diverted to where the badgers had their sett. I leaned on a post beside the ditch and gazed across at the fresh earth round one of the sett mouths, not really thinking of anything. The light was dying rapidly but you could still see some detail. All at once I found myself gazing at a shape which had appeared as if by magic. There was no movement that I could remember; the creature just materialised at the edge of the entrance hole. It was a young badger, lacking the bulk and defined colours of its parents, paler coated and with creamier facial markings. It only stayed above ground for a few seconds but it was enough to make me want to see more. So for the next few nights expeditions were made down to the sett as light was fading.

It was a marvellous time of year. Blue skies during the day, separated by a few light showers, brought crystal clear nights still balmy enough to be comfortable. A huge harvest moon towered off to one side, silvering the fields and giving enormous, elongated shadows.

Waiting for the badgers was almost as exciting as seeing them. A great deal happens out in the anonymous dusk. One evening, while it was still quite light, a kestrel swooped down and plunged into one of the entrance holes for a moment, only 30 feet or so from us watchers. Another evening a heron flew over from the east and pitched in the upmost branches of the oak tree before vanishing into the blanket of the night. It was surprisingly noisy on these still evenings. The heron kronked its way across the fields. A curlew bubbled, lapwings squeaked and owls hooted softly. Cows erupted into a succession of bellows, as if the end of the world had come. There was never a silent moment.

As it became darker it was more difficult to pick out shapes or surroundings in spite of the silver path of the moon. The surrounding vegetation threw shadows which seemed to move. My eyes strained and my imagination started to bite. The occasional little creature ran across the ditch edge, a vole dashing for shelter or some unknown predator on its hunt. When the badgers did appear they performed their usual magic, appearing in front of my eyes without apparent movement. Without the distinctive black and white pattern on the head they would have been impossible to see in these conditions. Presumably the colouring allows easy contact in poor lighting. The photographs I took on those few nights of perfect weather were not perfect, nevertheless they represent memories of a fascinating and happy glimpse into lives running parallel to ours, yet not often seen.

Badgers are large creatures, their bodies as big as a medium-sized dog, tremendously powerful in the hind quarters, yet they move around largely unobserved. One evening they were clearing out bedding and a huge amount of activity could be heard underground. Sounds of dragging were interspersed with scrabbling and little grunts. I imagined them heaving and straining to bring out the old bedding, dried and stale, from far below. It appeared that there were two or three badgers foraging round above ground, hidden in the vegetation, collecting new bedding and taking it down below. Perhaps the most marvellous thing about badgers is the realisation that they have been in residence for longer, perhaps, than our houses. Long may they continue.

That old sett has been the dogs' favourite walk for a long while. They rush over to the corner of the field and have a sniff as a matter of routine. One year I noticed a patch of well-mown lawn outside the sett, close to a newly dug entrance. I wondered what it was but did not give it a lot of thought. Then one day the mystery was solved. Brock bounded over and then backed off, looking intently at the lawn-like patch. I saw something red, heard a yelp from Brock and a squeal from the entrance to the hole. There was a fox-cub facing towards us, then backing slowly down the hole. The lawn, perhaps 6 feet by 4, was where a litter of cubs had played each evening. We came back a few days later and found the herbage growing again in ragged tufts, soon it was just like the rest of the field. Mother fox had moved the litter to another one of her holes, disturbed to think that her secret had been penetrated.

One year we had a very hard winter and the rhynes froze solid. Boys skated on them, or rode their bicycles along the ice during the day. Then it rained heavily on the frozen ground, bringing quick floods, as there was no way for the water to escape. The water froze once more and stayed iron-hard for a couple of weeks. Snow fell and stayed powdered and loose to blow with the wind and drift to fill rhynes and ponds, then it blew harder and the powder twisted into fantastic shapes along the rhyne banks, but left the frozen water clear. It was a time of intense cold and showed the place in a quite different light. During the period when the snow lay in a blanket a few inches deep over everything, it revealed an amount of activity which we had not previously noticed. There was a tightly woven network of tracks crossing and recrossing everywhere, with particularly heavy traffic along the banks of the rhynes and at certain favoured crossing points.

It is great fun to take a field guide to tracks to see if you can decipher the messages of the tracks. As with many illustrations in books, it quickly becomes apparent that 'your' tracks are made by creatures unknown to the writers! Some are quite unrecognisable, others seem obvious; they are exactly like the drawings in the book. Then you realise that the creature you believe it to be is unlikely to be present in such numbers!

I was particularly interested to see otter tracks crossing and recrossing Old Rhyne. Here was proof positive, something I had seen myself, rather than relying on research findings.

That particular year it stayed frozen and white for some time. One day I took the two dogs out for a walk. Brock thought it was marvellous and ran in huge, widening circles. He was visibly delighted, rolling in it, sniffing the deeper drifts and tearing everywhere at high speed, for he was still in the early stages of what we euphemistically called training. We were standing in the middle of the moors, watching him rushing round, when he stopped for a moment and then tore off at high speed in a straight line. Soon he was out of sight, then reappeared, moving steadily towards us, nose down, following some obviously strong trail. What was it? A hare perhaps, or possibly just another dog? No. Far in front of him, running at a leisurely pace, was a bright red fox, brilliant against the blue of the snow in the half-light.

It paused by the edge of Old Rhyne, looked back and saw Brock thundering up. It gathered itself, seeming to flow like liquid across the ice, and set off at high speed across the field and up towards our house. Brock made a valiant effort but lost out to the fox in sheer speed.

One April, Romey and I went out early one morning, deliberately leaving the dogs behind. We hoped to catch a few early birds and animals afield before too many people were around. The part by the 'deserted' village has always fascinated us and by 6.30 we had reached the place where the drove runs beside the woods. Not being a naturally early riser, this seemed like the crack of dawn to me, but my wife was quite awake and observant. She noticed something red-brown in the grass of the field. We thought it might be a roe deer, of which there had been rumours of sightings for some time, but it was a fox, playing with something hidden in the grass. Luckily the wind was blowing away from us and there were no noisy dogs to give us away. I fitted the camera onto a monopod and set up ready for a shot. Then, to our astonishment, the animal started trotting towards us. It paused when the motor-drive whirred, then came on across the ditch with an effortless bound, stopped a moment on the track just by us, and then trotted on. It all happened so suddenly we could not believe it.

The picture is not a masterpiece but it is treasured beyond many. It is one of my more vivid memories: a wild creature within a few yards of us. We were standing quite still, but in the middle of the drove, in full view. By dint of various chemical wizardries I was able to extract some sort of an image from a mere shadow on the negative I obtained in that grey early light.

It was in this same area that we saw the first signs of roe deer in the area. It must have something to do with the fact that it is the more enclosed part of the moors. Scrubby woodlands surround the 'deserted' village and the other side of the drove has much more enclosed fields, with heavily wooded raised banks, which are wide enough for a herd of cows to feed among the trees. It is a secret area, not used much by villagers or visitors, empty except for farmers visiting their stock or the occasional fisherman walking down to the North Drain.

One day we were exploring and one of the girls called us over. She pointed to a slot in the mud beside some shallow pools, among a grove of slender alders. Although we could not be sure, as it was not clear and fresh enough, I had a feeling in my heart that it was a roe. I kept that feeling alive over the years. After all, Dorset was not far away and was alive with roe. They were known to be spreading everywhere. Why not Tealham? For a number of years we had visited Northumberland and seen a great many roe up there. We became familiar with the ways of these seemingly delicate, but tough, little creatures, and the more I thought, the more convinced I was that roe would be seen on Tealham sooner or later.

Then one morning my wife was walking the dog in much the same place and he disturbed roe twins which floated through some bushes and over a rhyne. After that we heard reports of their presence from many people. They seemed to live over where we had seen them originally, around the 'deserted' village and further up, onto the edge of the hills, bordering Sand. Since then roe have taken over the area, with regular sightings all over the moors. They are said to be solitary creatures but seem to have changed their habits in these parts. Last winter a herd of 14

Roe deer in the early morning.

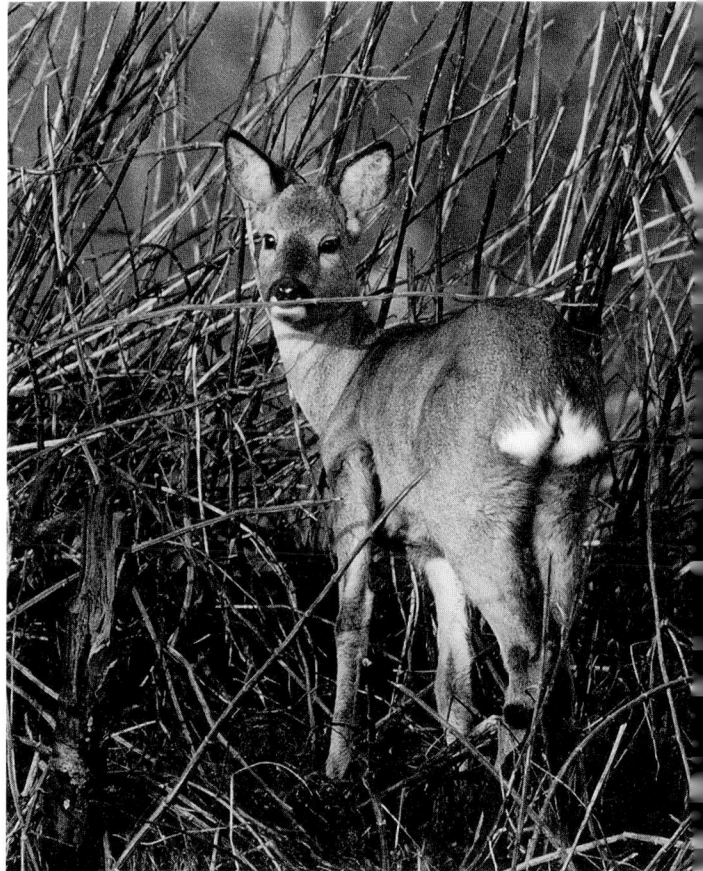

roe were seen regularly on one part of Tadham, feeding and moving together.

Roe are some of the most delightful and beautiful creatures around and add greatly to our enjoyment of the countryside here. Since most of the agriculture is based on grassland, they can do little damage and so can be enjoyed by everyone. All those who have seen them have mentioned it with excitement and pleasure.

Finally I should mention what must be one of the most numerous and obvious mammalian moorland inhabitants – the mole. It is rare to see the creature itself, but some fields seem to be more molehill than open ground. The soft peat soil, with water often only a few inches below the surface in the spring, seems ideally suited to these velvet creatures.

Brock, who is one of the friendliest and gentlest of dogs, has one abiding passion. He is a fervent and successful digger of moles. This started when he was a small and enthusiastic puppy and has continued to this day. He seems to have a way of detecting mole movements. I had always thought of them as scentless animals, difficult to detect underground, but he makes a dash for a particular molehill and starts digging furiously and has had some success, although he never harms the moles. The first came when he was little. He rushed over to a molehill, pranced round it, full of bounce, and then started biting and clawing at the loose earth. A flow of soil, divots of grass and a lot of noise showed his progress. Suddenly there was a swirl and something flew up and out. Brock stood there, looking down at it with wagging tail. Clearly he had no idea what to do with the completely unharmed mole, which lay winded on the earth for a moment before digging its way into the soft peat to disappear in seconds.

Insects and other creatures
All that water on the moors brings with it a rich harvest of insects. In recent years some of them appear to have diminished somewhat, as main ditches are cleaned out more clinically, but there is still an abundance of insect life and many interesting species are seen here which are found less often elsewhere.

All that water and rough ground brings a rich harvest of insects. The beautiful elephant-hawk moth, a lovely pink in colour.

The ditches have always been a rich source of wildlife, from fish to water-beetles. Although the cleaning process has changed and reduced the populations of some species, we are told that others have benefited. The important thing is that a variety of different stages of ditch, rhyne and drain cleaning is maintained, and this seems likely, because there are so many miles of them under such varied ownership.

A recent scientific study of the invertebrate fauna of Tealham and Tadham ditches, by James Stephen, recommended that *'the ditches should be cleaned on a cycle between one and three years, the cycles should be asynchronous, (especially in ditches of close proximity) so that a mosaic of different age class ditches results'*. If adopted, this regime should give an environment suitable for the maintenance of a diverse and healthy invertebrate community.

It is dangerous to talk about changes to populations on the basis of even a number of years' observation but there is some evidence that the variety of dragonflies is increasing on the Levels. My own interest in these splendid creatures is too recent to do more than point this out, but others who have watched the area over many years are sure that there is a spread of new species into the area.

Dragonflies have been described as bird-watcher's insects because they are so easily watched, so visible and colourful. They vary from tiny threadlike damselflies to the largest hawkers, brilliantly coloured and up to 3 inches long. The season starts with the first glimpse of the large red damselfly – a misnomer if ever there was one, as it is only $1\frac{1}{2}$ inches long and slender as a needle. In early May they appear in the nettles on the edge of the rhynes and among the lower leaves of the hawthorn bushes. Seen under a camera's macro-lens, they are far more than just red insects. The thorax is shot with metallic gold, as are segments towards the end of the tail. Their wings shimmer like gossamer in the new light of spring.

The last dragonflies are to be seen at the end of October; they are common darters, middle-sized creatures, with a most distinctive fluttering flight, which always seem to return to the same spot when hunting. The male is red and the female a golden beige. One late autumn evening I walked the dog down the enclosed drove on Tadham Moor and we were preceded by a cloud of golden-pale darters, as numerous as midges in July, fluttering weakly up with each step we took. They rose in waves in front of us, their wings glistening as they caught the low golden rays of the sun. A couple of cold days later and the drove was empty of life. Where were all the bodies?

Among the unusual dragonflies found here is the white-legged damselfly, which is pale, with distinctive legs, tiny and delicate. In the right spot, you may come across the banded agrion, brilliant in metallic blue or green, with a dark band across the wings of the male. The sight of a couple of males dancing in display above a slow-flowing rhyne is unforgettable. They are like images of Tinkerbell from Peter Pan – delicate, as though a puff of wind would blow them away for ever. Looking closely at the colour and brilliance of the body, I am amazed that anything so exotic exists away from the tropics. It is truly a living jewel. The wonderful thing about a close-up lens is that it brings this unexpected and unseen world into view. Many insects are seen to be amazingly beautiful, with glowing eyes, delicately drawn patterns on wings and needle-sharp hairs fringing their legs, etched as if with a diamond.

Tiny, jewel-like. common blue damselflies are found widely on the Levels.

Common hawker emerging from its exuvia. Prior to that the larva lived as an underwater predator.

The smaller damselflies in particular repay closer scrutiny. The emerald damselfly has spread recently from the Mendips down to the lowland rhynes. The male is metallic emerald, with a bronze thorax and a chalk-blue segment towards the end of the tail, while the female is largely bronze, sometimes with a tinge of pink. The red-eyed damselfly is another interesting species, which may be seen on water-lily leaves on the North Drain. This is rather larger and heavier than the emerald, with ruby-coloured eyes which contrast with a generally black body. Damselflies rest with their wings laid back along the tail so they appear as slender as tooth-picks.

The larger hawkers, chasers and skimmers sit with their two pairs of wings spread wide, making them seem even larger. Common and southern hawkers, brilliant in green, yellow and blue rings, are to be seen all over the moors in midsummer, often hawking up and down the droves or in the shade of bushes. As you walk along a drove they can quite unnerve you with the mechanical rattle of their wings as they storm past on their beat. They appear to pay little attention to people unless their movements are obviously jerky or aggressive towards them. I have spent a lot of time trying to photograph the southern hawker. This handsome green dragonfly seems capable of flying for ever without respite. When it does settle it can be as wary as a kitten at one moment and completely relaxed the next. Eventually you may be able to approach

The perfect adult common hawker resting on a sedge.

within a few inches to watch the eyes shifting their gaze from side to side, the head turning with them, vigilant yet unworried by your presence. Then it is possible to pick out the individual facets of the lenses and scars on the surface of the eyes. It may seem a strange thing to say but I often feel the 'personality' of the creature as I sit glued to the eyepiece and gaze at its magnified features.

At the end of 1990 there was a great invasion of what at one time was a rare dragonfly, the migrant hawker. The first time that we saw one was a great event, but soon we were brushing aside sightings as though they were of no consequence. This was unfair by any standard, as they are extraordinarily beautiful and vividly coloured creatures. The male has a deep blue ground-colour, overlaying black segments on the body and brilliant blue eyes. The thorax is a distinctive brown. The female has this same brown shade as her ground-colour, but her eyes are green. They fly more weakly than the other hawkers and are quite distinct once seen and identified for the first time.

The same year started with a considerable number of another unusual species – the hairy dragonfly. Although this creature lives up to its name, it is not dissimilar to the migrant hawker in colouring, though with even bluer eyes. The two species are distinguished immediately by the quite different

The eye of an adult southern hawker, showing the many facets which give it such keen eyesight.

seasons they occupy. There are signs that they too are on the increase and, perhaps, extending their range.

The largest British dragonfly, the emperor, has also had good years recently. It is a creature of tremendous energy, hunting tirelessly up and down a rhyne for long periods, appearing reluctant to settle in the open. This beautiful dragonfly has a more uniform appearance than the hawkers, which all look as if they are ringed like a tubular club-scarf. The male is powder blue with a green thorax, while the female is predominantly green.

Finally I must mention a species which is generally rarer yet relatively common on the moors: the ruddy darter. The male is a rich, deep red, with a distinctive waisted body, and flies with glittering wings from a set point in his territory. He is often to be found sunning himself on a bare patch of peat, setting off the brilliant colour of its abdomen admirably. One summer I found an even rarer species in the area. The red-veined darter has distinctively-coloured veins on the leading edges of the wings and is extremely handsome as well as scarce.

Darters are tiny creatures, although they rest with wings spread like the much larger hawkers. Their flight looks weak, but they appear to have little difficulty in catching small flies and other creatures. When it is particularly hot, they sit with their tails reaching for the sky in an effort to reduce the surface-area absorbing the direct rays of the sun. It is strange to see a row of tails pointing to the sky like needles in a pincushion.

Many species of butterflies may be seen along the droves or on the edges of the rhynes. On a hot day it seems as if the surface of the ground is in continuous movement. Gatekeepers, small tortoiseshells, meadow browns and speckled woods are the commonest varieties. The brimstone changes instantaneously from brilliant yellow in flight, to the appearance of a fresh green leaf as it closes its wings. The camouflage can be so effective that it vanishes from view completely.

The increasingly rare marsh fritillary is to be found off one particular drove. I was delighted to be shown a whole patch of their caterpillars hidden in gossamer patches, like spiders' webs, on devil's bit scabious, their food plant.

Another find was a patch of nettles almost hidden beneath colonies of small tortoiseshell caterpillars in every stage of existence from tiny black larvae to large, nearly full-grown caterpillars with yellow streaks along the flanks.

In the varying habitats of meadow, woodland and drove, a number of the smaller butterflies may be found, often in large numbers, including small blues, small and large skippers, looking strange with their stepped wing positions when at rest, small coppers, brilliant against hawkbit, and brown argus. In early spring the orange-tip dances over the fields of its host plant, the cuckoo flower or lady's mantle, which is so characteristic of the moorland season, while later the wall brown is to be seen spread out on warm stones,

The delicate orange-tip which depends on the plentiful cuckoo-flowers on the moors.

Small tortoiseshell drinking the nectar with tis long tongue which curls back like a watch spring when not in use.

basking in the sunshine. This latter butterfly seems to be strengthening its position in the area.

Grasshoppers and crickets have also caught my eye in recent years. Many are so well camouflaged as to be invisible until they move. Under the close-up lens they assume quite different personalities, armoured knights of impregnable appearance, shielded by coats of chitin, as heraldic as any medieval lord. Among the interesting species found locally are large and lesser marsh grasshoppers. The former is a handsome creature, with yellow and black striped knees, well over an inch in size, and extremely rare. Grasshoppers are

207

tricky to differentiate, particularly so because their colour varies with that of their habitat. However there are various characteristics which distinguish one from another, and which can be seen without hurting the animal. One is the pair of marks on top of the thorax. Some are parallel, others less so and some strongly divergent.

A number of crickets are to be found in the area, including the short-winged conehead, the bog bush-cricket and the dark bush-cricket. Grasshoppers have short antennae, while bush-crickets have very long ones which look extremely fragile and vulnerable, often extending to twice the length of their body. The female cricket has a great curved blade like a scythe extending behind; this

One of the many mimicking insects to be found in this area which is so rich in habitat. The wasp-beetle can readily be mistaken for its more painful conjener.

ovipositor is for inserting its eggs into the ground or vegetation, while the male looks short and squat without this appendage. The smallest of the clan are the ground-hoppers, some dark and squat, others striped and attractive.

Mayflies, beetles, moths, flies, wasps and bees are found everywhere. This miniature world repays study but requires getting down to its level. I spent some fascinating hours watching solitary digger wasps going to and from their burrows in a peat bank one day. They were most beautiful little creatures, half the size of a normal wasp and brilliantly coloured. It was strange to see how their appearance changed when they closed their wings. Although these seemed transparent they altered the whole appearance of the creature as they folded over the back: from a black-bodied wasp with brilliant gold rings, they changed to a much more muted and subtle golden-colour. Although they are described as solitary wasps, they breed in dense colonies, but keep to their own separate holes. Social wasps breed together in a single hole or nest.

One speciality of the Levels is the raft spider. It is one of Europe's largest spiders and is found near, though not always in, water. It lives among surface vegetation and will dive in to chase its prey. It is notable for the fact that the female, which has a body up to $\frac{3}{4}$ inch in length, is often seen carrying a large cocoon beneath her, which holds her eggs. We are always proud to show this handsome chocolate-coloured spider off to visitors. There are hosts of other spiders out there including orb spiders, wolf spiders and jumping spiders. The vegetation is full of them and many are well worth examining. Some are as delicate and beautifully-tinted as the flowers in which they live.

I cannot emphasise enough the delights of getting out a hand-lens and taking a closer look at the life all around. Often the smaller it is, the more colourful and jewel-like.

AS THE SEASONS GO BY

Seasons are more important in the country than in a town. In the city centre you can largely avoid weather; it passes you by. You are never far from shelter, so it is only a temporary inconvenience.

Not so in the country. Winds whistle past the windows, unprotected by high rise blocks or offices in rows. The whipping trees sing and then scream with its force. It is direct, elemental. Shelter may be far off and life must be adjusted to it. Sun, rain, and snow impinge directly on country people, forcing them to alter their ways to suit each new circumstance. Unexpected changes in the overall pattern – early winter or cold and delayed spring – may affect the whole course of life for weeks on end, bringing with it actions which are quite beyond the control of the individual. A late, cold spring does not mean just keeping the heat on later. It may be that the garden never fulfils its promise that year, or that cattle are unable to get out onto the fields at their usual time, involving expensive extra feeding. A drought is something that is seen and felt out in the country. Water may be cut off for part of the day and have to be fetched from standpipes in the nearest village or delivered by tanker.

For these reasons one notes with intensity the pattern of the seasons and any changes which occur. This chapter chronicles one view; others may see the same weather, the same changes in a quite different light. The separate viewpoints may be coloured by houses differently exposed to the wind, by the length of time spent outside or by temperament. Although the obvious difference is between town and country, there is nearly as much variation between village and country cottage. The village may offer almost as much protection from the elements as the town and can offer a similar artificial separation from the reality of what is happening outside. Snow may be a real problem if you live in a house, as we do, where high winds and quite moderate snowfall bring drifts. Roads within and around the villages are cleared quickly and effectively, except in the severest conditions, but the lane

Winter, and the fields run with water. Streaks of silver, and wider lakes and pools, quilt the landscape.

211

to a remote cottage or remote farm is not treated with such urgency.

I see the seasons vividly and with great affection. Sun and rain interchange with bewildering rapidity. The light alters from moment to moment and from hour to hour. Rarely does it stand still. It is mobile, contrasting brilliance with flat, grey nothingness, rain in the sunlight with leaden skies. This is a special part of England's charm, made the more noticeable on returning from the tropics or the desert, where weather settles in for long periods of sameness – blue skies may not seem so attractive on the twentieth day without any variation!

Winter

Many people think of spring as the start of the year. I feel that this event is better represented in our corner of Somerset by winter. It is the season of renewal, of life reappearing as the rains start to fall on the summer-parched moors. Birds stir again in the fields after a long absence and their movement is vivid against the shining silver runnels of water lying in the fields. Yet the browning grasses and dying rush-stubble camouflage them as they pause to feed. Winter is a time of paradoxes.

It comes on insidiously. Days gather in; frost whispers under the car tyres; the air crackles sharply in the faint breath of morning. These signs herald the start. But the most significant feature at the beginning of winter is the long wetness of continuously falling rain, sufficient to make you feel it has set in for ever. Only the hardy, or those who have to, set out for the fields in this weather. Others sit it out indoors with hot crumpets, jam and butter, beside a roaring fire. The raw dampness of early autumn chills the bones and makes you feel colder than you really are. The house walls absorb the heating without taking off the chill and it remains miserable. Later, those thick cottage walls act as storage heaters, evening out the heating and keeping the air dry.

Sometimes the rain continues for weeks on end, a slackening or stoppage of the drizzle quickly being overtaken by more grey, chilling deluges. Perhaps the most depressing feature is the dark, dank greyness of the landscape where all light seems to have been sucked out.

Then one day you wake up to find it has stopped. The sun lightens and brightens the world again. The fields run with water. Streaks of silver, and wider lakes and pools, quilt the landscape below. The moors are alive with birds. Dunlin, snipe and lapwing wheel above; others, in dark rows, perch on tussocks still standing above the water surface. It is a magic place, transformed overnight from dull, even-coloured pastures to a wild and unpredictable landscape, constantly varying in colour. Glittering highlights and reflections show the areas of open water.

Winters are warmer on the Levels than in many other parts of Britain. That is not to say that they cannot be extremely cold and even dangerous at times. But on the whole they are shorter, milder and less extreme. Rarely do we see snow for more than a day or two a year.

In early winter we settle down to a long period of damp. Roads are wet for weeks on end and mud covers everything. Cattle are driven from one soggy

Snow comes but rarely. When it does we enjoy the inevitability of the car being stuck within our lane and enjoy walks in an unfamiliar landscape.

field to another and their routes cross or follow roads in their twice daily passage from field to milking bail. During the winter a spring runs continuously at the top of our access road and carves runnels down the sides of the road. This spring licks further at the mud and cowdung, spreading it across the tarmac, so that the car may be clean when it comes off a wet motorway on the trip from London, but it is filthy within moments of hitting the road below the house.

When snow does come, it brings chaos. Because the land is so flat, and the sheltering elms have long gone, snow drifts across the roads and fills the lanes with great rapidity. With the wind in a particular direction, our lane has

Woodcock, taken from the bathroom window, feeding in the soft ground under a sheltering hedge one December day.

214

been known to fill to hedge level after only a few inches of snow – and we are trapped. Snow being rare, the devices to clear it are rarer still and we rely on a friendly farm tractor coming down the lane. My own digging is useless against a wind curling and licking across the moors and piling in the soft powder faster than I can remove it. So, on the occasional day when it happens every year or so, we sit back, enjoy the inevitability of it and take long walks in unfamiliar surroundings. Even if the lane is full, there is access by foot up the hill and down on to the moors.

As the years roll by, it is clear that drainage is having its effect. Flooding now occurs less frequently and lasts for shorter periods. Even so, water and flooding remain significant factors in life here. Winter is dominated by the waterlogging of the soil. Birdlife reflects this. The area is typical of semi-marsh habitat. Centuries old, unbroken, unimproved, permanent pasture, wet for at least part of the year, supports a flora lost over much of the country. This is what has built up the special character of this small area, a character which remains to this day. The whole combines to offer a mixture of plant and insect life which continues to attract wading birds, ducks and other creatures which prefer traditional wetland conditions.

Winter on the moors is a special delight. The light, the sounds and the feel of the countryside vary continuously. They change from hour to hour as well as from day to day. Skies are huge and alter continually under the influence of strong wind systems. Add to this the fact that we are on the western side of the country, where a clear blue sky rarely persists for more than a few hours, and it is clear that the canvas is bound to be varied and interesting.

The landscape is a fascinating one, with sudden changes in light. It may change in a few moments from a dull, overall leaden grey to the brilliance of a spotlit stage, highlighting a line of willows in the distance. Or a black, stormy background may dramatise the brilliance of sunshine, gilding the bright-cold lappets of floodwater and highlighting a golden fringe of reeds marking long-submerged ditches. Mist, rain, sleet and storm clouds are part of life here. They cannot be ignored or dismissed.

Before the end of year the weather fluctuates, but could be described generally as dull and greyness prevail. For days on end it is overcast, with intermittent drizzle. It is the in-between season – the off-season when the colour and sparkle of autumn has left us and the real, crackling-cold brilliance of enjoyable winter has not yet arrived. It is a time when bones ache and the heating has not yet permeated the walls and made the house cosy. It is dark, damp and bone-chillingly cold. Getting up is a misery. This is the time when those who are faint-hearted about country living question their decision to live there.

Often Christmas is the turning point. You wake one morning to brilliant blue skies, ice films the rhynes and frost lies in the dark hollows of the garden. Although it is cold outside there is a warm glow in the sun. Cheeks and faces burn and breath smokes in the sharp air. It feels good to be there, to be alive and able to look out across the great expanse of the moors. Days like that bring their own magic and, sometimes, great flocks of duck and waders from afar.

Sunsets are superb if the day remains clear. Rising mists, curling up from the rhynes as the sun goes down, only affect the surface layer. The sky remains crystal clear but of varying shades. Sometimes, on a really cold day, the blue of the sky darkens until it is almost black at the top. The horizon may turn pink, then red, until darkness falls. On other evenings the cloudless sky glows orange – a quite extraordinary effect. The most spectacular sunsets occur when a heavy cloud bank rolls over, leaving the lower part clear and cloudless. As the sun drops, the dying rays tint the bottom of the clouds, flushing them with pinks and reds, emphasising the roundness. Some of the most exotic evening effects occur when a sunset such as this falls over part-flooded moors. Clouds and colouring reflect in the bright water, silhouetting the grass and rushes which grow up through it or fringe its edge. With a flight of wigeon taking off, leaving an impression of dark bodies and liquid double-whistles, it is the perfect setting for a Peter Scott landscape.

From this Christmas turning point, winter comes to life. The weather

varies considerably. It is never safe to assume that the cloudless blue skies of morning will remain until the afternoon walk. A grey and rainy morning may clear in a matter of minutes to give shafts of sunlight against midnight-black skies. Sometimes the transformation is so rapid and unexpected that you feel you must be dreaming.

It is a time of excitement, as is any time of change. The colours, textures and atmosphere of the country alter continually. Fields film over with water. Runnels and flashes extend down the moors, outlining ditches that are almost hidden, only the faintest of depressions on the surface. Further rain fills the rhynes and they spill over. The face of the moors changes as the silver water spreads across as far as the eye can see. They become an inland sea, glistening, silver, fringed with pale beige dead reeds and outlined with a lace

Sunsets are superb, particularly when a cloud bank rolls over after a clear, damp day. This picture shows one of the few houses out on the moor itself.

217

of grass running across the high points. It looks deep enough to float a ship. In fact it is so flat that the film of water may be insufficient to support a canoe, except in certain hollows.

Each day brings changes to the wildlife population. Sometimes the moors are echoingly empty. These are the raw, grey days of wind and drizzle, and the birds seem to hate them as much as we do. They stay away until a quick break in the weather may bring in thousands of lapwings. They appear from nowhere and fill the skies and fields for a day. But when the next day dawns, calm, green and bathed in diffuse sunlight, they have disappeared once more. A drive round the boundary of Tealham in winter brings both rewards and disappointments. Frost lying in the hollows may reveal snipe feeding at the damp edges of every rhyne, while on an apparently identical day a few days later, there may be nothing – the place is empty once more.

I fancy that the birds and animals are even more put out by a blanket of snow, though perhaps they do not suffer so much as when the moors freeze solid. A combination of icy winds, sub-zero temperatures and snow can be deadly to less-hardy southern creatures. In such weather it is not unusual to find their gossamer-light carcasses lying out in the open fields, starved to death.

How is it that birds appear to react to changing circumstances so quickly and effectively? A few days of unusual weather, such as rain followed by heavy flooding, soon attract hordes of waders and duck. Where do they come from? What is so much more attractive here than in their normal feeding grounds? How do they find out about our particular piece of countryside? Do they have scouting parties out all winter looking for those perfect feeding grounds, or are they following some long inborn tradition? However you look at it, there appears to be an efficient form of bush telegraph.

It is often possible to predict changes in the bird population days before they take place. Heavy frosts bring clouds of snipe into the damp, warmer patches in the fields. Flooding sees the arrival of wigeon, shoveler and pintail to join greatly enlarged flights of resident teal. Dunlin, ruff and hordes of lapwings come from nowhere when the floods are dying down, when all that is left are silver runnels

The winter landscape is one in which shape and quality is determined by the presence of water.

lying across the debris of grass in the soft, waterlogged fields. A really hard snap results in the disappearance of all except the mute swans, which are powerful enough to forage in most conditions.

The unpredictability of winter is what makes it exciting. The sheer beauty of the changing light makes you hunger for more. This low, flat landscape, redeemed by its low fringe of surrounding hills, is enchantingly beautiful as the changing light illuminates it, darkens the surrounds or highlights gates and rhynes. The winter landscape is one in which shape and quality are determined by the presence of water. Without water it would revert to a flat expanse of uniform green – pleasant, but without that magic quality.

219

Spring

In recent years winter has tended to edge out gradually and springs are wet and cold. Older people talk about how the warmth used to spread in from the south-west as May arrived. Now the new season seems to be announced by changes in plant and animal life rather than perceptible alterations in warmth. This goes to prove that nature's seasons are governed principally by the duration of light and dark, rather than soil warmth, although some of our garden flowers suffer through appearing too soon in relation to the weather.

Lapwings take advantage of the slightest improvement in conditions to display over the meadows, performing fantastic aerobatics to the sounds of tearing silk from their over-stressed wing feathers. Their eerie, penetrating cries are very much part of the spring scene. Kingcups appear on the banks of rhynes and ditches. One meadow on Tealham is unusual in that the kingcups cover the whole area, instead of being restricted to the water's edge; the field is a riot of rich gold for weeks on end. Normally these plants keep to the margins of the rhynes where they find the damp condition their roots crave.

Grass loses that dull, dirty, late-winter look and takes on a brief, vivid green before assuming the browner herbal hues of summer pastures. The first buds swell up on the trees, burst and feather out into the new, infinitely beautiful leaves of spring. The first of these is the pussy willow. As the first catkins appear and open out into a wonderful filament of soft, feathery stamens, bumble bees appear as if by magic. It does not seem to matter how cold it is, as soon as a glimmer of sun appears, the murmuring of bumble bees fills the air around. Then bee and willow transform the atmosphere into the joy of summer to come. It is one of the golden moments of the awakening year.

Bumble-bees appear as if by magic.

Sometimes this first spring gesture may seem like a hollow joke. Hail may be falling, with winds screaming across the open spaces, and it can actually seem colder than at any other time of year. Ice-cold and scarlet-nosed, I have watched fascinated as some enterprising bumble bee buzzes from nowhere to the first feathers of pussy willow.

Long, wet springs compress the seasons. When at last the warmth starts to make itself felt, it does so with a rush. Duckweed clouds the water in the ditches, like a dusting of green confetti. Buttercups, early orchids and cowslips mist the upper meadows and ring the edges of the moors. Then follows that wonderful period when cuckoo flowers cover the moorland pastures with a shimmer of palest lilac. Fields are briefly chequered with wonderful patterns and colours – brilliant pale green grasses, strong, dark green clumps of rushes and all the shades of other herbs. One of my most vivid impressions of this time is of a snipe, richly coloured in a bracken and black mixture, with white eye-stripes, standing head erect among a riot of flowers: ladies smock, celandine, buttercup and others, set against the many greens of early spring. The bird looked as if it was crowned with flowers.

Before we realise it, it is really spring and the birds are busy nesting. Rooks sway high up in the few remaining clumps of dead elms, or struggle with new nests in tall swaying poplars. Herons are also at their nests early in the big wood near Blakeway. As the weather warms up, ditches become populated with anxious grey creatures peering intently at cold green and peat-black waters. They are waiting for the faint movement which means another mouthful, perhaps a wriggling eel. With nests full of gangling youngsters back in the wood, there is a desperate need for unending supplies of food. As the season moves on, it seems they are forced to fly further afield to find sufficient food. We see little parties of two or three herons flying over the house, apparently on their way to Cheddar Reservoir.

At the same time comes the first flush of leaves; osier and alder scrub glows with amazing brightness. Birches are infused with the most delicate pale green pastel haze which spreads along the copses and the edge of the

North Drain. Hedgerows start with palest yellows and pinks of the first leaves, before they harden into the uniform green of summer. In some years, the first pale, delicate and bronzed oak leaves are devoured by thousands of brilliant, metallic-turquoise weevils. They swarm over them until only skeletons of the leaves remain – then they vanish. Another crop of leaves grows, which are left alone. The tree does not appear to suffer a check from this.

At this time of year trees are at their most interesting. Some, notably ash and walnut, remain bare until much later. But for a short while every tree shows its own individuality. The shades vary subtly and each variety is quite distinct from the next. By midsummer they will have merged into one continuous green, dusty and anonymous, but now they are of every pastel shade, the variations delicate and light, but with some strong colours even at the start. Flushes and ripples of palest green appear and run along the woods and copses, as if washed with watercolour. The hedgerows feather out earlier. At first almost imperceptibly, just a hint of green here and there, preceded by the dazzling, hard white of the blackthorn, then one day you become aware that they are all green. At first one can distinguish the individual tints of hawthorn, blackthorn, elm and elder, but then they merge together into the long lines of familiar green, which seem uniform to our eyes and exist only on the edges of our consciousness.

At the end of spring – or is it the beginning of summer, I am never sure? – May blossom comes out in all its glory and warms the hedgerows with its creamy heaviness. Its profusion is part of the general lushness. This is the time when plants, animals and insects are all intent on the propagation of the species. May blossom is at the very centre of this activity. Its flowers buzz with insect life; the scent hangs heavy and renders us soporific. The nectar leaves insects half-drunk with its potency and it seems to be the very fount of fertility, a shrine to new life and the future. The long boundary hedges froth with white which rapidly deepens to rich cream and eventually takes on a pinkish tint before the petals fall. The blossom smothers the green, so that the hedges look like ships in full sail, bowling down the lanes.

Around the same time, other parts of the moorland hedging are covered with clusters of cream flowers and the air is pungently scented; elder is in full bloom. This tree has always been important to countrypeople. In some parts it is considered unlucky to cut an elder tree down. If this is so, gardeners round here must incur their fair share of bad luck, as elder grows with great persistence and the plant seeds itself in considerable numbers.

Elder has always been an important medicinal and food plant. The old books tell of the ointments and cordials that can be made from it. It is said also to keep flies away from a house when planted close to the walls. No doubt this is partly due to the acrid smell of the leaves, though at blossom time this repulsion apparently loses its potency. The beautiful panicles of flowers attract their own large population of nectar-drinking insects.

The flowers make a delicious, delicate wine, with a flavour which can only be likened to one of the most expensive of Alsatian wines, *Gerwurztraminer*. It also makes the most refreshing 'champagne', but beware! The bottles tend to burst unless they are kept in cool cellar conditions. We used to keep ours in a barn with a corrugated iron roof. One year my wife was passing near a couple of screw top cider bottles full of this concoction when they burst, with a noise like the end of the world and the splinters of glass cut through her corduroy trousers, luckily without scratching her. Elderflower champagne is ready in a fortnight and has a low alcohol content. It is one of the most refreshing drinks ever invented for a hot summer day.

Surplus elderflowers also may be turned into a delicious syrup which makes up into a popular and tasty squash. The syrup keeps for several weeks if prepared correctly. Finally, when the berries are ripe in late summer, you can make one of the finest red fruit wines around. The only problems are the large quantity of berries needed and the amount of work separating them from their stalks. The drink must be kept in bottle for several years if it is to lose that characteristic rough elder taste and round off into a smooth, elegant wine. Then it is superb.

As spring merges into summer, a long succession of birds arrive to mark

223

the passing season. Warblers flit around the undergrowth from the end of March on, many arriving in the dark days of April. Swallows, exhausted from their long flights, are seen singly, then in pairs. The first arrive in mid-April, and by mid-May they are sitting in rows on the fences round the fields.

The cuckoo is generally a little later. For a week or so, the call of these strange birds is heard everywhere. Like ventriloquists they seem to hide the direction of their voice. Then bright flashes of colour pinpoint yellow wagtails in their breeding plumage, as they dive and twist for insects off their headquarter fence-posts.

On virtually the same day each year – generally 3rd May – I see the first whimbrels. Their arrival point is usually the same field each year. They visit us for a week or two in their long migration and are gone again. Their arrival marks the passage of the year more clearly than almost any other event.

Summer

I visit the moors less often in summer, as the garden demands more time. When I do get out, however, my concentration seems to be greater. Summer horizons are smaller. Fully leaved trees cut the view, circumscribe the limit of vision. In winter the eyes travel out to great vistas, even from our modest elevation. You feel the need to walk on and on, to see what is around the next bend or beyond the horizon.

Not so in summer. Hedges, and leaves, shrubs and flowers, confine the eye and obliterate the memory of what is beyond. It is a time of waiting and watching; of looking at detail and the micro world so close by. The art of cottage gardening is to provide a fresh surprise around each corner; to open up a new but confined vista and encourage the onlooker to explore that in

Swallows, masters of the air, most welcome of all spring arrivals.

224

detail before moving on. The summer landscape works in the same way. Spaces which appear at first sight to be open, close in. Meadowsweet and willowherb fringe and restrict the view.

The long droves which divide the moor into sections, providing a freeway to remote fields, are edged with beards of long grass, nettles and yellow iris. The centres of these wide, unmade tractor-ways which run between the roads, were originally just plain peat and soil but are filled regularly with debris, stones and any other substance which will provide a hard surface. Peatland droves subside, form waves and then collapse into deep pits. Filling these is a continuous business. The smoother droves make marvellous gallops and they are the best way of getting away from the roads and into the heart of the moors where remote fields sleep, hidden from outside eyes, where unexpected woods and copses are found.

Access to remote parts is one of the greatest boons of life on the moors. The wonderful green meadows and ploughlands of the shires and the home counties are to be appreciated from afar, not walked among. There most farmland is inaccessible, with field leading into field through gateways, often locked and with notices banning trespassers. Out on our moors anyone is free to roam into their heart along the droves, although most are not recognised rights of way. The droves are kept in good condition by the various owners – those farmers who must use them to reach their fields.

The space between open drove and ditch, untouched by cattle and too soft for galloping ponies, carries the natural mixed herbage of the region. It is tangled, strong-smelling and untouched by spray or sickle, colourful, but not as varied as a Devon bankside. Occasionally it is mowed when the ditches are being cleaned out in their regular cycle, but otherwise it is left to grow naturally. Alder bushes and willows appear in some places. Many are cut down again as ditches are cleared, but some are missed and grow beyond interference, becoming a permanent part of the landscape. The droves are mostly exposed and open. One of the most surprising aspects of the moors is this very openness for, although Tealham is a place of cattle, there is little shelter. Cattle live out

On Tadham Moor there is a covered drove, a secret place of hanging trees and fern-covered banks, where flowers colour the undergrowth.

in fields without trees, without anywhere to get out of the wind or the sun. In those few fields with a corner of tall poplars and thorns, the ground beneath the trees is worn down with constant use and mired with cowpats. This shortage of trees is not traditional. It is a feature of modern times; a reflection of the costs of trimming and hedging, of Drainage Board policies and the high costs of labour.

Out on the moors the countryside varies more than is apparent at first. Below the house, it is a patchwork of open fields split up by ditches and dissected by the long, straight, reflecting line of the North Drain. On the eastern part of Tealham it is more remote and distinct. Visitors are rarely seen. Boggy tracks lead into the centre and some parts have areas of low-lying scrub. Here some droves are deliciously cool tunnels of green, with peat-brown tracks beneath, soft and springy like cliff-top turf. Oak, birch, alder and sallow tangle and mat on either side.

Seen close up, this summer hedging is a riot of colour. Like a box of jewels it is made up of an infinite variety of colours, shapes and patterns. Many of the components are very ordinary – plants to which you would not normally give another thought. But under a magnifying glass they assume a different aspect. For example, briars in flower are quite beautiful. Their petals are as delicate as any rose, their individual stamens beautifully formed, exquisite, host to numerous bees and other summer insects seeking nectar. There are a number of species of blackberry and their flowers range from deep pink to those with dead-white, matt, crinkled petals which look as though the colour has been sucked out of them.

Entangled in the hedge-bottom are the flowers of other plants. Tufted vetch, with prehensile, seeking tips and purple pea-flowers, twines in among everything. Here and there in the tangle are the yellow snap-dragon blooms of common toadflax. Umbelliferous plants are an essential part of the mixture, although Queen Anne's lace and hogweed tend to stand out beyond the bank's tangle, often in bare patches at the edge of the trackway, forming a lace curtain of delicate and rare beauty. Valerian is similar in appearance but softer, its flowers in a loose bunch. It is tall and elegant and the flower heads are flushed with touches of pinks and mauve. Herb robert, yarrow, ragged robin and many others help to make up the tapestry of the hedge under-storey.

Some of the greenest fields, delightfully secret and hidden, are to be found bounded by raised banks which are wide enough to support more than hedges. Some have small woods on top, with broad cattle tracks running up the middle. Foxholes curl under ancient roots and tawny owls sit quite still in the ivy covering the larger trees. Some of these trees are undoubtedly old but none is of any great size.

The ground is a few inches higher in these fields. One would expect a drier, browner sward in midsummer, but in fact it maintains its miraculous greenness, as the plant mix has less sorrel and other coloured herbage. The topsoil may also be deeper, holding the moisture better, so it does not dry to the hard and impermeable shield of the true peat soil.

Sitting on the bank, hidden from the open moors, with the all-pervading and pungent scents of damp soil and oak leaves, it seems a completely different world to that of winter. Then the same place is soft and treacherous and the whole surrounding moorland can be seen through the bare trunks and twisted branches. The curtain of grasses is cut down and flattened, and you are exposed. But in summer the leaved branches hide the view. The dark, heavy smell of the soil fills the air and the consciousness, defying movement or thought. Why do anything other than absorb that which surrounds you? The summer heat sucks out the damp from the ground, making the air heavy, yet also intensifying the scents all round. Above the earth-smell, the air is permeated with the heavy odour of damp grass, hints of subtle herbs and the strong, cloying perfume of wild honeysuckle.

Outside sounds – tractors, distant roads and aeroplanes from Bristol Airport – are muted, and disappear completely in high summer when the greenery is at its most dense. Instead, local noises intensify. Rooks caw in the high treetops, driven from traditional elm, now dead and gone, to old and twisted birches, where their nests increase in size and weight each year. Pigeons coo soporifically. Wrens rustle in the depths, sometimes bursting into violent song. Warblers utter little sibilant notes, visible for fractions of a second as they peck and feel their way in frantic haste through the mantle of leaves.

Occasionally, there are moments of sheer magic. A pair of curlew appear, circling and bubbling as they serenade each other. But even that miraculous sound is cut off as they drop over the far curtain of the banks to bob and curtsy in the open field beyond.

North, beyond these secret fields, lies a more open area. The hedgerows are raised on banks. A path wanders along the top of one of these. It twists beside roots and alongside fallen branches. You have to duck and weave to get by, but it continues all the way to the edges of the North Drain. Who would use such a path? Why is it so well-worn? Then a company of milking

Lords-and-ladies are found under the trees, or among the banks. Sometimes it is possible to see some of those creatures which are in turn dependent on them.

cows is seen standing beneath a group of trees, swishing their tails and keeping out of the heat of the day. From the piles of droppings around, it is clearly a favourite place. Those gentle and patient faces look at us with interest and then resume their chewing. We hear their movements and soft blowings for some while after we move out of sight.

Close to this part of the North Drain, separated from the water by a broad stretch of lawn-like turf, is a patch of alder carr which looks to my mind exactly like a piece of primeval Canada. It is probably what much of the area would have looked like in the past. Water lies in shallow pools the whole year round. Within these pools grow multi-trunked alders, like umbrellas, twisting and interlinked. The edges are a chaos of fallen trees, hollow willows and twisted undergrowth. It is possible to walk through or round the shallow pools, for the bottom is hard. There is little vegetation, except for some grass and this remains short and trimmed. Elsewhere it is a matter of penetrating dense jungle. A great variety of creatures lives in and around this small area.

One day one of my daughters was climbing an old willow and flushed out a tawny owl from deep in its daytime roost. I don't know who had the biggest fright, the owl or Jessica, as she peered down the hollow in the centre of the trunk. Woodpeckers, cuckoos and numerous small birds have also been seen there. Last winter the carr was a favourite haunt of little flocks of siskins which remained for much of the colder period. There is an extremely tame robin who lives in the undergrowth nearby.

Late summer shows up one of the greatest changes of recent years. The roadside verges and rhyne edges are regenerating after years of unremitting cutting and spraying. Councils can no longer afford to do more than the bare minimum necessary for safety. Where it used to be considered essential to mow the edges and keep them like rough lawns, however inappropriate that may be in the deep countryside, this is no longer possible. We had forgotten how beautiful uncut, untreated verges could be.

This change has taken place gradually. The road below us has rhynes on either side, plus a couple of yards of rough verge. For years it has only supported a mixture of grasses. They are now interspersed with patches of colour. Rust-red spikes of dock line the inner edge. Meadowsweet blossoms creamy-rich and heavy-perfumed in the full heat of deep summer. After the frothy glory of the Queen Anne's lace in spring, the umbels of hogweed, valerian, angelica and hemp agrimony nod stiffly in the breezes. Ragged robin, cranesbill, knapweed, marsh woundwort, purple loosestrife and two or three varieties of willow-herb bring a patchwork of colour as the seasons move on. Down in the rhynes, duckweed, arrowhead, flowering rush, frogbit and water-crowfoot flower and spread to add beauty to the particular time of year.

One special feature of these parts is the cutting of certain of the wider verges for hay. This provides valuable feed for one or two smallholders who would otherwise be short in winter. The tractor runs down the road in early evening, scissoring away with a quiet but insistent chatter. The vibrating blades cut through the ripe grass with a continuous sibilant hiss and it falls neatly into rows. Later that week the rows are turned and, later still it is baled and carted away, often late into the night. One lot is stored in an old cottage which has not been lived in for many years, but which is put to good use now; it is full of sweet-smelling hay and the fabric is kept in good order by George, the farmer. The cottage is so small, and the amount of land that goes with it so negligible, I cannot see it again being occupied in spite of a splendid position part-way up the hill.

Further over, on the lower road to Mark, the verges provide hay and are also grazed. A patient cow and its equally patient owner wander quietly along the edge of the road, putting grass and herbs to good use. It is one of the sights which sum up the peace of our countryside.

In recent years grass cutting has gone on for most of the summer. There was once a definite gap between cutting for silage at the beginning and for hay at the end, but this is no longer the case. Silage-making is a movable feast. The initial flush of spring grass is grazed by cows impatient to get at fresh greenery after a winter of hay and silage. After a period of regrowth the first cut for silage takes place. The grass is mown when it is still reasonably young but has bulked out well, before it goes to seed. In essence, silage is grass which has been preserved by compressing it and excluding air, although the process may be aided by chemicals which prevent the grass spoiling if conditions within the clamp are not perfect.

The cutters are out as soon as the weather permits, with great jets of grass blowing up into the wire mesh trailers which carry it to the clamp for storage. Throughout the summer these trailers are a feature of life on the moors. They trundle along the roads and droves in streams, barely keeping up with cutting and clamping. At the clamp, the grass is tipped out and another tractor rolls over it to compress it before the next load arrives. Cutting goes on all day. Food and drink are taken out to the workers and everything else takes second place.

Silage seems to be part of the scene for much of the early and midsummer period. The high water-table, combined with judicious management of the sluices, aids long and sustained growth. Productivity is high. The seasons become blurred, as silage making runs into hay making. You notice one day that the cut grass is being left and turned – hay time again!

Hay is an even more demanding master. Silage can be made when the weather is comparatively poor, whereas hay requires time to dry or it is spoiled for good. If it cannot dry, it will go mouldy or, in extreme cases, ignite spontaneously. Fortunately, the weather is often better here than in the rest of the West Country. The flat moorland has a very low summer rainfall, which makes up for heavy rains in the autumn and late winter. The overall precipitation is no more than that of East Anglia – quite different from the hilly parts around us, which have normal West Country rainfall. In summer we see the thunderstorms and rain following the rim of hills which surrounds the area, but no rain falls on the moors. In fact, summer

Hay is a demanding master, taking precedence over everything when the weather is right.

drought is one of the problems we face in most years in our garden on the side of the hill, but the moorland does not suffer because the water-table is artificially adjusted, according to need. It has the best of both worlds, sunshine and wet roots for its grass.

When the weather and time are judged right to start cutting, nothing is allowed to interfere with it. Mowing goes on until midnight and starts again as soon as the dew is off the ground. Because the farms are small and machinery is expensive, contractors do much of the work. Otherwise it may be undertaken within a group of farms, by machines bought as a co-operative venture. Lots are drawn for the order of cutting and everyone prays for a long enough spell of just the right weather to complete the total acreage.

The fields look white and vulnerable for a while after cutting. If it continues dry and warm, this whiteness persists for two or even three weeks; if wet, it becomes flushed quickly with the palest green and gradually assumes a lawn-like finish. It is a glorious time of year.

The white, shaven fields attract great hordes of young birds. They appear as if by magic. Brown young starlings feed together, scare together and take flight together. They are knitted together by some special bond, flying and living as one, like a flight of waders on an estuary. Young lapwings arrive suddenly, at first in dozens, then hundreds and sometimes by the thousand. They feed steadily across the pale surface, parti-coloured and obvious, still keeping that special distance between birds which is so characteristic of the species. By contrast the starlings pour across the surface like some viscous liquid, bundling up together, fighting, pushing and shoving, bad-tempered and bad-mannered. Small flocks of other birds also glean the open field, of which linnets are perhaps the most colourful.

Hares do not appear to like the pale surface, although they lie much of the time in open fields, and vanish for a while. Sometimes a cut coincides with the flowering time of some special species; the white stubble may set off a fringe of southern marsh orchids, like jewels in the tangle of colours along the rhyne edges. Years ago the field would have been red and pink with orchids,

Lapwings arrive suddenly, at first in dozens, then in hundreds.

but now the rhyne sides are the only places where they survive.

As June moves into July, and then August, a whole series of changes occur on the moors. The grass goes through various stages of coloration and the green fringes on the edges of the rhynes change dramatically as different wild flowers dominate. In early June they are yellow with wild iris, then comes the pink-red of willowherb and finally the blowing cream panicles of meadowsweet fill the air with their sweet, heavy scent. The grass starts the summer, after the cuckoo flowers have finished, as a patchwork of dusky and bright greens. Gradually a dusting of buttercup-gold appears, which is then tempered with patches of rust-red sorrel growing freely among the tall grasses. In July the sward is red-brown. From afar, it may look dry and dusty, but in reality it is rich and succulent and cattle relish it.

Grass is a plant which is easily ignored. Seen close to, through the sharply-defined field of a macro lens, it is beautiful, varied and of a great many shades other than green. Some grasses are feathery, arching and delicate.

Others are white, or black, with great clusters of seed cascading from the heads. Razor-sharp or soft as down, curving and blowing in the wind or stiff and straight, there are an enormous number of varieties. The best way to observe or photograph them is lying down, so you are on the same level, while they are illuminated from behind. This shows off the tiny hairs and bristles which catch the light as if cast in gold. It may show also a variety of tiny insects which base their life on grass and its pollen. This pollen causes great problems for hayfever sufferers but it is a beautiful and essential substance. At certain times of the year, an animal walking through a field will push up great clouds of it which sparkle and hang in the sun.

In July the birds are still singing. Larks and pipits ascend into the heavens, their bodies vibrating with the passion of their song. Young and old yellow wagtails flash and dance in the sun as they feed from their observation posts lining the roads. Little flocks of linnets twitter and trill their way across the open spaces, undulating in flight. The last few calls are heard from the curlews, not quite as pure and liquid as earlier in the year.

Then in August all sound ceases. The last snipe stops drumming. The moors are silent, still, empty. All the songbirds vanish from sight and sound. Lapwings may occasionally erupt from the now-desolate, empty fields, but there is none of that joyful spontaneity which normally characterises their flight. The year is dead. Even the tractors go into hibernation once hay-cutting stops. Life seems to vanish from thicket and field. Where do they all go? Is there some form of bird-Ramadan, a time of fasting and abstinence?

Autumn

But in early September the season changes again. Slowly and subtly something happens. The Indian summer may go on into late October, but an inner sense of change seems to be felt before then. The trees, which have weathered in late summer into dull, drab, dirty-green shapes, dusty and indistinguishable from each other, begin to colour. Some drop a few early leaves and reveal part of their skeletal shape. Others show a tinge of yellow on one side. The various species become distinct once more. Ash is clearly different from oak, chestnut and sycamore. The process is slow; in some autumns the trees stay in this new state – faintly coloured, with slightly less foliage – until late November, before shedding all their leaves in the last glorious stages of autumn. In other years the process is compressed.

Days shorten. Firesides beckon as the air catches in the throat in the evenings, clean but cold. It is a time of change, of excitement. The smell of autumn is one of the sharpest and most evocative scents in the world. It is a curious odour of damp and soil and leaves mixed up together, a primeval, earthy smell which seems to presage the changing season. This scent is the true precursor of winter,

Autumn, when mists rise up from the moors as the evenings start to gather in.

a feeling deep within the senses, touching a hidden part of the consciousness.

Autumn is when mists rise from the rhynes in the early evening. In many ways it is the most exquisite of seasons. Spring is beautiful everywhere in Britain, lush and yet delicate, heartrending in its freshness and renewal, but here autumn brings out the importance of the rhynes and ditches, showing a totally different world.

In autumn, and sometimes in spring, the mists come down over the moors as the evening starts to gather in, and again as temperatures change with the wakening day. They creep across and confuse the landscape. Sound is muffled, but an occasional mournful pipe from a golden plover, or the sharp wail of a lapwing, sometimes escapes to the orchards above. At times the mist plays tricks with acoustics and the sounds are magnified; one hears the full babel of conversing birds as if they were next door. Looking down from above, all that can be seen is a great rolling white plain with the tips of bushes and the heads of cattle projecting above it. The cloud thickens and increases in height above ditches and rhynes, so that walking cattle may vanish from sight, then reappear some yards on. From face level, the mists appear even more mysterious.

The evening starts with a slight chilling in the air. Within minutes a haze of mist forms on one side and just above the water in a ditch. It thickens and rises, and the tips of the grasses and rushes disappear into it. The tube of vapour rolls along the ditches, until their positions round the fields are quite distinctly defined. If it is a really chilly evening, contrasting with the last remaining daytime warmth of an autumn sun, vapour starts to rise all over the ground. Cattle may be seen with their bodies apparently missing, absorbed by the mist, only their legs and heads visible. I remember walking down one evening and stopping by Old Rhyne to lean over the gate. It was a magical scene. The Friesians were still out in the field and the mist swirled round their legs as they walked, almost the entire length hidden by the vapours. Above each ditch the mist thickened into a tunnel well over head height. The animals lacked substance, like ghosts materialising in a dream. Their images flickered and wavered, their body colours reduced to pastel shades. The willows looked as if they had been pencilled in with a pale grey-brown, very soft chalk.

Sometimes I look out in the early morning and see this same scene, but with a different quality of light. It is even more mysterious and unreal – alien, but peaceful. John Buchan wrote about 'mysterious pagan groves of ash trees' – places where time has stood still and strange forces from the past seem to hold sway even in a later age. Tealham Moor has something of the same feel, although it is friendly, not malevolent as in the Buchan groves. The mind fills with thoughts of a different era, of events long past. The ghostly blanket of white is difficult to comprehend at first. When part of the mist blows away for a moment and reveals the ground beneath the canopy, it is as solid and substantial as ever. The mist rolls across once more and the mystery returns, with just the tips of trees appearing through swirlings of mist which whiten the moors into the distance.

It is possible to imagine anything at times like this. It is easy to look down and see King Arthur and his companions trotting across a track through the marshes, on their way to Glastonbury and the Isle of Apples. You can almost hear the whinnies of the horses and the clash of metal on metal, together with the creaking of leather. The cries of a far-off bird are like the sounds of men calling to each other as they ride. Autumnal mists bring strange fancies which are difficult to dispel.

The grasses in the uncut areas of scrub and along the droves whiten and sharpen against the dark soil. The last of the wild flowers lose their coloured heads. The year is dying, even if it takes its time about it. Or is it the renaissance, the time when a new year is revealed as the old layers are peeled away?

Flocks of small birds appear out on the darkening moors. Linnets, goldfinches and many pipits crowd the tall vegetation of the verges and rhyne edges, picking at the great bunches of seeds still hanging ripely from the plants. Goldfinches prefer thistles, the rest take whatever is on offer. Others feed in the torn-up area where cattle have been standing as they try to shelter from the worst of the wind. This is the season of gales and the wind has a sharp, frosty, cutting edge which always seems so much worse in comparison to

The grasses fringing the ditches whiten and the last of the flowers lose their coloured heads. Farmers get on with the routine jobs of autumn such as pollarding willows.

balmy summer breezes. Lapwing flocks appear and rapidly increase in size, dark-winged, infinitely manoeuvrable and filling the skies in the periodic 'frights' with which they are so afflicted during these shorter days. They appear in their myriads, sometimes only staying for a matter of days. At other times they remain for much of the winter – often favouring a different set of fields from those of the previous year, as if bored with the same old surroundings. At the very end of autumn they are joined by golden plover in their hundreds. In the still of the evening their soft piping is soothing; a contrast to the restless, wild cries of the lapwings.

The equinox brings wild and windy weather to all parts, but we seem to notice it here particularly. Gales scream across the wide open spaces, broken only by a few wildly whipping willows and ragged thorns. These winds bring with them the start of the rains, which may continue, on and off, for weeks on end. This is the time when the drought is forgotten and the great sponge of the moors renews its heart. At first the hard crust of the peat withstands much of the deluge and there is considerable run-off. The runnels fill with water, silver-streaking the fields. The ditches and springs run. The sound of water is everywhere, trickling, running, rushing along. Then the summer-hard crust starts to break down. The peat beneath begins to melt into its winter consistency and absorbs more and more water. Further downpours vanish into the ground without any problem, although signs of the weather are seen in turgid ditches, running springs and ponds coming back to life. Drainage pumps start to run again after the silence of late summer. Then, quite suddenly, after a couple of days of heavy rain, the sponge can absorb the surplus no more.

Long runnels of water appear in the fields, following the lines of ancient drainage. They may stay, varying in depth and intensity, for the whole of the winter. The ground is like a huge reservoir which cannot be filled any more without overflowing. Any surplus must be pumped away or it will bring the water table above the surface and flood the whole area, forming a great inland sea.

So, the year comes back to the starting point. The land renews its resources for the following spring and we who live here settle down to a few months of peace. Few outsiders venture out on to the water-streaked moorland during winter and we are able to wander widely without seeing anyone other than some farmer fetching hay for bullocks on the higher ground. Tealham and Tadham revert to their ancient possessors, the wild swans, wailing lapwings and great hordes of fieldfares and redwings which pour in from Scandinavia. Teal hurtle across the wild pastures and herons flap down lazily to fish the quiet rhynes. A whisp or two of snipe are found in suitable hollows and by peat-edged ditches.

Of all the seasons this is best; the start of it all, the renewal of resources but also the time of contemplation and of memories.

FARMING AND CONSERVATION

Nothing stands still. The pressures of making a living, if nothing else, force people to expand their activities, use their resources more efficiently and try to squeeze more out of what they already own. These pressures are as apparent in deepest rural Somerset as they are in the largest city. Now we are a part of a greater Europe we also find ourselves facing pressures from outside. In some cases these may be of benefit, as with grants to preserve a way of life or improve communications. In other cases they may be damaging, as in the Common Agricultural Policy (CAP), which has encouraged overproduction of many products.

It is important that this change is not ignored. We must examine evidence of change, discuss the damage being done to a way of life and look in more detail at what might happen in the future. Is anything more needed? Is it possible to bring together people with apparently differing aims and see if solutions may be found for the most pressing and immediate problems? All this needs airing and public comment. It is not enough to leave it to common sense on its own. It has already been proved that this does not work; there are too many pressures, particularly economic ones, to enable common sense alone to produce the right solution. There are a great many factors involved – farming, leisure, the preservation of our ancient heritage, and wildlife, to name but a few. People must realise the issues and debate the mix with goodwill to produce that most British of solutions - a compromise.

As far as Tealham Moor is concerned, recent changes have been for the worse, but all the evidence points to a growing awareness of the problems caused by previous actions and a determination to put them right. Only the future can tell whether this optimism is justified. At least it will have been documented for our descendants to make judgement. Will they look over a moor which is still farmed and which abounds with the wealth of wildlife we remember from the 1970s? Or will it be a prairie, devoid of wildlife and farmed by two or three organisations, with the aid of machinery rather than people? Let us look at the present situation, what the Government is already doing and what it might do in the future.

Sites of Special Scientific Interest and Environmentally Sensitive Areas
Gradually it is being appreciated that many of the traditions of the past were not as foolish as people imagined. Areas like medicine and farming have evolved into the high-tech era, yet there are signs that both are taking a fresh look at the past. Alternative or traditional medicines have returned. Farmers are looking at the potential for minimum-cost farming rather than the previously fashionable feeding for marginal returns.

Previous wisdom said that the permanent pastures of the Levels must be improved by drainage and reseeding. Doubts have been cast on this approach, but whatever the result, times have changed and there is now no imperative for continually increased production. A second reduction in the milk quota has taken place and set-aside payments are available for those who wish to take them up. The way is open for the 'lowest-cost' theory to be put to its test here on the Levels.

The arrival of machinery eased the work of the farmers but has also led to

SSSIs, places where unusual plant and animal populations exist.

actions which despoiled the countryside. This did not appear to matter to the Government while food production was all-important. Now this philosophy no longer obtains. There has been a realisation that some aspects of the old ways were worth retaining or even bringing back. The problem is how to encourage these aspects, and at the same time pay for them, while enabling the farmer to make a living from his land.

In the early 1980s, a great many SSSIs were identified around the country. These covered places where unusual plant and animal populations existed, where the last remnants of some beleaguered species hung on, or where special conditions still obtained which had vanished elsewhere. Large areas of the Somerset Levels, including large portions of Tealham and Tadham Moors, were designated SSSIs. Once a site had been notified, it was possible to come to a voluntary arrangement, through the Nature Conservancy Council (NCC, or English Nature), to be paid to retain present methods of farming and cultivation or to undertake certain beneficial changes, without losing profitability. Many of the sites are on wetland and part of the agreement is for these to remain undrained, although this is something the owner or tenant can only partly control. He can undertake not to underdrain the particular fields or install pumps but he cannot control the basic water table set by the IDBs and the NRA. The most important factor is that no more of this land can be 'improved' – drained, ploughed or reseeded – without consultation. If the site is of particular significance, and the farmer will not agree to a management agreement, then the NCC can take him to court and, ultimately, purchase the piece of land compulsorily at a fair market valuation. This is, however, a step which they are reluctant to undertake.

An SSSI is a specific field or site, and a farm may contain more than one SSSI, which may be the subject of separate management agreements, possibly at different levels of payment.

Under the original Act establishing the process for identifying SSSIs, the fact that sites were to be notified had to be publicised ahead of the actual formal notification. This had a disastrous effect, especially for one block of land on the western side of Tealham. Farmers saw the coming notification as the beginning of restrictions on their way of life, of bureaucracy dictating how they were to farm – it should be remembered that this was before everyone had woken up to the serious long-term implications of the food surpluses in Europe. Plans were put afoot to drain a block of botanically-rich land on Tealham immediately. These plans were approved by the Ministry of

Drainage of a patch of botanically rich ground on Tealham went ahead when the imposition of future restrictions was notified.

Agriculture and the scheme went ahead. In fact the plan was drawn up with the help of the Government's own advisory service, ADAS, through their local office, which approved of the scheme and endorsed its benefits, despite pleas from the NCC.

In this particular case, the object of the drainage was said to be to enable machinery, cattle and milk bails to get out on the land even at times of heavy rain, not to reseed or promote arable crops, since in its normal, undrained state, poaching of the land can be a major problem in wetter times.

The farmers' action provoked an instant reaction. The NCC visited the farmers and asked them to stop, but contracts had already been signed. A letter followed, again requesting that the action should stop. Agreement was then apparently reached at a meeting but, when the officials next arrived, the work had been completed. A further letter followed from the NCC, saying that the 76 acres of moor ground under question had been made subject to a Section 29 Order from the Ministry of the Environment, under the provisions of the 1981 Wildlife and Countryside Act. This was designed to call a halt to everything, to give a breathing space for both sides to consider their actions again and was to last for nine months. After that, it was hoped, a spirit of compromise would lead to the drawing up of a management agreement which would suit everyone. It was widely believed by the Ministry that time would show the benefits to be obtained by both farmer and countryside and this view has been vindicated as the years have gone by. Unfortunately local farmers were not convinced at the time.

Looking back, it is almost certain that both sides would now prefer that this course had not been taken. Certainly the farmers were ill prepared for the consequences. Inexperience in their respective roles and powers, problems of scientists dealing with small farmers and a new and untested Act, with some silly provisions about prenotification in it, all contributed to a hasty taking of stands. To the horror of the farmers, they were virtually stopped from using the land and all their actions were put under control of the NCC. The NFU intervened and meetings were held on the moors. It was pointed out that the proposed restrictions would make it impossible to make a living and eventually a more workable agreement was reached.

Over ten years have elapsed since then and the area is still subject to control under Section 29, as the initial five-year agreement has not been renewed by the farmers. What has this meant to them?

The original agreement was less restrictive than I had imagined. The private pumping of this section of the moors was allowed to continue, even though that was what originally brought on the Order. Apart from that, there were restrictions placed on stocking, cultivations and the use of fertiliser. It was a flexible agreement. Its restrictions and terms depending on the botanical value of the ground, and varied from field to field. Stock would not be allowed onto the fields until 1 June, although special circumstances might alter this date to 15 May.

"We are not allowed to roll or harrow the ground in spring, or to plough or reseed in any way," I was told. "No chemical sprays may be used, except where approved for specific problems. Also, there is a limit to the amount of farmyard manure which may be applied. One of the advantages of a pumped and drained field is that you can get a muck-spreader onto the field at all times, which makes it ideal for spreading straight off the yard. In fact, this makes running a farm much easier – one of the hoped-for advantages when the drainage was first planned."

Compensation was paid for the restrictions placed on these farming activities and it seems that the farmers did not suffer financially from the Order. The problem is the very British one of hating to have personal liberty restricted. What hurts them is not being able to do as they like with their own fields, perhaps make changes and improve the ease of farming. There is always someone overseeing their activities.

The main bone of contention is pumping. Records kept since it began, show that fauna and flora of the fields and deep-drained ditches have all but vanished and the breeding population of birds on the open moor has declined to virtually nothing. This is precisely the situation that the Order was designed to prevent. It is interesting to note that grass yields and the feeding value of the area also appear to have declined steeply. So it seems no one has gained.

A further Section 29 Order was placed as a result of another farmer refusing to face up to SSSI status, but for a very different reason. Although his land is not a part of the official Peat Production Zones that were drawn up by Somerset County Council, he wanted this land designated as such. If this had been agreed he would have been sitting on a valuable piece of land and would no longer be subjected to a management agreement

The fauna and flora of the deep-drained fields have all but disappeared. Hen reed-bunting on thorn.

under an SSSI. After several court hearings and appeals, the NCC applied to buy his land compulsorily at a fair valuation. The counter appeal was based on a claim that it was much more valuable, since it was peat ground, although there appeared no evidence to support this. The case was finally resolved in 1991, after several years, with the High Court ordering the landowner to sign a management agreement, which has since taken place.

So all has not gone smoothly in the transition, even on such a small area as Tealham and a few years ago the Tealham and Tadham Farmers Association was formed to represent the views of everyone on the moors. It was formed when the introduction of high water levels in the area was first mentioned and has held a few infrequent meetings, which have been attended by a representative from the MAFF. As someone involved told me recently, "It has sometimes put its foot down when perhaps it shouldn't but it does make a valuable contribution in promoting local farmers views." From MAFF point of view it gives a single point of contact and acts as a general sounding board for the owners and tenants of the land.

In conversations with local farmers I have come across a general belief that some of the major conservation groups are far too intransigent in negotiations. There is no spirit of compromise or discussion. As somebody said, "They want nothing less than the whole pie." Many believe that these organisations pay no attention to the fact that people have to make a living off the land, but press on, confident of the power of their huge membership figures. This is leading to a hardening of attitudes, which benefits no one. Conservationists should aim for a situation where people continue to make their living off the land while giving the best opportunities for wildlife, rather than one where birds take precedence over everyone and everything.

Since the original SSSIs were designated, further developments have taken place. In 1984, the whole of Tealham and Tadham Moors became part of one of the first six ESAs designated in England and Wales. These were set up under Article 19 of EC Regulation 797/85. The criteria set for these are that ESAs should be:

Payments under the Environmentally Sensitive Area scheme are made to any farmer in the area who undertakes certain methods of farming and restrictions. Lapwings on the moors.

- *of national environmental significance;*
- *whose conservation depends on the adoption, maintenance or extension of a particular form of farming practice;*
- *in which there have occurred, or there is a likelihood of, changes in visiting farming practices which pose a major threat to the environment;*
- *which represent a discrete and coherent unit of environmental interest; and*
- *which would permit the economical administration of appropriate conservation aids.*

Here in Somerset the ESA covers both the Brue Valley and Sedgemoor proper, on the other side of the Polders. It was officially set up in April 1987. Under this scheme, the Ministry of Agriculture is encouraging farmers to adopt, or continue, methods of agriculture which will achieve conservation as well as agricultural objectives. In return, they receive annual payments depending on the severity of the restrictions or the extra work involved. Interestingly, in addition to grassland preservation, broad-leaved woodland management, the preservation of barns and dry stone walls can also come into the scheme.

The farmer voluntarily enters into a long-term agreement to meet the conditions set out in a management plan. This sets out to *protect natural habitats, particularly on grazing land and wet meadows, to maintain landscape and archaeological features and to encourage the retention and management of broad-leaved woodland'*. This is a remarkable statement and promises to be a pilot for designating ever larger parts of the countryside under the same scheme. The fact that it is a European Union project is significant and should ensure that it will have a long life – long enough, it is hoped, to achieve some solid objectives in conserving parts of Britain which have been vanishing at far too rapid a rate recently.

The difference between the SSSI scheme and ESAs is that while SSSIs are the subject of individual management agreements, the ESA is a blanket agreement. Anyone farming within its boundaries is entitled to apply and the rate paid is standard for a particular area. By early 1988 40 per cent of the usable area (excluding roads, buildings etc,) had been taken up by farmers participating in the scheme. By 1994 this had risen to over 53 per cent. If a farmer obtains payment under an SSSI he is not entitled to an ESA payment for the same land, but an individual farmer may have some land covered by ESA and other by SSSI agreements.

Since actual payments have been received, there appears to have been a general acceptance in the farming community of both the need for the changes and the method of compensating people for being frozen in a moment of time, so to speak, but just before the SSSI scheme, things started to become nasty round the countryside. The farmers of West Sedgemoor, in particular, were up in arms about 'infringements of personal liberty'. It became so bad that effigies of various people were burned, including that of the local representative of the NCC. Farmers and their official representatives had not yet accepted that life was changing for everyone in the agricultural world and that the problems previously faced by industry would also affect them . The golden age of subsidy, surpluses and protection was over, but not everyone saw that in the early 1980's. The farming lobby was still extremely aggressive, confident that no government would do anything but encourage their undoubted efficiency.

A local farmer buttonholed me one day. "You want to watch it, with your views round here."

"What do you mean?" I asked, astonished.

"Pushing they SSSI things to farmers so we can't farm our own land properly."

It turned out that I was being confused with the local NCC man, who had a similar name – he who had been burned in effigy elsewhere. I explained that it was not me; I was only a bystander – nothing to do with Government or indeed taking any stand in the matter. Indeed I felt that the affair had been so badly handled that my sympathy lay with the farmers at that stage. One farmer in particular, who later suffered from the Section 29 Order, was especially interested in wildlife and loved the countryside with great intensity, but he was indignant about the way things were going. In the end I put a notice in the local paper, disclaiming any connection with the NCC or the events out on the moors. This saved further unpleasantness.

At about this time milk quotas started to take the steam out of the situation and this easing of tensions continued when the first payments started to arrive under the SSSI scheme. Although delays in the receipt of payments kept the problem alive for longer than was necessary, people came to realise that this time the problems of surpluses would not just go away. It was a new situation and perhaps they were luckier than the majority of farmers elsewhere, to whom no help was given. Many of the smaller farmers liked and believed in the traditional type of farming on the moors. Change was something forced on them, and it was not relished by everyone. Now the new schemes offered a chance to continue as they wished.

In the years that have passed since these changes were instituted, attitudes have altered. By 1994, eighteen agreements covered 640 acres of SSSI on Tealham and Tadham while over 30,000 acres of the total area designated an ESA on the Somerset Levels and moors has been taken up and payment received. The schemes have become a fact of life and a recognised – and important – part of farm income. Indeed the way things are shaping up in the EU, I believe that the ESA and SSSI schemes may be the agents for keeping many farms solvent in this area, as well as achieving their other aims.

Attitudes to this vary, as is only to be expected. We British are an independent and, some would say, bloody-minded lot. We do not always take kindly to being directed to do something by officialdom, however good the case. Farmers are amongst the most independent of us all. I have talked to people who are for, and others who are against, the schemes. One told me that he had taken up the ESA payment because, although it puts some restrictions on him, the money makes up for them. Another was quite clear that he would never accept payment under ESA. "I believe in heavy fertilising and like to get my cattle out early. It's up to me how I decide what should be done with my own land." Yet another was against the payment for the very reason that it involved no change to his farming at all. "I'd feel I was cheating the Government if I took money for that." The question is, will the loss of profit arising from the eventual and inevitable withdrawal of conventional subsidies be met by increased intensification on marginal lands? ESAs allow the choice, but SSSIs do not, for certain methods of intensification are not allowed on SSSI-notified land.

Another farmer has both ESA and SSSI payments coming in, on different pieces of land, "but I only signed up for the lower payment under ESA. That suits my methods well. The higher payment places too many restrictions and would change my methods considerably." The payment he receives is really for retaining present methods. The margins he needs to make a living, at a

253

time when they are being squeezed by reduced subsidies on animals, are preserved by the ESA payment. Without that he would have been forced to increase the intensiveness of his enterprises and this, in turn, would have affected wildlife badly – something he would not have liked to see.

So the payments made so far have achieved part of their objectives. That they have not achieved them completely is due to another factor, which is covered neither in SSSI management agreements nor in ESA stipulations – the water table. The first set of ESA payments concentrated on farming methods over which the farmer had control – cultivations, fertiliser applications, stocking intensity. Water was an outside factor not mentioned in the original terms, in spite of the fact that the land was farmed and looked as it did because it was a wetland. Unfortunately the whole area continued to dry out and change its nature, in spite of the gains arising from the ESA scheme, and looked less and less like a wetland each year that passed. Much concern was expressed generally about the loss of wildlife and the changing landscape.

Notice was taken of all this and in 1992 the whole ESA scheme was revised and up-dated, taking into account the feelings of farmers, conservationists and the general public concerning the future of the Levels. The most important difference from the previous scheme was that an upper tier of payments became available for allowing the collective raising of water levels in blocks of land. At last the importance of water levels had been recognised in an official payment scheme which would determine the future of the area. It was a moment of supreme importance to the survival of the Levels and moors in any recognisable form. The MAFF leaflet explaining the scheme is quite clear in its expectations, as well as the methods required to obtain these grants:

Farmers entering the scheme are expected to farm in sympathy with this special environment. The ESA payments are available in three tiers depending on the intensity of the restrictions required, payment rising as these become more demanding.

TIER 1. Purpose: *'To maintain the Somerset Levels and Moors ESA landscape and grassland.'* Payment £50 per acre.

The requirements include no ploughing or re-seeding and precise restrictions on the use of artificial fertilisers. No fungicides or insectices may be used and weedkillers are restricted to certain weeds and particular techniques. No liming is allowed and the ditches must be maintained mechanically, not by sprays. Perhaps most important of all, 'for the appearance of the landscape, hedges, trees and pollarded willows must be maintained in accord with local custom', while no draining or under-draining may be undertaken.

At last the importance of water-levels has been recognised in the new schedule of ESA payments.

Water levels to remain as under present regime, with at least 6 inches in ditch bottoms in winter.

TIER 2. Purpose: *'To enhance the ecological interest of grassland'*. Payment £81 per acre.

Requirements include all those of Tier 1 plus restrictions on harrowing and rolling in spring and summer, with further restrictions on the use of fertilisers and weedkiller. Grazing is subject to set periods in the summer and there are instructions on mowing times and methods.

Water levels to remain in summer much as at present and to have at least 12 inches of water in winter ditches.

'A further payment' of £32 per acre is available under Tiers 1 and 2 if splashy conditions are maintained in winter with a water table of less than 12 inches below the field surface in summer.

TIER 3. Purpose: *'To further enhance the ecological interest of grassland by the creation of wet winter and spring conditions on the moors'*. Payment £162 per acre. 'These flooded conditions can only be attained in coherent blocks of land where these water levels can be maintained independently of the rest'.

Requirements are those for all of Tier 1 and much of 2, plus no mechanical operations between spring and mid-summer, fertilising confined to home-produced cattle manure only, with restrictions on amount, and no silage making. No sheep are to be kept on the land and density of cattle kept low, with no early stocking.

Water levels: In summer ditches must be less than 12 inches below field level and the fields held in a splashy condition throughout the winter.

PUBLIC ACCESS TIER. Purpose: *'To provide new opportunities for public access for walking and other quiet recreation'*. Payment £274 per acre.

A further payment has been made available recently, for strips to form access routes. The payments will be in addition to other ESA payments on the land.

There are also grants available for 'capital works', to enhance the land or meet the conditions laid out for the ESA payments. Among others these cover planting and laying of hedges, planting and pollarding of willows and conversion of arable back to grassland. Grants are also available for various imaginative schemes, such as improvements to herb-rich meadows and creation of ponds or scrapes, as well as the necessary works on sluices to maintain high water-levels.

The first two tiers are similar to the arrangements in force up to the autumn of 1992 and of proven value. The important new factor for conservation of wildlife and landscape is Tier 3, and the supplementary payments for Tiers 1 and 2, which require the maintenance of splashy conditions from 1 December to 30 April. These should bring in once more the huge numbers of birds for which the area was famous, maintain the unique plant and invertebrate life on the Levels and give us back the magic of its silver-streaked fields in winter. The whole programme should also lead to the return of the lost breeding bird population.

In 1994, MAFF announced that the total take-up of ESA, under the new scheme so far, was over 30,800 acres from 837 applications. This is some 7,400 acres more than in the previous period.

As long as the payments are seen to be fair farmers will take them up in some numbers. Some will never do so, regardless of amount, for they believe in the freedom to choose for themselves. Further objectives can be achieved in the future, by careful selection of payment against requirement, now the principle has been accepted in the countryside and by its people. After that it is a question of bargaining to achieve a mutually acceptable compromise.

I talked about the Tier 3 agreement with one local farmer who has not taken up this or any other ESA payment, because they have a twenty-one year SSSI agreement on the land. While this does not pay anything like the rates of the ESA, it has security of tenure. The ESA agreements run for much shorter periods that are not as attractive in an uncertain future. He remarked that if it were possible to add some ESA Tier 3 payment for water management to the existing length of SSSI payment then it could be acceptable, even though it would preclude sheep, which are currently important to him.

I am told that the income from ESA payments, plus returns on that type of farming, should exceed the income from more intensive methods. Only time will demonstrate this to a sceptical rural community who are also concerned about the long-term commitment of Government. Present agreements are for ten years, with a break point after five.

Trees and ditches

Willows used to line all the tracks and roads out on the moors, most of which were ancient cattle droves long before they were tarred. For instance, the main road separating Tealham from Tadham Moor is still called Jack's Drove. Tradition says that a reason for the willows was to mark the course of the droves when the land was flooded; they were vital safety markers where ditches were soft and could quickly drown anyone who might fall into them in bad weather. Willows also provided materials for pea-sticks, fencing posts, thatching spars and hurdles but, for the modern farmer, they are simply something else to be trimmed, another drain on labour. For this reason I am particularly delighted that tree replacement, trimming and pollarding are requirements under the ESA agreement. The money helps compensate farmers for the very real costs involved in preserving one of the countryside's most loved features.

However, to compound the current problem of a dwindling number of trees, the Lower Brue Drainage Board talks about regulations which ban trees being planted or allowed to grow within several feet of the banks of viewed rhynes and drains. In the old days willows were planted deliberately, hard by the banks of these rhynes, because the roots helped stabilise the ditches and prevented the banks collapsing with time. Nowadays the ditches are cleared by machine and everything is subordinated to ease of use and speed of clearance. River Authorities throughout the country have taken this argument and changed the faces of our rivers, streams and waterways. It is said that one of the major reason for the decline of the otter is that its natural homes, holts beneath ancient tree roots by the water, have been destroyed methodically and progressively throughout much of the country. A compromise, whereby trees are planted on one side of the ditch only, would seem a sensible solution which would meet everyone's needs and objectives.

Canalised rhynes may be easier and quicker to clean out but they also let water down river extremely rapidly. This may be fine to relieve flash floods but it also lowers water levels too quickly. The surroundings of a river used to act as a vast sponge, letting water out slowly throughout the summer. Now the upper reaches no longer act as reservoirs for dry periods. It is true that farmland becomes drier earlier in the spring but it can also lead to a quicker move towards drought conditions in the summer.

One of the problems is a reducing number of trees.

One thing I hate is the use of flail cutters on hedges, which destroy and rip without thought and where it appears to be too much trouble to stop the machine and leave a sapling to grow into a tree. Many of the hedges round the edges of the moor are squared-off, featureless and treeless now. Periodically the council gives away saplings to plant out, but there is a simpler solution. Ashes grow naturally in many of the hedges, but few are allowed to develop to take the place of the many elms which were removed as Dutch elm disease hit us. Ash grows fast, can be pollarded if poles are required and burns even when green. It is one of the toughest woods and is native to these parts. But it seems that it is easier to hedge without obstruction – or thought for the future.

I have often wondered why we do we not use hedges as sources of income, as on the Continent. It costs little to leave native trees to grow, and they will be valuable in years to come. The Government is promoting forestry as an alternative income for farmers. But rather than covering the countryside with a dark blanket of conifers, is it not worth thinking of using the hedgerows more effectively and helping to reduce the huge deficit we have in timber? Indeed, it is worth asking why farmers do not take advantage of this free resource without needing subsidies. If the Belgians think it worthwhile to grow poplars for timber in their field boundaries and hedges, in very similar country to ours, there must be money to be made from such an enterprise.

Apart from the income, there are other advantages. Birds and animals will flourish, shade will be provided in the fields and the beauty of the landscape will be greatly improved. One of the things I find most difficult to understand is why there are so few trees on Tealham Moor and on the western part of Tadham. Cattle are the traditional inhabitants of these moors and I cannot imagine that they do as well out in all weathers as they would if some shelter were provided. A treeless expanse is not traditional to the area, in spite of the comment made by a member of the NRA in 1990. He was asked at a meeting why they planted no trees along the banks of Somerset drains and rhynes. He answered that it was traditional. A voice came from the back, "It's only traditional for you. Our rivers always used to have trees along them. It's just so long since you cut them all down that you can't remember them." There was an uneasy silence before the man moved on to something else.

This increase in treelessness is a recent phenomenon and the bareness continues to spread in the locality. One has only to drive round other wetland areas to see rows of pollarded willows providing shelter and materials for garden and farmyard. Why not here?

Even those trees which do exist used to be neglected. Then, a couple of years ago, to everyone's delight, a firm was contracted by Somerset County Council to pollard all the roadside willows on the moor. How nice to know that someone is at last taking care of this important aspect of the rural landscape.

It is excellent that tree maintenance is a requirement of the ESA payment, but few people plant trees to complete the landscape. It would help if more farmers planted where there are gaps, or made up rows which have long vanished. One farmer has done so on the western boundary of Tealham, and he also regularly pollards the original trees. They really bring the landscape to life and he is to be congratulated on his work. It is possible to obtain grants to assist with these costs and they should be actively encouraged. Nothing is more suited to a moorland scene than a long line of pollarded willows adding perspective to the boundary ditch.

Ditch clearance has changed radically in the past few years. In the past, Mr Cliff Fear cleared many of them, partly manually, partly with the gentle help of an old tractor-mounted rake. Many were cleaned out on a cycle of three years, allowing plants and animals to flourish in the intermediate years, while the ditches held water like a sponge after heavy rain. He was a part of the moorland scene and continued in the old ways until his death. This sad event proved to be the watershed in the management of ditches in the area. It brought with it an end to the old manual ways and a change in the regime of clearance. The differences may not seem significant until they are looked at in the context of other changes in water management. For instance, modern-style machine cleaning produces square sides to the ditches, while manual clearance preserved sloping edges. The latter are much kinder to young birds,

Treeless droves and ditch edges are not the tradition. A covered drove on Tadham Moor.

and waders are able to walk right down to the water and probe into the muddy edges – a small advantage but important for long-term conservation.

Since then, clearance of viewed rhynes seems to have become more frequent and certainly more thorough. It is done with a digger and is considerably more brutal than before. Instead of clearing weeds and growth down to the previous ditch bottom, it appears to be policy to dig a bit more, a bit deeper each time. Little except pond-weed grows in some rhynes now. When it rains, they flush down like someone pulling the chain on a lavatory. Not only has the ditch cleaning become more intensive, but it is also accompanied by the removal of trees and self-seeded bushes on the bank side.

The argument about trees and clearance seems to be a local one. In most other parts of the Levels, willows grow all along rhynes. They are a part of the character of such country, marking the water boundaries of fields. They are regularly pollarded and suit the landscape. On Tealham, however, they appear to be seen as unnecessary obstructions which upset the speed of the ditch-cleaning operation. Trees act as lungs. They cool the atmosphere and enable us to breathe the right mix of elements. The tropical rainforests are not the only trees which contribute to this. Britain has the lowest tree cover in Europe, so we could also do our bit. The ravaging of our hedges in recent years, the death of so many elms from disease and the effects of acid rain are surely worth countering.

While I have the greatest sympathy with local farmers and the difficulties they are facing – and let no one underestimate these – I am sometimes surprised at their lack of awareness of the value of good public relations. For example, in 1973 we lost most of the large standing timber when Dutch Elm disease killed off all except the youngest growths of elm. Little regrowth has occurred since, although some of the hedges are surviving under the mess of brambles which took over. Within a year or so the countryside completely changed its appearance, yet little planting has taken place locally to replace these ancient giants. Even sadder is the fact that practically no ash or hedgerow maple saplings have been allowed to survive in the annually-flailed hedges.

263

Ditch clearance has changed radically in the last few years. Kinder methods of yesteryear have been replaced with mechanical dredging, often carried out in an insensitive manner.

Most of those that have grown are in privately-owned hedgerows, not those on farms. This ought to give pause for thought.

With the lack of roadside trees on the moors, and the neglected willows, it is no wonder that some people feel that farmers do not care about the countryside in which they live.

Tree planting and preservation, a higher winter pen, less sensitive methods for initiating pumping, less rigid attitudes by the local Drainage Board – which is controlled by farmers – and encouraging people to understand what goes on in the countryside, should all be major priorities. The way to keep the countryside free for those who own and live in it is to anticipate public opinion, to work towards what the majority expect and hope for, by looking for improvements which can be undertaken at little cost.

By enlisting the aid of people with a deep and passionate interest in the countryside, mountains can be moved. The farming community should try and obtain their help, rather than looking on them as potential foes. Each has broadly the same aim, to enjoy a familiar countryside, even if for apparently differing reasons.

Conservation measures

Conservation is a frequently used word nowadays. To the working farmer, conservationists may often be seen as busybodies interfering in the country which they do not own or even live in. The word 'conservation' may imply the threat of restrictions where none existed before, a change from the freedom to farm as they wish to doing only what 'they' out there allow. To others it may signify a bringing down to earth of the whole farming business, the return of a recognition that there is more to the countryside than just producing food.

There are two sides to the problem and they need reconciling. There is little recognition of the right of the farmer to make a living, of the effort that goes into their farms and the sheer hard work involved in making that living. Often one has the impression that the incomer sees farm land as a great open space for walking and picnicking, a place where the farmer spends time deliberately closing footpaths, dirtying the roads and putting bulls in fields where they, the public, would like to walk. Some of the conservation bodies, which ought to know better, seem just as ignorant of the outlook, aspirations and indeed humanity of the farmers. They tar them all with the label 'barley baron', without seeing that small-scale farming is a precarious and lonely living. Small farmers, who are in the majority round here, do not always approve of what is said in their name, or the changes in practice forced on them by pressures from outside. Uninformed, prejudiced comment from incomers will only serve to harden attitudes. No one, in whatever walk of life, likes others telling them what to do. How much more so if they feel that

265

There is a need to encourage preservation of saplings within the hedgerows. Ash grows naturally in many, and hedgerow maple could also be encouraged to bring back cover.

266

a lot of half-baked rubbish is being talked by those who do not have to feed their family from the land.

The gulf between these two points of view is often extremely wide. It is vital that it is bridged and that a broad interchange of views takes place, leading to mutual understanding. Otherwise a period of strife will develop which will not help anyone.

I hope that this new understanding may be starting to develop round here, but it is going to take a long time to bring all interests together. In 1979, before the troubles started, when the Somerset Trust for Nature Conservation (STNC) bought its first reserve on Tadham Moor, they were careful to involve local farmers and gain their sympathy. The committee responsible for running the new reserve consisted of a local farmer's son, a well-known dentist/bird-watcher, an STNC permanent officer and myself. We showed farmers what was happening and what was planned, and listened also to their views.

When we first bought the land, we made it known that it would still be available for grass-keep and that basic methods of farming would remain similar to those which had been carried out here for generations. Nobody seemed concerned about the new ownership or the plans. The Chairman of the Wedmore Preserving Club – the local farmers' communal rough-shooting organisation – and one or two of the more senior farmers were taken round and shown the ideas we had for improving the ground for breeding birds and keeping the various plants of interest. They seemed impressed in spite of the fact that we also announced a ban on shooting on the STNC ground.

This spirit of involvement and sympathy with local views has not always continued so harmoniously. Some conservationists have behaved insensitively and sometimes arrogantly. They must realise that farmers own the land and are proud of their custodianship of it, but their prime aim is to provide for their families. The aims of wildlife conservation must be combined with the preservation of peoples' livelihood. A successful landscape and countryside is one where the various interests have come together, discussed their various requirements and produced a plan for the future. Inevitably this will be a

267

compromise – what in life is not? But it will help preserve the two arms of the countryside, people and wildlife.

The STNC's first purchase was quite small, just under 10 acres. Since then, the land it owns in this area has risen to around 100 acres, so a good start has been made. It had been hoped to build up a single block of land in the most botanically and ornithologically interesting land, on the north-eastern part of Tealham. This has proved difficult, however, and acquisitions have been in four distinct blocks. It was difficult to know what to do in these circumstances, whether to wait only for the best of all the fields and take years to build up any sort of holding, or to buy land which is interesting but not in the ideal location in relation to what we had already. It is a classic dilemma. The STNC has taken the view it is better to try and establish themselves in the latter manner and hope that the network can be completed in the fullness of time.

The STNC has a particular objective which is not always appreciated by the outside world: it aims to preserve conditions for the benefit of wildlife and plants in the area. The emphasis is on the wildlife, rather than on people being able to see that wildlife, although naturally it aims to achieve that too where possible. For there is no doubt that it is necessary to enthuse people in order to gain support. But not everyone agrees with the philosophy of keeping people out in favour of the wildlife. Some people locally, and others involved in conservation positions elsewhere in the country, feel that every effort must be made to involve people, to let them see what is being preserved, and why. This involvement should not be restricted to Trust members only but ought to be extended to the general public. They are the new members of the future who will help raise the money so necessary to purchase and run the reserves. This is a fresh point of view which appears to be gaining ground. I am very much in favour of this approach, as I have seen open access in action in Holland, where it has been most successful in changing peoples' attitudes to the preservation of wildlife.

One of the dangers is that a conservation body may purchase an area and treat it as if it were one or two scientist's private domain. Birds and animals are very much more resilient and tolerant than we give them credit for, as witness the wildfowl flying in to Slimbridge each day in the winter. Unless there is a good reason for keeping people out – for example, in a particularly sensitive nesting area or where there is danger of rare plants being trampled – people should be let in unhindered. It is only by increasing people's interest that nature will be conserved for the future. More interest from people means increased pressure for Government assistance, pressure to pass suitable legislation, extra grants and more subscriptions to help purchase new reserves.

In spite of this minor dissent, over detail rather than aims, I feel the STNC does a remarkable job through its acquisition and running of so many reserves. It deserves all the support it can obtain. It buys up land which either has unique properties at present or which, by changes in farming, land use and layout, could be enhanced to the benefit of the wildlife. The money for the purchase comes from a variety of sources. In the case of the first field, money was provided by the STNC, the World Wildlife Fund, local fund raising and the Pilgrim Trust.

What happens to the land once it has been bought? First, the Trust carries out botanical, geological and other surveys, to see just what assets and problems there are. Arrangements are made to let the grass keep when appropriate but, on Tealham, firm rules have been drawn up as a part of the letting. Perhaps the most important of these is that cattle are only allowed onto the land from 1st June to 31st October . Tealham is classed as a wetland area and part of the objective is to encourage the breeding of wading birds which like these conditions. May is the month when young snipe, curlew and redshanks are hatching. The winter strictures are to encourage tussocking of the grass, vital for the following year's breeding birds, and to clear the ground for possible artificial flooding. Winter bird-visitors are as important as the breeding population.

The ground is let for grass keep only. It is to be mown and then the remains grazed. In some cases, it is specified that only light grazing should take place but the particular regime is determined by the special characteristics of each field. No artificial fertiliser or raw slurry is to be put on the ground, only rotted

The first pumping into the Somerset Trust block of lands on Tealham, following presentation of a pump to the Trust by the CEGB.

straw-based manure. No cultivations are allowed – no rolling or harrowing and quite definitely no ploughing or reseeding.

The small blocks of land so far obtained are difficult to control in an environmental sense. Neighbouring drains and ditches have a disproportionate effect on the STNC fields, simply because they are such a major part of the area. In the meantime, efforts are being made to raise the water-level artificially by whatever means possible. Anything which helps to trap water inside a pen when ditch levels fall helps. Modifications are made in various ways. Field gutters are blocked at the ends to ensure that they do not run into ditches. Extra feed ditches may be dug where, for instance, the reserve fields back on

to the North Drain. These are then fitted with one-way flap valves so that water can enter when the Drain is high, but is unable to run out when it falls again. Each flush of water is retained within the field system. The warden on the RSPB reserve in West Sedgemoor reports that simply damming certain ditches so that the rhynes brimmed over in the winter, held sufficient water to moisten the fields right through to the end of the breeding season.

With permanent winter flooding over a reasonably sized block of land, the ground should stay soft right through to early June and offer an ideal habitat for wintering waders and swans, and near-perfect conditions for wader breeding. Trials have also shown that it provides optimum growing conditions for local grasses too.

But despite the designation of SSSIs and the ESA, those fields with ancient sward going back untouched into history are changing their herbage content as the ground dries. Fewer species of grasses and flowering plants are found than a few years back and this in turn has affected the bird population as has been proved in a series of studies carried out by the STNC and by the RSPB on Tealham Moor. In the winter of 1974/5 flocks of up to 1,400 dunlin were seen on the moors; in 1990 no more than fifteen. The ground is becoming too hard for their small and slender beaks to penetrate, as they feed on creatures in the first inch of soil. Previously the moor ground provided ideal conditions for the wading birds, with a semi-liquid soup in the upper few inches and a full population of easy-to-reach invertebrates. Flocks of over 1,000 snipe, surely an indicator for the area, have reduced to the occasional 300 at peak over the whole area. Ducks come in only rarely now and peak flocks of 70 or more Bewick's swans, staying for weeks on end in the early 1980s, have been reduced to brief visits of a few birds at the beginning and end of their season.

RSPB surveys carried out in 1977, 1983 and 1987 showed the total number of breeding waders had halved. Since then the curve of the decline has increased. John McGeogh, who has kept detailed records for years, has shown that breeding snipe numbers halved between 1985 and 1990, while curlew stopped breeding altogether. These may seem insignificant numbers and of little

'It has been clear for many years that these last attempts to drain our wilder places are neither cost-effective nor do they fit in with the public will.'

consequence to someone whose living from the land may be endangered and is struggling to continue. The point is that the figures also coincide with a reduction in farming productivity on the moors, particularly the underdrained areas. The various changes do not appear to have achieved their desired improvements.

But figures do not give the real picture. They do not seem yet to show a catastrophic situation. The real change becomes apparent only when one looks at how many birds and other creatures one can actually see in the various seasons of the year. Fifteen years ago a winter drive round the roads of the moors was an adventure. I would see ruff, dunlin, golden plover and teal close to as I drove round. Flights of waders and duck whistled overhead. In summer, snipe ticked away on roadside posts and curlew called out on the meadows; now, the fields are silent in summer and spring. It is rare to hear a snipe drumming and it is a long time since I have seen one on a roadside post. It is an event to pick out the shape of a snipe crouching down by the road edges as winter frost bites. For much of the time the main or only inhabitants are crows. It is no longer an area in which to enjoy spectacular displays of wildlife. This is the visible effect of changing drainage policies. At present it would be difficult to take an outsider round the moors and justify payments under the ESA scheme on the grounds of preserving wildlife and habitat. These are the facts which have to be faced.

Since then much necessary action has been taken by the Government, through its payments to farmers, to retain methods of agriculture sympathetic to the countryside and to preserve the permanent pasture. The new ESA Tier 3 payments have enabled one block of STNC land to be included in a larger area which has been flooded this winter. Water lies in the runnels and the soil is heavy with moisture permeating every pore. Here the various changes of the past few years will be reversed and conditions revert to what used to pertain. Time will show the benefits to wildlife and, it is hoped, to productivity of the grass. While further increasing the sizes of such water-controlled blocks is also being explored by the authorities.

Part of the answer lies with these Tier 3 payments but only positive action on water management policy as a whole can prevent continuing deterioration of the rest of the Levels. This is up to the NRA and their interpretation of their responsibilities to wildlife and conservation in the area. It is our responsibility to remind them of that duty and to insist on it being implemented.

ALL OUR FUTURES

Depressed about the apparently inexorable drying of the moors at the time, I went to see the person in charge of NCC activities on the Levels in the critical period of 1991. I emerged some hours later feeling more heartened and have since realised that this interview took place at a watershed in the affairs of this part of the country and is worth reporting in full.

Since then the NCC has changed its name to English Nature and Brian Johnson has gone on to deal with another knotty problem, peat extraction. Perhaps most importantly, new ESA payments have come into force, taking water-levels into account at last.

Dr Brian Johnson, a very practically-minded scientist and also an enthusiast for the potential of wetland meadows, is a wetland and grazing marsh man through and through, having been brought up on the Kent marshes, lived in the Fens and spent eight years living on Derwent Ings, the great Yorkshire peatland. He is as interested in and knowledgeable about local and national farming techniques as about wildlife. I cannot think of a better accreditation both to the cause of conservation and country life.

I went to see him to try and obtain another perspective on life on our moors, this time from the scientific viewpoint: dispassionate, rational and not tainted by emotion. I certainly obtained this perspective but underneath, there was also an enthusiasm for the area, its people and way of life. This cheered me considerably. The human face of science is not always easy to find.

I had not realised before that the NCC is involved on both sides of the fence. Although it has many scientists working on conservation, it also employs land-agents and is very much a part of the agricultural scene. Through these people, it is aware of current farm profitability, bank policies and farming methods. I felt this to be particularly important in such times as these, where change is hitting the farming world with increasing ferocity.

It is important to see how this body fits into the scheme of things. I cannot do better than quote their own official description of their work: 'The NCC is the body responsible for advising Government on nature conservation in Great Britain. Its work includes the selection, establishment and management of National Nature Reserves...and...Marine Nature Reserves; the provision of advice and dissemination of knowledge about nature conservation; and the support and conduct of research relevant to these functions.' Perhaps most important of all, it is responsible for identifying and arranging the management of SSSIs on behalf of the government.

There are 17,300 acres of SSSI on the Levels and moors and the NCC deals with over 900 owners and occupiers in connection with them. It is the largest piece of farmland notified in the whole of the United Kingdom. In 1991 240 management agreements existed between owners and the NCC. On Tealham and Tadham Moors there were 2,267 acres of SSSI in early 1991 and twenty-five agreements covered around 590 acres of this area. This has been increased to over 640 acres in 1994.

The NCC owns over 740 acres of the moors and Levels, of which 69 acres are on Tealham/Tadham and all this land has been designated as the Somerset Levels National Nature Reserve. Where possible it looks for blocks of farmland which are hydrologically separated from adjacent land, so they can be managed independently from the surrounding farmland with regard to the water table. Its holdings at Moorlynch and King's Sedgemoor fit this description. The land on Tealham/Tadham is used mainly for research and is a fascinating example of how vital this type of work can be.

The plot is devoted to to a unique scientific analysis of the effects of fertilisers on herb-rich meadows on peat. This is the first such experiment and has yielded some fascinating results already. Perhaps the most interesting is that the control plots – natural unimproved sward without fertiliser – are placed among the top third of *all* British grasslands, however treated and of whatever nature, in terms of measurable energy which can be used by an animal productively. It shows the natural grassland is highly productive already and would become even more so if the water table were higher. It is significant is that these trials are funded by the NCC, MAFF and the Department of the Environment together. This promises that full official weight will be given to the findings.

'The Nature Conservancy Council is the body responsible for advising Government on nature conservation in Great Britain.' Bewick swans taking off on Tealham.

Why do the IDBs continue to push the merits of drainage? The IDBs see their role as protecting the interests of all their members. In the case of one district this might include, say, two arable farmers. But grass and arable crops on the same peat ground have opposing requirements. Native wetland grasses require a high water table throughout the year, arable crops need it low. The IDBs are said to believe that they might be sued by the arable farmers if yields were noticeably reduced as a result of a high water table, whereas no one can prove loss of yield for grassland. So a fine British compromise - which is leading to the gradual loss of our Levels - keeps the water table as high as possible, but consistent with the needs of the arable farmers, even though they are in a considerable minority, owning less than 6 per cent of land on the Levels.

Farmers often see reseeding as their saviour. It has been said that only by reseeding the drained ground could it be made to pay – drained ground which has not been reseeded has been markedly less productive to date. But reseeding has proved to be difficult to achieve. Because of climatic conditions on the moors, grass will not germinate satisfactorily, or flourish thereafter. Grass germinates best in autumn, and the moors are particularly dry at this time. Draining the land and leaving the existing wetland grasses simply reduces yields, as they need moisture at their roots to give of their best. When land has been under drained, it will shrink and compact as much as 12 inches in the first year and over 40 inches in two years. This is another problem which is not always considered fully. When over-flooding occurs it is noticeable that the drained areas inundate first and retain water longest, because they are so much lower.

Dr Johnson is convinced that the arable farmers in this part of the world already see that their operations would be uneconomic in a free market. In the view of the NCC it would be good value for money to persuade these farmers to leave arable and convert back to grassland, then the problems faced by the IDBs would be solved at a stroke. There is a precedent for such payments in the Norfolk Broads.

The Levels can be said to serve many interests and functions: nutrient removal; ground water recharge; agriculture; wildlife habitat; recreation;

leisure and tourism. 'Suitable' agriculture may be defined as either the most efficient, or the optimum for natural water levels – two very different interpretations. Retaining natural water levels, and minimising costly pumping, will give the lowest base costs. In a nation which already over produces most agricultural products, the argument for 'improving' land does not hold water, especially where it involves the destruction of something already regarded as desirable for other reasons. However, each function does not have to stand on its own. Assessment of the Levels must be based on their value when the mix of functions is optimised.

In Brian's opinion the situation presaged a massive change in the future of farming. Already few beef farmers can rely solely on beef for their income. There is a huge increase in production of sheep, which will have its inevitable effect on prices and production. But milk is still profitable and looks the most suitable long-term farming enterprise for the Levels, even with further reductions in the quota. If water levels were raised, and the ground reverted to the conditions of the seventies, then milk production costs should be lower here than in other parts of the countryside, as less or no extra fertiliser would be required to support the grass yields.

Fortunately it appears that the current situation on the moors is still reversible. It has been proved that it is possible to take a completely dried up area of peat and wet it again to convert it to its previous state. The NCC bought 400 acres on King's Sedgemoor, some of which was under drained arable land. Within five years it was classed as 'semi-improved', having previously been 'improved'. Thirty-five species of plants had increased to 60. The next step is to raise the water levels and bring the birds back. The NCC thinks long-term and this reserve is designed to conserve wildlife in perpetuity.

Treated water will not effect this change. It is necessary to use raw river water, which has the requisite natural dispersants to enable it to penetrate through the surface and into the pores. One experiment by the STNC indicated that an impermeable crust could be formed below the surface, but other cases show that the process of drying-out can be reversed. Martin Mere in Lancashire is a good example of a wetland rescued from unfavourable conditions.

Although the condition of the fields can be restored fairly quickly once current practices of drainage change, danger to the bird population comes if a local reservoir of breeding birds is no longer available from which new populations can spread back into the areas. It has been shown that birds are traditional in their behaviour. Recolonisation takes place far more rapidly if there is a local breeding reservoir, than through attracting visiting birds to fill the same void. On Tealham this is becoming problematic. For instance, if the present rate of decline is projected forward, breeding snipe should be extinct on Tealham by 1994. The NCC predicted from their records that breeding lapwings would vanish from King's Sedgemoor by 1991. They actually disappeared in 1990. Snipe and many other waders are specialised feeders and need water within 20 cm of the field surface to obtain food in normal spring and summer conditions.

The summer water table is not dependent only on the water-level in the ditches. As the winter pen is currently kept so efficiently low by extremely effective and free-flowing ditches and drains and powerful pumps, so the soil has dried out as a whole. This lowers the water table permanently. There is no doubt that the low winter and spring pen is the real problem when considering the future and productivity of the moors.

What have been the landmarks which have promoted these changes on Tealham and Tadham? The Gold Corner Pumping Station completely altered the pattern of flooding in the Brue Valley and caused desiccation of the Catcott area. The North Drain Pumping Station had a further huge effect on Tealham and Tadham, taken in conjunction with the widening of the North Drain. Total automation of pumping, with very high capacities, has completed the picture. Between them they changed an area which was dependent on outside conditions, and which maintained the water levels normally at field level during the winter, to one which could be controlled completely in all except the most extreme conditions. With the aid of the pumps it would have been possible to change the area from permanent grassland to a largely arable culture. Only the changing requirement for arable crops and the arrival of the SSSIs prevented this taking place. The NCC is determined not only to stop the deterioration of the Levels but actually to restore them to the conditions suitable for wetland wildlife. This involves considerable change.

The winter pen was introduced in 1976/7. If machine automation was to work it was necessary to set a definite level to which to pump. At present this level is set considerably below mean field level. The NCC is now recommending that the winter pen should be set at mean field level until the end of April or the beginning of May. It has been proved that as soon as the grass grows in these conditions, evaporation and transpiration will clear the ground of water and give easy access for livestock. The ditches can be kept as full as one likes after that.

The NRA set up a committee to report back in April 1991 on future water level management. The NCC was represented on this committee and was determined that sense and legality should prevail. They say that present pumping regimes go against the spirit of the agreements signed by the Government at Ramsar in Iran in 1973 and ratified in 1976. This Convention on Wetlands of International Significance was designed to preserve internationally important wetlands and promote their 'wise' use. The whole of the Somerset Levels and moors, of which Tealham and Tadham are part, is a special protection area which will be put forward to the Department of the Environment for ratification as a 'designated' area – one of the greatest importance. So far nearly 400 such sites have been notified, from 45 countries, which reflects the potential importance of our area in world terms.

Another interesting fact came to light in 1990, one which will have a considerable impact on future decisions and operations. IDBs had assumed that they had complete power over drainage in their areas, as had the bodies which used to be responsible for water control before the privatisation of the water companies. In fact it appears that the real power lies in the hands of the NRA Flood Defence Committee. This body is similar to a local authority in powers and duties. It is responsible for water movement in the whole of its

The Levels can
be said to serve
many interests...
agriculture,
wildlife habitat.
The North Drain
in high summer.

catchment area. This committee is appointed and not elected. Members are put forward from each of the local authorities involved, MAFF and the NRA. The NRA can therefore over-rule the IDBs, if it is acting in the interests of all people who have a stake in the moors. It has two special responsibilities: a mandatory duty to further nature conservation and a discretionary power to drain. It appears therefore that nature conservation can take precedence over drainage in the way the NRA acts in performing its statutory duties – quite a revolutionary concept in the light of previous assumptions.

Faced with a drying wetland, the NCC is not prepared to sit back and see the SSSIs deteriorate further, or even stay as they are. They are determined to see the wetland restored. It has been calculated that if the trend towards the conversion of the Levels to arable had continued to its logical conclusion – as looked likely before the introduction of SSSIs – it would have cost the Treasury three times as much to dispose of surpluses as it does in ESA and SSSI payments. Thus there are agricultural, economic and conservation arguments all pointing in the same direction. It is significant that in 1990 there were many more complaints from farmers about low water levels than about high ones. Farmers on North Moor actually petitioned against their own IDB.

Early entry to the moors used to be important to farmers because there was a shortage of fodder. This is no longer true. Dairy and beef herds have declined, while sheep have increased, but may soon be faced with over production. The problem in recent years has been that farmers want the moors to be as predictable as the rest of their land, where timing can be judged within days each year. Wildlife cannot cope with conditions like that and the moors do not give their economic best under such circumstances.

Dr Johnson told me there is no doubt also that the drying of the moors has led to a dramatic fall in productivity. This is due to two factors. First, the lowering of the water table means that the natural grasses of the area cannot exploit the moisture properly. The growth is less dense as some plants die off. Farmers believe that they can make this up with artificial fertilisers, but this will become increasingly uneconomic as the price rises in real terms. And secondly, a decrease in deposition of silt, which was always considered to be a good natural fertiliser.

Another factor to be considered in the future is the greenhouse effect. There is no doubt that a steady process of warming, however minute, has lead to the sea-levels rising over the past hundred years or so. This has virtually no effect on sea-defences at the coast – a rise of a few centimetres makes no difference. The real effects occur with storm surges into the funnels of estuaries and rivers, and the continual raising of inland flood-banks, such as those on the Parrett. In future the costs of this will have to be weighed against the real economic alternatives of agriculture, tourism, water-charging, wildlife and the multiple uses of the moors.

To summarise the views of the NCC. The raising of water-levels in general and the winter pen in particular would be better for wildlife, agriculture and the population of the area as a whole. If the inevitable change to arable had taken place, as seemed certain before the declaration of SSSIs, then the character of the place would have changed completely. It would have altered from a rural economy, dependent on a great many small farmers, to a few huge properties owning thousands of acres. This would have changed the character of the villages, reduced rural jobs considerably and certainly lost much tourist potential.

Most importantly, the NCC feels that the argument for common sense and self-preservation, for those who work on the moors and Levels as well as the wildlife, is gaining ground.

What about the position here on Tealham? How is this likely to look in the future?

The NCC sees the eventual restoration of flooding on Tealham and a doubling of breeding bird populations within a few years. Many farmers in the area now understand that they cannot make a living off farming alone for much longer, but living off farming and SSSI/ESA payments presents a different, and altogether happier, picture. Either farmers must pass on the methods and secrets of traditional moorland farming to the next generation or they risk bankruptcy. The choice is as tough as that. But hope is there. The worst period of indecision could be over.

It is interesting to look back from the end of 1994 to the observations made during this interview. Little has fundamentally changed in the meanwhile, though Tier 3 payments should be the start of a sea-change in attitudes to the long-term future of the moors. In a recent article in ADA Gazette, MAFF talked about the new concept of drawing up a Water Management Plan for an area, which sounds an exciting new approach. This places emphasis on the need to take a positive approach to managing levels in an area, based on farming, conservation and other needs, rather than accepting the status quo. This sounds as if it is nearing the ideal situation, where the winter pen will be more generally raised in those areas where this makes sense.

I can only hope that this view is not over-optimistic. There is a long way to go still.

I continue to find Tealham in all its moods one of the most enchanting places I have ever known. The light varies continually, the fields change their tapestry through the seasons and the view is always of water gleaming somewhere in the picture. There is a feeling of history, peace and space which is increasingly difficult to find in this crowded island. At times the moor is dramatic, with dark storms a background to sunlit fields and glinting ditches, at others delicate and pastel-tinted. May we all be strong enough in our will to retain this enchantment for our successors and as a very special environment for its wildlife.

Tealham in all its moods is one of the most enchanting places I know.

ACKNOWLEDGMENTS AND THANKS

People

It is impossible to confine a list of acknowledgments and at the same time make it comprehensive. So many people have helped me try and understand Tealham and Tadham Moors, and have passed on their history, and talked about the characters who lived and worked on them in the past. They have told me about how the countryside has changed and how they view those changes. I have talked with people over a drink, listened to them chatting over a cup of coffee and absorbed the vanishing ways and stories, which will soon be forgotten unless recorded.

Among those who have helped more consciously and directly are a number of key figures. They include Mrs Hazel Hudson, painstaking historian of Wedmore; Stanley Tucker, Christopher Duckett and Alan Banwell, who kindly consented to be interviewed and who dug deep into their memories. I have particularly fond memories of the late Roland Duckett, Christopher's father, who helped introduce me to the wildlife on the moors, by way of his fields out on Tadham. With him I first saw a newly-hatched curlew wobbling on over-long legs.

I am especially grateful to our neighbours, John and Doreen Duckett, who looked after us when we first came here and have told us so much about being brought up and farming on the moor. Their kindness can never be re-paid.

Dr Brian Johnson of the Nature Conservancy Council was always courteous and helpful when I put my many queries. John McGeogh, the bird-watcher who probably knows most about the wildlife on the moors, gave me friendship, access to his findings, as well as many tales about the creatures he has seen. We worry together about the changes we have observed.

Dr Kiff Hancock helped me to understand the policies and methods of the Somerset Trust for Nature Conservation while both the National Rivers Authority – Wessex Region and the Lower Brue Drainage Board patiently explained how they operated and their responsibilities.

I trust I have reflected all these views accurately. I have tried to present a broadly-based picture of history and what is happening now, attempting to present the different attitudes and interpret them fairly. My only bias is to hope farmers and wildlife should be able to live together, so each can make a succesful livelihood on the same piece of land.

BIBLIOGRAPHY

There are many more books on Somerset than these shown here. The County is blessed with many authors who have admired it. But these represent the core from which I drew knowledge and added it to my own findings and interviews.

1. *A History of Somerset* – Robert Dunning/Somerset County Library, 1987.
2. *A History of Somerset* – Robert Dunning/Phillimore, 1983.
3. *A History of Wedmore* – F.J.Pearce/Private, 1971.
4. *Archeology of Wetlands* – John Coles/Edinburgh, 1984.
5. *Avalon and Sedgemoor* – Desmond Hawkins/David and Charles, 1973.
6. *Domesday Studies* – Rev. R.W.Eyton/Reeves & Turner, 1880.
7. *Old Mendip* – Robin Atthill/David & Charles, 1964.
8. *Prehistory of Somerset Levels* – J.M.Coles & B.J.Orme/Somerset Levels Project, 1982.
9. *Story of Somersetshire* – W.R.Richmond/Wake & Dean, 1905
10. *The Draining of the Somerset Levels* – Michael Williams/Cambridge University Press, 1970.
11. *X11 Hides of Glastonbury* – Ray Gibbs/Llanerch Enterprise, 1988.
12. *Wedmore's Moors and the Enclosure Acts of the 18th Century* – Cuthbert Rose/private, 1982.

INDEX